1/21/94

R
920.03
Bio

Biography Today

Profiles of People of Interest to Young Readers

1993
Annual
Cumulation

Laurie Lanzen Harris
Editor

Omnigraphics, Inc.

Penobscot Building
Detroit, Michigan 48226

Laurie Lanzen Harris, *Editor*
Cherie D. Abbey and Margaret W. Young, *Contributing Editors*
Barry Puckett, *Research Associate*

Omnigraphics, Inc.

* * *

Eric F. Berger, *Vice President, Production*
Laurie Lanzen Harris, *Editorial Director*
Peter E. Ruffner, *Vice President, Administration*
James A. Sellgren, *Vice President, Operations and Finance*

* * *

Frederick G. Ruffner, Jr., *Publisher*

Copyright © 1994 Omnigraphics, Inc.

ISBN 1-55888-345-2

Printed in the United States

Indexed in
CHILDREN'S
MAGAZINE
GUIDE

Contents

3

5

Preface

Biography Today is a publication designed and written for the young reader—aged 9 and above—and covers individuals that librarians tell us that young people want to know about most: entertainers, athletes, writers, illustrators, cartoonists, and political leaders.

In its first year (Volume 1, 1992), *Biography Today* was published four times. Beginning with Volume 2, 1993, *Biography Today* will be published three times a year, in January, April, and September. We have made this change to adapt our publishing schedule more closely to the school year. Despite this change in frequency, the total number of pages will change only slightly. We had initially planned to produce four issues of approximately 100 pages each; now we plan three issues of 125-130 pages each, with a hardbound cumulation of approximately 350 pages.

The Plan of the Work

The publication was especially created to appeal to young readers in a format they can enjoy and readily understand. It is available as a magazine and as a hardbound annual. Each issue contains approximately 15 sketches arranged alphabetically; this annual cumulation contains 42 sketches. Each entry provides at least one picture of the individual pro-filed, and bold-faced rubrics lead the reader to information on birth, youth, early memories, education, first jobs, marriage and family, career highlights, memorable experiences, hobbies, and honors and awards. Each of the entries ends with a list of easily accessible sources designed to lead the student to further reading on the individual and a current address. Obituary entries are also included, written to provide a perspective on the individual's entire career. Obituaries are clearly marked both in the table of contents and at the beginning of the entry.

Biographies are prepared by Omni editors after extensive research, utilizing the most current materials available. Those sources that are generally available to students appear in the list of further reading at the end of the sketch.

This annual cumulation contains a special Appendix featuring updates for those people covered in Volume One whose careers have changed significantly since we included them. These individuals include Colin Powell, who stepped down from his position as Chairman of the Joint Chiefs of Staff, and Thurgood Marshall, who died in the past year.

Indexes

To provide easy access to entries, each issue of *Biography Today* contains a Name Index, General Index covering occupations, organizations, and ethnic and minority origins, Places of Birth Index, and Birthday Index. These indexes cumulate with each succeeding issue. This annual cumulation contains the cumulative indexes, with references to both the individual issues and to the cumulation.

Our Advisors

This publication was reviewed by an Advisory Board comprised of librarians, children's literature specialists, and reading instructors so that we could make sure that the concept of this publication—to provide a readable and accessible biographical magazine for young readers—was on target. They evaluated the title as it developed, and their suggestions have proved invaluable. Any errors, however, are ours alone. We'd like to list the Advisory Board members, and to thank them for their efforts.

Sandra Arden	Troy Public Library Troy, MI
Gail Beaver	Ann Arbor Huron High School Library and the University of Michigan School of Information and Library Studies Ann Arbor, MI
Marilyn Bethel	Pompano Beach Branch Library Pompano Beach, FL
Eileen Butterfield	Waterford Public Library Waterford, CT
Linda Carpino	Detroit Public Library Detroit, MI
Helen Gregory	Grosse Pointe Public Library Grosse Pointe, MI
Jane Klasing	School Board of Broward County Fort Lauderdale, FL
Marlene Lee	Broward County Public Library System Fort Lauderdale, FL
Judy Liskov	Waterford Public Library Waterford, CT

Sylvia Mavrogenes	Miami-Dade Public Library System Miami, FL
Carole J. McCollough	Wayne State University School of Library Science Detroit, MI
Deborah Rutter	Russell Library Middletown, CT
Barbara Sawyer	Groton Public Library and Information Center Groton, CT
Renee Schwartz	School Board of Broward County Fort Lauderdale, FL
Lee Sprince	Broward West Regional Library Fort Lauderdale, FL
Susan Stewart	Birney Middle School Reading Laboratory Southfield, MI
Ethel Stoloff	Birney Middle School Library Southfield, MI

Our Advisory Board stressed to us that we should not shy away from controversial or unconventional people in our profiles, and we have tried to follow their advice. The Advisory Board also mentioned that the sketches might be useful in reluctant reader and adult literacy programs, and we would value any comments librarians or teachers might have about the suitability of our publication for those purposes.

Two New Series

In response to the growing number of suggestions from our readers, we have decided to expand the *Biography Today* family of publications. *Biography Today Author Series*, to be published in mid-1994, will be a 200-page hardbound volume covering 20 authors of interest to the reader aged 9 and above. The length and format of the entries will be like those found in the regular issues of *Biography Today*, but there will be *no* duplication between the two publications.

Kings, Queens, and Leaders of Africa will be the first volume published in the new *Leaders of the World Series*. This 200-page hardbound volume, ready in mid-1994, will cover between 30 and 40 leaders of Africa and will feature historical as well as modern figures. The biographical entries will be similar in format and content to those found in *Biography Today*. Please see the bind-in card for order information.

Your Comments Are Welcome

Our goal is to be accurate and up-to-date, to give young readers information they can learn from and enjoy. Now we want to know what you think. Take a look at this volume of *Biography Today*, on approval. Write or call me with your comments. We want to provide an excellent source of biographical information for young people. Let us know how you think we're doing.

And here's a special incentive: review our list of people to appear in upcoming issues. Use the bind-in card to list other people you want to see in *Biography Today*. If we include someone you suggest, your library wins a free issue, with our thanks. Please see the bind-in card for details.

And take a look at the next pages, where we've listed those libraries and individuals who received free copies of Volume 2, Issues 1-3, for their suggestions.

Laurie Harris
Editor, *Biography Today*

CONGRATULATIONS!

Congratulations to the following individuals and libraries, who received a free copy of *Biography Today,* for suggesting people who appeared in Volume 2:

Audubon School
Dubuque, IA
Lois Hirsch

Alberto Bender
Marshall, TX

Birney Middle School
Southfield, MI
Laura Schiller

Blue Island Public Library
Blue Island, IL
Deborah A. Beasley

Central Junior High School Library
Oklahoma City, OK
Bobbie Frisk

Central Middle School Library
Dover, DE
Brenda Maxon

Citrus High School
Inverness, FL
Gloria Moore

City of Inglewood Public Library
Inglewood, CA
Kay Ikuta

Clearwater Public Library
Clearwater, FL
Jana R. Fine

Alina Degtyar
Kew Gardens, NY

East Liberty Branch Library
Pittsburgh, PA
Amy G. Korman

Eastover Elementary School
Charlotte, NC

Eastway Junior High School
Charlotte, NC
Linda Johnson

Ela Area Public Library
Lake Zurich, IL
Lynne Schwick

Eureka Springs High School Library
Eureka Springs, AR
Alice McNeal

Linda Eveleth
Valencia, CA

Exposition Park-Bethune
Regional Library
Los Angeles, CA
Jerry Stevens

Franklin County Library
Rocky Mount, VA
Shirley A. Reynolds

N.L. Gallop
Santa Rosa, CA

Glen A. Wilson High School
Hacienda Hts., CA
Cindy Kirkley

Glencliff High School
Nashville, TN
Janie R. King

I.M.S.
Riverside, CA
Christine M. Allen

Jefferson Middle School
Grand Prairie, TX
Lynn Witherspoon

11

Johnson County Library
Shawnee Mission, KS
Debbie McLeod

J. David Kopp
St. Louis, MO

Livaudais Junior High School Library
Gretna, LA
Deborah Conn
Joseph Young

Livonia Civic Center Library
Livonia, MI
Barbara Lewis
Kimberly Koscielniak

Mansfield Public Library
Mansfield, MA
Janet Campbell

Monteith Elementary School
Grosse Pointe Woods, MI
Barbara Harwood

Moriarity Middle School
Moriarity, NM

North Miami Beach Library
North Miami Beach, FL
Sylvia Freireich

Northwest Regional Library
Tampa, FL
Susan Oliver

Paris High School Library
Paris, TX
Glenna Ford

Ben Pennewell
Lawrence, KS

Percy Julian Junior High
Oak Park, IL
Ella Pappademos

Quachita Parish Public Library
Monroe, LA

Robert Frost Middle School
Granada Hills, CA
Dr. E. Sinofsky

Selinsgrove Area
Middle School Library
Selinsgrove, PA

Southern Door Elementary/
Middle School Library
Brussels, WI
J. Davis

Theodore Roosevelt High School
Wyandotte, MI

Hue Tran
Garden Grove, CA

University City Public Library
University City, MO
Marilyn Phillips

Wayland Free Public Library
Wayland, MA
C. Behr

Wells Academy High School
Chicago, IL
Q.E. Jackson

Wickliffe Public Library
Wickliffe, OH
Jeanne Schimmelmann

Wiley Elementary School
Hutchinson, KS
Tyler Gates

Maya Angelou 1928-
American Writer and Performer
Author of the 1993 Inaugural Poem,
On the Pulse of Morning

BIRTH

Maya Angelou (MY-uh AHN-juh-loh), the noted black writer who was chosen to read her poetry at the Clinton presidential inauguration in January 1993, was born Marguerite Johnson on April 4, 1928, in St. Louis, Missouri. Much of the information about her colorful life comes from her own autobiographical writings, which are sometimes imprecise about dates and details. The second child of Bailey and Vivian (Baxter) Johnson, she had a brother, Bailey, Jr., one year older, who referred to her as "Mya Sister," a name that eventually evolved into the Maya of today.

The family lived first in St. Louis and then moved to Long Beach, California. When little Bailey was four and Maya was three, their parents' marriage ended. The children were sent alone, by train, to live with their father's mother, Annie Johnson Henderson, in rural Stamps, Arkansas. Fortunately, as they reached the South, other black passengers took pity on the children and shared their box lunches with them.

YOUTH

Grandmother Henderson quickly became "Momma" to her little charges, and the strength and wisdom she imparted to them restored a sense of security they had lost when their parents divorced. The children were reared in the segregated world of the pre-war South. Annie Henderson kept a country store in Stamps, with modest living quarters in the back. There, young Maya and her brother enjoyed the simple pleasures of childhood—and learned to work, to study, and to pray. Maya discovered also, as Lynn Z. Bloom wrote in the *Dictionary of Literary Biography,* "what it was like to to be a black girl in a world whose boundaries were set by whites." Annie Henderson, proud and honest, was a force in her small community. Sharing a home with her and their handicapped Uncle Willie, the children were able to absorb the protective love and rich religious traditions of their heritage, while accepting the grim realities of life for Southern blacks.

Maya's ten-year stay in Arkansas was interrupted when she was seven and she and Bailey went to live in St. Louis with their beautiful, glamorous, and worldly mother. The bustling city life excited Bailey, but frightened his little sister. Deep trauma came to Maya at the age of seven and a half, when she was raped by her mother's boyfriend. Maya was absolutely devastated. When the rapist was found kicked to death (possibly by her uncles) after her court testimony, she believed, wrongly, that she was responsible for his murder. She stopped talking to anyone except her beloved brother for several years. The two of them returned to their grandmother's home, and Maya shut herself into a world of books and the soothing sounds of the spirituals she heard in Momma's church. She remained mute until Mrs. Bertha Flowers, a gracious, educated woman whom she still refers to as the "aristocrat of Black Stamps," encouraged her to read aloud, thus helping her to regain confidence and pride.

Angelou revealed as recently as a dozen years ago that "There isn't one day since I was raped that I haven't thought about it. . . . I have gotten beyond hate and fear, but there is something beyond that."

After Maya's graduation from eighth grade, she and Bailey again went to live with their mother, now remarried and living in San Francisco. The innocence and order of their childhood was behind them as they met and mingled with the colorful characters who moved in and out of the rooming house run by Vivian and her new husband. Maya later spent a disastrous summer vacation with her own father in Long Beach. After a physical attack by his girlfriend, she ran off and found shelter in a junkyard commune inhabited by a racially mixed group of homeless children.

"From this experience," writes Nancy Shuker in a recent biography, *Maya Angelou*, "[she] gained an abiding knowledge of herself, of her own resources, and a strong tolerance for other people's differences." Maya returned to San Francisco after a month with a new determination to take charge of her own life. "Adults had lost the wisdom from the surface of their faces," she remembered. "I reasoned that I had given up some youth for knowledge."

EDUCATION

Angelou's early schooling was in Stamps, where she graduated in 1940 at the top of her eighth-grade class at Lafayette County Training School; she also attended Tousssaint L'Ouverture Grammar School when she lived with her mother in St. Louis. When she and her brother moved to San Francisco, she attended George Washington High School. She also earned a scholarship to California Labor School and began studying drama and dance there. She became pregnant during her senior year and gave birth to a son at the age of 16, one month after her graduation from Mission High School's summer program in 1945. As Angelou tells it, "I'm often asked, 'Why did you end the book [the autobiography *I Know Why the Caged Bird Sings*] with the birth of your illegitimate son?' And I tell them I wanted to end it on a happy note. It was the best thing that ever happened to me."

Although Angelou's formal studies ended there, she is a self-educated woman with broad literary and cultural interests. She holds more than thirty honorary doctorates from such schools as Smith College, Mills College, and Lawrence (Kansas) University.

FIRST JOBS

Angelou held her first job while still in high school. It was in the midst of World War II, and with so many men away in service, women were finding employment in traditionally male jobs. Maya Angelou, still a girl and temporarily out of school after her frightening experience while visiting her father in Long Beach, was one of these. She managed to get around the age requirements and was hired as San Francisco's first black and first woman streetcar conductor. Later, with only a high school education and a baby to support, she took a succession of other jobs, as a cook in a Creole restaurant (which she knew nothing about), as a cocktail waitress, and as a madam for prostitutes. At this lowest point in her life, she also experimented with drugs.

"For a few months," writes biographer Shuker, "Maya straddled two different worlds. In the one, she was . . . living outside the law, wheeling and dealing with people in the underworld. In the other, she was a hard-working, church-going, devoted and responsible mother. Within this [latter] world, she also had an intellectual and artistic life. She took modern dance lessons and she read."

Perhaps hoping to create a more stable home life, in 1950 Angelou married Tosh Angelos, a white man of Greek descent; it is from his surname that her own is derived. Their different races were an issue from the start: her mother strongly disapproved, and strangers stared whenever they went out in public. Their marriage ended in divorce in less than three years.

CHOOSING A CAREER

The love of dancing and the breakup of her first marriage eventually led Angelou into a stage career. While entertaining in a local bar, she was discovered by show-business people from the cabarets around San Francisco. Soon she was a celebrity in the city's artistic colony and received a scholarship in 1952 to study dance in New York. She then joined the European tour of *Porgy and Bess*, singing in 22 countries, in opera houses and concert halls that she could only have dreamed about before. As she traveled, she taught modern dance in Rome and Tel Aviv and learned new languages. She is now fluent in six languages, including Fanti, a West African tongue.

Although she loved touring with the cast of *Porgy and Bess*, Angelou missed her son. She returned to the U.S. and worked as a nightclub singer, mostly on the West Coast, except for a brief period living in a houseboat commune with her son and four others. In 1958, though, her work took a new direction, as she relates here: "I didn't seriously think of writing until John [Killens, a social activist and author] gave me his critique. After that I thought of little else. John was the first published black author I had really talked with. (I'd met James Baldwin in Paris in the early fifties, but I didn't really know him.) John said, 'Most of your work needs polishing. In fact, most of everybody's work could stand rewriting. But you have undeniable talent.' He added, 'You ought to come to New York. You need to be in the Harlem Writers Guild.'" By 1960, Angelou moved to New York, joined the Writers Guild, and began to learn to write.

CAREER HIGHLIGHTS

Since that time, Angelou has had an amazingly varied career in the arts, including singing, dancing, acting, producing, editing, and writing, in a host of forms. In New York, she started out by appearing in off-Broadway plays, including the award-winning *The Blacks*. With Geoffrey Cambridge, she wrote, produced, and appeared in a revue, *Cabaret for Freedom*. It would be the first of several to come. With a growing interest in social causes, especially civil rights, Angelou was appointed by Dr. Martin Luther King, Jr., to serve as northern coordinator for the Southern Christian Leadership Conference in 1960. By this time, she had formed a relationship with the South African revolutionary Vusumzi Make, and she and her son soon moved with him to Egypt. There in Cairo, in 1961, she employed still more of her creative talents as associate editor of the *Arab Observer*, the first woman editor there. She took a trip to Ghana with her son Guy as he started college, planning to stay just long enough to help him settle in. On their third day there, Guy had an automobile accident and broke one arm, one leg, and his neck. Angelou stayed on in Ghana, helping Guy through his recovery. She then took a job from 1963 until 1966 as assistant administrator at the School of Music and Drama at the University of Ghana and feature editor of the *African Review*. During these years, she contributed to Radio Ghana and the *Ghanian Times*.

In 1966, Angelou returned to the United States to resume her writing career and to record the poetry that she had begun to write. Encouraged by novelist and essayist James Baldwin to write about her fascinating and complex life, she responded with *I Know Why the Caged Bird Sings*. The first in her series of five autobiographical works, it was published in 1970 to immediate popular and critical acclaim. With her recent celebrity as a speaker at the Clinton inaugural, *I Know Why the Caged Bird Sings* has enjoyed a renaissance, earning it a place on the current *New York Times'* best-seller list for paperbacks.

A BROADENING PRESENCE

Drawing on her considerable talents, Angelou continued to act, to write screenplays, television scripts, and poetry, and to direct and produce. She was nominated for a Tony award in 1972 for her role in the stage presentation *Look Away*, and in 1977 won an Emmy nomination as best supporting actress for playing the grandmother, Nyo Boto, in the TV movie *Roots*. Angelou became a TV narrator and interviewer and, in every medium, acted as a representative of the black experience. She received academic appointments as writer in residence at the University of Kansas (1970), and distinguished visiting professor at the universities of Wake Forest, Wichita State, and California State in Sacramento, all in 1974.

Angelou was appointed by former President Gerald Ford to the American Revolution Bicentennial Council (1975-76), and she also served on the Presidential Commission for International Women's Year (1978-79) during former President Jimmy Carter's term of office. In 1981, Angelou was given a lifetime appointment as the first Reynolds Professor of American Studies at Wake Forest University in Winston-Salem, North Carolina, where she now resides. She continues to write and to lecture.

Recently, she received an even greater honor by being chosen to write and deliver the ceremonial poem, *On the Pulse of Morning,* for the inauguration of Bill Clinton as forty-second president of the United States.

Of all her writings, Angelou's autobiographies are perhaps the best known. Although many commentators describe these volumes as uneven in quality, readers have enjoyed their painfully honest portrayal of a modern black American woman's search for identity and self-expression—what writer Lynn Z. Bloom describes as "Angelou's odyssey—psychological, spiritual, literary, as well as geographical." Critical response to her poetry has been mixed. Typically characterized by strong rhythms and short lyrics, her poems depict social issues and daily problems common to contemporary life for American blacks. Her works are vividly brought to life in her own powerful stage performances. Taken together, Angelou's autobiographies, poetry, and other writings have guaranteed her place as one of the foremost voices in contemporary American literature.

MARRIAGE AND FAMILY

Angelou once said, "I will say how old I am, I will say how tall I am, but I will not say how many times I have been married. It might frighten them off." She is vague when asked about specifics of her personal relationships; she prefers not to discuss them. Yet she recognizes that others do discuss them: "They honor the coward who stays in a murderous and abusive relationship," Angelou says. "They herald that as something wondrous. But in every marriage I went with everything I had. Humor. Intelligence. Honesty. Faithfulness. Good appetites for everything. But if it didn't work, I never stayed."

She was first married in 1950 to Tosh Angelos; their marriage broke up within three years. In the early 1960s, Angelou lived with South African freedom fighter Vusumzi Make, first in New York and London, later in Egypt, but they were never legally wed. Angelou was also married, from late 1973 to 1981, to Paul Du Feu, a writer and carpenter.

Maya Angelou has one son, Guy Johnson, whose given name was Clyde but was changed to Guy, at his request, when he was an adolescent. Guy Johnson was educated at the University of Ghana during the time he and his mother made their home in Africa, and he now lives in Oakland, California, where he is a poet and also a personnel analyst for the city. Angelou has a grandson, Colin Ashanti Murphy-Johnson.

MAJOR INFLUENCES

Angelou's life was shaped by three female role models—Annie Henderson, the grandmother who gave her love and a sense of duty; Bertha Flowers, the "aristocrat of Black Stamps" who opened up a world of language and culture; and Vivian Johnson, the mother who gave her the courage to face challenges and to whom Maya, at last, gave unqualified love in return.

SELECTED WORKS

AUTOBIOGRAPHY

I Know Why the Caged Bird Sings, 1970
Gather Together in My Name, 1974
Singin' and Swingin' and Gettin' Merry Like Christmas, 1976
The Heart of a Woman, 1981
All God's Children Need Traveling Shoes, 1986

POETRY

Just Give Me a Cool Drink of Water 'fore I Diiie: The Poetry of Maya Angelou, 1971
Oh Pray My Wings Are Gonna Fit Me Well, 1975
And Still I Rise, 1978
Shaker, Why Don't You Sing? 1983
Now Sheba Sings the Song, 1987
I Shall Not Be Moved, 1990
On the Pulse of Morning, 1993

DRAMA

Cabaret for Freedom, 1960 (with Geoffrey Cambridge)
The Least of These, 1966
Ajax, 1974 (adapted from Sophocles)
And Still I Rise, 1976

SCREENPLAYS

Georgia, Georgia, 1972
All Day Long, 1974

RECORDINGS

Miss Calypso, 1957
The Poetry of Maya Angelou, 1969
An Evening With Maya Angelou, 1975
Women in Business, 1981

TELEVISION SCRIPTS

Black, Blues, Black, 1968 (series)
Assignment America, 1975 (series)
"The Legacy," 1976

"The Inheritors," 1976
"Afro-American in the Arts," 1977
"Sister, Sister," 1982
"Trying to Make It Home," 1988

HONORS AND AWARDS

Chubb Fellowship Award (Yale University): 1970
National Book Award nomination: 1970, for *I Know Why the Caged Bird Sings*
Pulitzer Prize nomination: 1972, for *Just Give Me a Cool Drink of Water 'fore I Diiie*
Tony Award nomination: 1972, for *Look Away*
Rockefeller Foundation Scholar (in Italy): 1975
Woman of the Year in Communications (*Ladies Home Journal*): 1976
Golden Eagle Award: 1977, for "Afro-American in the Arts" (PBS documentary)
One of "Top 100 Most Influential Women" (*Ladies Home Journal*): 1983
Matrix Award (Women in Communication): 1983
Essence Woman of the Year: 1992
Horatio Alger Award (Horatio Alger Society): 1992

In addition, Great Britain's National Society for the Prevention of Cruelty to Children has named its new London facility the Maya Angelou Family Center.

FURTHER READING

BOOKS

Angelou, Maya. *I Know Why the Caged Bird Sings*, 1970
----- *Gather Together in My Name*, 1974
----- *Singin' and Swingin' and Gettin' Merry Like Christmas*, 1976
----- *The Heart of a Woman*, 1981
----- *All God's Children Need Traveling Shoes*, 1986
Contemporary Authors New Revision Series, Vol. 19
Dictionary of Literary Biography, Vol. 38
Notable Black American Women, 1992
Shuker, Nancy. *Maya Angelou*, 1990
Who's Who in America, 1992-9?

PERIODICALS

Current Biography 1974
Ebony, Apr. 1990, p.44
Essence, Dec. 1992, p.48
New York Times, Dec. 5, 1992, p. A8; Jan. 20, 1993, p.B1

People, Mar. 8, 1982, p.92
TV Guide, Oct. 4, 1986, p.10
U.S. News & World Report, Dec. 14, 1992, p.22

ADDRESS
c/o Dave La Camera
Lordly and Dame, Inc.
51 Church Street
Boston, MA 02116

OBITUARY

Arthur Ashe 1943-1993
American Professional Tennis Player,
Author, Commentator, and Activist
First Black Man to Achieve #1 Ranking
in Professional Tennis

BIRTH

Arthur Robert Ashe, Jr., was born July 10, 1943, in Richmond,
Virginia, to Arthur Ashe, Sr., and Mattie (Cunningham) Ashe.
He had one younger brother, John, a stepsister, Loretta, and a step-
brother, Robert.

YOUTH

Arthur Ashe, Sr., was a superintendent for the city recreation department, and the Ashe family lived in a house that sat alone overlooking Brook Field, where Arthur Jr. spent so much of his youth. The house was isolated—they were five minutes from their nearest neighbor—and Arthur spent most of his early years in the company of his mother, a frail, quiet woman who taught him to read when he was five. She died of a stroke when he was six. When the little boy heard of his mother's death, he told his father "Well, Daddy, as long as we're together, everything will be all right." Arthur and his brother were raised by their father and a housekeeper, Mrs. Otis Berry, who stayed on with the family after Arthur Sr. married Lorene Kimbrough when Arthur was 12.

One of nine children, Arthur Sr. always worked hard at a number of jobs. In addition to his recreation department job, he started a landscaping company and also worked as a chauffeur and caterer as his young sons were growing up. He instilled in his sons the importance of hard work, discipline, and respect. Arthur Sr. knew it took exactly 10 minutes to get home from school—and young Arthur was expected to be home on time, every day, no excuses. It was a rule he never broke.

Ashe's cool temperament and dignified manner were also a result of his upbringing. "You don't get nowhere by making enemies," his father told him. "You gain by helping others. Things that you need come first. Foolishness is last." The courage, grace, and determination that marked Ashe's entire career were instilled by his dad. Later in his life, when the honors of a world-class tennis champion came his way, he said this of his father: "Nobody would be honoring me if Daddy hadn't raised me the way he had."

Ashe was able to trace his ancestry back to his great grandparents, who were all slaves. His father's father, known as "Pink" Ashe, was half Native American and half Mexican. Ashe also had two high-profile second cousins: boxer Archie Moore and actor Sidney Poitier.

EARLY MEMORIES

As the only black player in the all-white world of championship tennis, Ashe remembers being as "noticeable as the only raisin in a rice pudding." He started to play at the age of six, with "arms and legs as thin as soda straws." He played as much as he could, and often he'd watch the white kids play in Richmond's Byrd Park, where it was illegal for blacks to play.

Two themes run through Arthur Ashe's life: tennis and the struggle for racial equality. He had a segregated upbringing in Virginia, where separate facilities, from buses to tennis courts, severely limited the lives of black people. He attended all-black schools, and despite his early and obvious talent in tennis, had to break one racial barrier after another to succeed as a tennis champion. He remembered "the unmistakable impression left in black school children that there is not much they can do beyond being garbagemen or mailmen. You might be a policeman, but never a bank president, mayor, or chief of police. Every black kid I knew grew up feeling that certain jobs were off-limits and unattainable, that books and the Pledge of Allegiance said one thing, but once you left school, you had to live in a completely different set of circumstances."

EDUCATION

SCHOOL AND TENNIS

Ashe attended Baker Elementary School in Richmond, where he earned all As and Bs. At the same time, he was developing into a young tennis powerhouse. His first coach was Ronald Charity, a college student who noticed Ashe on the courts of Brook Field and who taught at the 17th Street Mission in Richmond. Ashe entered his first tournament at the age of eight, and although he lost, he learned that he loved to compete.

Ashe later came to the attention of Dr. Robert Walter Johnson, who took young black tennis proteges under his wing to give them a start in a sport that was long the domain of the white upper classes. Another of Johnson's

proteges, Althea Gibson, became the greatest black woman's tennis player to date. They competed in the American Tennis Association, the black equivalent of the USLTA (United States Lawn Tennis Association), which excluded black players. Ashe spent eight summers under Johnson's tutelage, beginning a winning streak in 1955 when he won the ATA 12-and-under singles and doubles. He dominated ATA championships from 1955 to 1963, and in 1960 and 1961 won the U.S. Junior Indoor singles tournament two years in a row.

Always an outstanding student, Ashe attended Booker T. Washington Jr. High and Maggie L. Walker High School in

Richmond. Before his senior year, he moved to St. Louis, Missouri, to train full-time with coach Richard Hudlin. He graduated from Sumner High School in St. Louis with the highest grade point in his class. At this time, he was the fifth-ranked junior player in the U.S.

His excellent academic and tennis credentials earned Ashe a scholarship to UCLA (University of California at Los Angeles), where he was coached by J.D. Morgan and Pancho Gonzalez. Gonzalez, one of the finest professional tennis players of all time, was the man Ashe later named as his only sports idol. In 1963, Ashe became the first black to be named to the U.S. Davis Cup team, and he also made his debut at Wimbledon. His record as a Davis Cup competitor set a record: from 1963 to 1978, he won 27 singles matches and lost only five. In 1965 he led UCLA to an NCAA championship in tennis.

Ashe graduated from UCLA in 1966 with a bachelor's degree in business administration. He later recounted how his proud grandmother focused on his achievements in the classroom, not the courts. "I'll never forget how proud my grandmother was when I graduated from UCLA," he recalled of this strong woman, once a domestic worker. "Never mind the Davis Cup, Wimbledon, Forest Hills. To this day she still doesn't know what those names mean. What mattered to her was that of her more than 30 children and grandchildren, I was the first to be graduated from college, and a famous college at that. Somehow that made up for all the floors she scrubbed all those years." In September 1966, he entered the Army Reserve, where he served for two years, as a lieutenant and also as an assistant coach at the U.S. Military Academy.

CAREER HIGHLIGHTS

EARLY YEARS

In 1967, Ashe won the U.S. Clay Courts singles, and in 1968, he again made tennis history as the first black man to win the U.S. National men's singles, the first black man to win the U.S. Open, and the first black man to achieve a #1 ranking in tennis in the U.S.

Ashe was an outstanding doubles player as well, winning the U.S. Indoors doubles with Stan Smith in 1970, the French Open doubles in 1971 with Marty Riessen, and the Australian Open doubles with Tony Roche in 1977. During these years, he also won the Australian Open singles title in 1970 and the WCT Championship singles in 1975.

WIMBLEDON

One of the finest moments in Ashe's career came in 1975, when he met Jimmy Connors, the brash, mouthy favorite, on the courts of Wimbledon. Ashe had always been known as a serve-and-volley player, whose powerful serve and stamina at the net wore down his opponents. But for the Connors match at Wimbledon, Ashe used a new strategy. He took Connors by surprise by varying his game, winning in four sets. His record for 1975 was an incredible 108 victories to 23 losses, and it led to his ranking as the #1 player in the world.

Ashe's cool, unruffled temperament, almost as much a part of his signature as his killer serve, offered a vivid contrast to Connors and his generation of tennis champions. Players like Connors, Ilie Nastase, and John McEnroe shunned the polite reserve that characterized the game before they arrived, and often made rude gestures and comments when a call didn't go their way.

The year following his Wimbledon win, Ashe suffered from eye and heel problems, plummeting to 257th in the rankings, but he made a stunning comeback to a #7 spot by 1979. But in July 1979, following a tennis clinic, Ashe suffered a serious heart attack. In December, he underwent quadruple bypass surgery on his heart. In April 1980, Ashe retired from tennis. He was named the captain of the U.S. Davis Cup team that year, and he coached the team to two consecutive championships, in 1981 and 1982, despite the continuing ill-mannered court behavior of Connors and McEnroe, whose unruly conduct reflected negatively on Ashe and on the team a whole.

ACTIVISM

Throughout his career, Ashe dedicated himself to encouraging minority children to participate in athletics, and he sponsored clinics in poor areas all over the country. He also encouraged blacks to achieve in school, advocating that communities "build more libraries than gymnasiums." A *New York Times* columnist paraphrased Ashe's approach this way: "the wise youngster should aspire as much to own the Chicago Bulls as to be a member of the team."

Eventually, the NCAA also made a more rigorous stand on academics and athletes. In 1989, they approved Proposition 42, which outlined minimum academic requirements for players to receive athletic scholarships. Some black critics found the ruling racist, because it denied black players without passing grades the ability to play. Ashe disagreed vehemently, claiming that black athletes should be able to meet the requirements and that "too many black athletes develop a hard-core cynicism that specifically de-emphasizes education and views athletic stardom as a worthy goal in and of itself." These athletes are encouraged in this attitude by schools and parents, said Ashe, who declared "If public school districts—even poor ones—can organize their sports programs to produce first-class athletes, then they can use the same organizational skills to at least produce second-class scholars."

His activism in support of equal rights extended to international affairs, and he got involved in anti-apartheid campaigns against South Africa. In 1969, he joined a players' group that protested South Africa's status as a competing nation in the Davis Cup. In 1970, he was banned from playing in South Africa. Also in that year, South Africa was barred from the Davis Cup, and Ashe spoke to the United Nations asking that South Africa be banned from the International Lawn Tennis Federation.

In 1973, Ashe made the decision to play in South Africa. He competed in the South African Open, against the wishes of many anti-apartheid groups who thought he and other high-profile black activists should continue to boycott the country. But Ashe chose to go, saying: "Ellis Park [in Johannesburg] will be integrated and I will be a free black man on display." He became the first black man to reach the finals of that Open. Afterwards, he visited the all-black township of Soweto, where he gave a clinic on an old, cracked public court. He was cheered by the people of Soweto, and one hung an amulet around his neck and gave Ashe a nickname: *sipho*, meaning "gift."

Some black leaders felt he wasn't militant enough. "I tried to reconcile it by weighing the immediate advantages of being more militant and out front with the longer-term benefits of continuing to break new ground. I was convinced—and I believe today—that most of the progress in the world, scientific or social or anything else, is made bit by bit. That is the way things work, and when you look back . . . quite a bit has been accomplished."

In 1983, Ashe, still suffering from heart problems, underwent another bypass operation. Around this time, he became a regular television commentator for HBO and NBC on their tennis broadcasts. In 1985, he was inducted into the Tennis Hall of Fame. Ashe was always an articulate speaker and a fine writer. He began a column for the *Washington Post* in 1978, was a regular contributor to *Tennis* magazine, and also published three autobiographies, *Advantage Ashe* in 1967, *Arthur Ashe: Portrait in Motion* in 1975, and *Off the Court* in 1981. In 1983, Ashe was asked to lecture on the history of black athletes for Florida Memorial College. His research for that course led him to embark on a six-year project in which he explored the history of blacks and athletics from 1619 to the present. The result was the three-volume *A Hard Road to Glory*, published in 1988. "The more I delved into it, the more emotionally attached I got to the information—especially with people I felt had undertaken heroic actions."

AIDS

Around the time of the publication of *A Hard Road to Glory*, Ashe noticed a numbness in his right hand. He was admitted to the hospital and underwent brain surgery. The operation revealed a brain infection, "toxoplasmosis," that indicated that Ashe had AIDS (Acquired Immunodeficiency Syndrome). He was sure that he had contracted the disease from blood transfusions he had received after his heart surgery in 1983. (Although all blood is screened today, it was not tested uniformly until 1985).

Wishing to protect his and his family's privacy, Ashe kept silent about his condition, except for close family and friends. But in 1992, *USA Today* got hold of the story and planned to publish the information regardless of Ashe's wishes. Ashe called a press conference in April 1992 and announced his condition to a stunned public. He expressed outrage and concern for the invasion of his family's privacy, particularly that of his five-year-old daughter, Camera. When he was momentarily overcome, his wife, Jeanne, continued his prepared statement: "beginning tonight Arthur and I must teach her how to react to new and sometimes cruel comments that have very little to do with her reality." The public responded with equal outrage, and *USA Today* was widely condemned for its handling of the issue.

The activist in Ashe emerged again, and he founded the Arthur Ashe Foundation for the Defeat of AIDS and began to speak out on the issue. He gave a speech at the United Nations on World AIDS Day in December 1992, a speech he considered to be the most significant of his life. He was taking a variety of drugs to help his body fight the increasingly debilitating disease and was in pain from his continuing heart condition. In January of 1993, he became ill with PCP, a form of pneumonia that often takes the lives of AIDS patients. After a brief recovery, he came down with PCP again, and died February 6, 1993. His final work, *Days of Grace*, deals with his struggle with AIDS and was published in the spring of 1993.

His legacy is summed up in the words of Donna Doherty, editor of *Tennis* magazine: "Arthur Ashe cast a spotlight across the paths of all he touched. He was eulogized as a prince, a hero, a Christ figure, an instrument through which higher powers work their mysteries. He used tennis as his platform to spring into the business of trying to right the wrongs of this world. He would want us to do the same: to see beyond the tennis courts that bring us so much enjoyment and learn to help others; to spend the time we have on earth making a difference, however small. It's the Arthur Ashe way."

MARRIAGE AND FAMILY

Ashe married photographer Jeanne Marie Moutoussamy on February 20, 1971. Their daughter, Camera Elizabeth, was born in December 1986. Both Jeanne and Camera have tested HIV-negative. Ashe has left Camera a series of letters to remember him by.

HOBBIES AND OTHER INTERESTS

After his retirement, Ashe played only a "social" game of tennis, preferring to play golf, which is less physically demanding. His contributions to charities were numerous, including the Children's Defense Fund and the United Negro College Fund. He also served on the boards of the Aetna insurance company and the USLTA and was past chairman of the National Heart Association.

WRITINGS

Advantage Ashe (with Clifford G. Gewecke, Jr), 1967
Arthur Ashe: Portrait in Motion (with Frank Deford), 1975
Getting Started in Tennis, 1977
Arthur Ashe's Tennis Clinic, 1981
Off the Court, 1981
A Hard Road to Glory: A History of the African-American Athlete, 3 vols., 1988
Days of Grace, 1993

HONORS AND AWARDS

ATA 12-and under championship: 1955
ATA 15-and-under championship: 1957, 1958
ATA 18-and-under championship: 1960
ATA men's championship: 1961, 1962, 1963
U.S. Hardcourts championship: 1963
NCAA championship: 1965
U.S. Clay Courts championship: 1967
U.S. National championship: 1968
U.S. Open championship: 1968
Australian Open championship: 1970
Wimbledon championship: 1975
WCT Championship: 1975
Tennis Hall of Fame: 1985
Sportsman of the Year (*Sports Illustrated*): 1992

FURTHER READING

BOOKS

Ashe Arthur, with Clifford G. Gewecke, Jr. *Advantage Ashe*, 1967
Ashe, Arthur, with Frank Deford. *Arthur Ashe: Portrait in Motion*, 1975
Getting Started in Tennis, 1977
Great Athletes, Vol. 1, 1992
Who's Who among Black Americans, 1992-1993

PERIODICALS

Current Biography Yearbook 1966

Ebony, June 1989, p.139; Nov. 1990, p.100
Esquire, Oct. 1992, p.101
Jet, Apr. 27, 1993, p.11
New York Times, May 7, 1992, p.A18; Feb. 8, 1993; Feb. 9, 1993, p.B9
New York Times Magazine, Aug. 31, 1986, p.26
Newsweek, Jan. 22, 1992, p.40; Apr. 20, 1992, p.62; Feb. 22, 1993, p.60
People, Mar. 6, 1989, p.243; Apr. 20, 1992, p.51; June 8, 1992, p.42
The Sporting News, Feb. 15, 1993, p.9
Sports Illustrated, Apr. 20, 1993, p.24; Feb. 15, 1993, p.12
Tennis, June 1992, p.19; Sept. 1992, p.20; Apr. 1993, p.110
Time, Apr. 20, 1992; Feb. 15, 1993, p.70

Avi   1937-
American Writer for Children and
Young Adults
Author of *S.O.R. Losers* and *The True
Confessions of Charlotte Doyle*

BIRTH

Avi (AH-vee) Wortis, who prefers to be called by his first name
only, was born in New York City on December 23, 1937. His father,
Joseph Wortis, was a psychiatrist, and his mother, Helen (Zunser)
Wortis, was a social worker. Avi has a twin sister, Emily, who is
a poet and critic, and a brother, Henry, who is a scientist.

YOUTH

Avi grew up in Brooklyn in a family that encouraged reading and storytelling. Two of his great-grandfathers were writers, and one of his grandmothers had been a playwright. He remembers his grandparents delighting him with stories, which inspired his own love of reading. According to family legend, at five he rushed into a room shouting "I can read!" and his appetite was filled with children's books, adult novels, even comic books. He recalls "watching, listening, reading: the natural education of a writer."

EARLY MEMORIES

Avi remembers being "shy, not into sports, but someone who loved to read and play games of imagination." He also remembers loving history from a young age, especially the era of the American Revolution. He later studied history in college, and many of his best-loved books are set in historical times.

While he was growing up Avi thought of himself as an outsider. He found solitude "enormously appealing. Now some of it was rationalization because I was isolated. But I remember wandering the streets intensely alone and happy."

EDUCATION

Avi was not a good student. Writing and spelling were especially hard for him. He remembers doing well in science, but dreading each Friday—the day of spelling tests. He wound up flunking out of the first high school he went to, largely because he could not write. He learned later that he suffered from dysgraphia, a writing dysfunction. His parents found him a different high school, a smaller one that emphasized reading and writing, and he also studied with a tutor. It was his work with his tutor that inspired him to become a writer, for though it was hard work, he was stubborn and determined to write well.

After graduating from Elisabeth Irwin High School, Avi attended the University of Wisconsin, where he majored in history and received his bachelor's degree in 1959. He developed a strong interest in the theater and stayed on at Wisconsin, finishing a master's degree in drama in 1962.

FIRST JOBS

Avi moved to New York after graduation and tried his hand at writing plays, without much success. He also tried writing a novel for adults, again without success. He recalls other jobs from this time in his life: "sign printer (sometimes with spelling mistakes), carpenter, theater coach, a whole host of jobs I never did with much satisfaction or success."

CHOOSING A CAREER

Avi was able to blend two of his loves—theater and reading—in a job he held at the New York Public Library Performing Arts Research Center, where he was on the library staff for the Theater Collection from 1962 to 1970. He enjoyed library work and attended Columbia University at night to study for his M.L.S. (Master's in Library Science), receiving his degree in 1964.

It was while working as a librarian that Avi began to write for children, largely because he had started to invent stories for his own young sons. "Only when my own kids came into my life did I start to write for young people. I was to find what I did best. Writing for kids has been the center of my life ever since. Kids, if you will, gave me my life."

CAREER HIGHLIGHTS

While he was establishing his writing career, Avi continued to work as a librarian. He combined his two careers from 1970 to 1986, working as a professor and humanities librarian at Trenton State College in New Jersey from 1970 to 1986, where he taught courses in research and children's literature. In 1986, he gave up his librarian job to become a full-time writer.

Avi's first titles, *Things That Sometimes Happen* (1970) and *Snail Tale* (1972), were for very young readers. He has since written successfully for a broad range of ages, from beginning readers through those in high school.

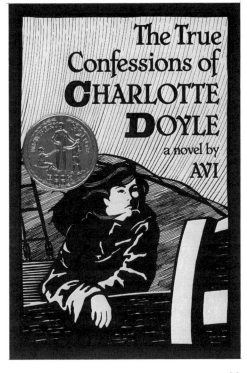

The style and type of his fiction also varies: he has written historical novels, notably *The Fighting Ground* (1984), set in the time of the American Revolution, and more recently *The True Confessions of Charlotte Doyle* (1990), set aboard a sailing ship in the nineteenth century. But Avi seems equally at home writing fantasy (*Bright Shadow,* 1985) or mystery (*No More Magic,* 1975, *Emily Upham's Revenge,* 1978, and *Shadrach's Crossing,* 1983). He is also a sensitive and funny writer of tales of contemporary life for young adults, which is confirmed by the success of such books as *S.O.R. Losers* (1984) and *Romeo and Juliet—Together (and Alive!)—at Last* (1987).

Of his historical fiction, *The Fighting Ground*, which won Avi the Scott O'Dell award, centers on one day in the life of a young boy. Jonathan, 13 years old, sees only the glamour of war and is eager to test his courage in the cause of the American Revolution. Through his eyes, the reader is introduced to the horrors of war as Jonathan is captured by Hessian soldiers. *The True Confessions of Charlotte Doyle*, which was named a Newbery Honor Book, is another of Avi's much-praised historical fictions. In it, Charlotte, 13, is returning to Rhode Island from England aboard a ship whose captain is a brutal madman. Charlotte's story is related in the first person, through her journal entries, and tells of her involvement in a murder and a mutiny, and how her experiences give her insight into her own family and its problems.

Avi's mystery titles include the popular *Shadrach's Crossing*, set in the 1930s and detailing a week in the life of 15-year-old Shad Faherty as he deals with smugglers, as well as with his family's poverty and sense of helplessness, in the Prohibition era.

Avi's funnier fiction includes *S.O.R. Losers*, about a group of seventh grade boys who are happy being artists, writers, and poets, and who have successfully avoided all the sports activities at their school, South Orange River Middle School. They are forced to play together on a soccer team, which inevitably loses all its matches, living up to their motto: "People have a right to be losers." South Orange River is also the setting for *Romeo and Juliet—Together (and Alive!)—at Last*, which tells how the friends of two shy but lovelorn middle schoolers arrange for their first kiss—in a slapstick version of Shakespeare's famous tale of star-crossed lovers.

Avi has great respect for his readers: "I hold a strong belief that most young people are as emotionally complex as adults. Some, I dare say, are more complex." His writing is equally complex, and his young readers admire his believable characters, the tightly written, suspenseful way he tells his tales, and the humor and wit he brings to his fiction. "What I always seek is a good, suspenseful story, rich in emotions, contradiction, irony—a story that grabs, makes you want to race to the end. At the same time I'm working hard to make the characters and ideas stay with the readers long after the last page."

Avi's readers are eager to know how he gets the widely different ideas he uses in his fiction, and Avi has this to say: "Because I have always read a great deal (still do), I have taught myself to think about people, circumstances, events, not in terms of singular occurrences, but in the context of evolving narratives that contain beginnings, endings, tensions, and locales. This means I am never without ideas."

In terms of structure, Avi prefers the novella form: longer than a short story, but not as long as a novel. After trying (and failing) to write an adult novel, he discovered that the novella form suited his talents and his purpose: "I love the book you can swallow in one long drink," he says of the form. "[The novella] has concentration and complexity but also a kind of directness."

Writing is hard work for Avi, and he rewrites his stories over and over again, working toward a balance in the rhythm of the words in a sentence, in the development of the plot, or in the creation of a character. "I remain enthralled with the idea and act of writing, the capture of ideas, the design of plot, the finding and shaping of words, the struggle to discover the real truths that lurk within the hearts of imagined souls."

Avi's deep respect for his audience is conveyed in the books he writes, as well as in his thoughtful reflections on his readers: "Give [kids] a world they can understand and they will read you. Give them a world that expands, or better, defines, their often unspoken, often hidden perceptions and extraordinary sensibilities, and they will embrace you."

MARRIAGE AND FAMILY

Avi married Joan Gabriner in 1963. They had two sons, Shaun and Kevin, who are now both rock musicians. They later divorced. He then married Coppelia Kahn, who has one son, Gabriel, from a previous marraige.

HOBBIES AND OTHER INTERESTS

When he's not writing, Avi enjoys photography.

ADVICE FOR YOUNG WRITERS

"I think reading is the key to writing. The more you read, the better your writing can be. Listen and watch the world around you. Try to understand why things happen. Don't be satisfied with answers others give you. Don't assume that because everyone believes a thing it is right *or* wrong. Reason things out for yourself. Work to get answers on your own. Understand why you believe things. Finally, write what you honestly feel then learn from the criticism that will always come your way."

SELECTED WRITINGS

Things That Sometimes Happen, 1970
Snail Tale, 1972
No More Magic, 1975
Captain Grey, 1977
Emily Upham's Revenge, 1978
Night Journeys, 1979
Encounter at Easton, 1980

The History of Helpless Harry, 1980
Man from the Sky, 1980
A Place Called Ugly, 1981
Sometimes I Think I Hear My Name, 1982
Shadrach's Crossing, 1983
The Fighting Ground, 1984
S.O.R. Losers, 1984
Bright Shadow, 1985
Wolf Rider, 1986
Romeo and Juliet—Together (and Alive!)—at Last, 1987
Something Upstairs: A Tale of Ghosts, 1988
The Man Who Was Poe, 1989
Seahawk, 1990
The True Confessions of Charlotte Doyle, 1990
Nothing but the Truth, 1991
Blue Heron, 1992

HONORS AND AWARDS

Best Book of the Year (British Book Council): 1973, for *Snail Tale*
Edgar Allan Poe Award (Mystery Writers of America): 1976 runner up, for *No More Magic;* 1978 runner up, for *Emily Upham's Revenge;* 1984 runner up, for *Shadrach's Crossing*
Children's Choice Award (International Reading Association): 1980, for *Man from the Sky*
Christopher Award: 1981, for *Encounter at Easton*
Scott O'Dell Award: 1984, for *The Fighting Ground*
Boston Globe-Horn Book Award for Fiction: 1991, for *The True Confessions of Charlotte Doyle*
Newbery Medal Honor Book (American Library Association): 1991, for *The True Confessions of Charlotte Doyle*

FURTHER READING

BOOKS

Children's Literature Review, Vol. 24
Contemporary Authors, New Revision Series, Vol. 12
Gallo, Donald R., ed. *Speaking for Ourselves: Autobiographical Sketches by Notable Authors of Books for Young Adults,* 1990
Helbig, Althea K., and Agnes Regan Perkins, *Dictionary of American Children's Fiction, 1960-1984: Recent Books of Recognized Merit,* 1986
Roginski, Jim. *Behind the Covers: Interviews with Authors and Illustrators of Books for Children and Young Adults,* 1985
Something about the Author, Vol. 14
Twentieth-Century Children's Writers, 3rd ed., 1989

PERIODICALS

Booklist, Jan. 15, 1992, p.930
Bulletin of the Center for Children's Books, Oct. 1989, p.27
Horn Book, Jan.-Feb. 1992, p.24
New York Times Book Review, Sep. 11, 1977, p.30
School Library Journal, Jan. 1973, p.116
The Writer, Mar. 1982, p.18

ADDRESS

15 Sheldon Street
Providence, RI 02906

Kathleen Battle   1948-
American Opera Singer

BIRTH

Kathleen Deanne Battle was born August 13, 1948, in Portsmouth, Ohio, to Grady and Ollie (Layne) Battle. The youngest of seven children, she has three brothers and three sisters. Portsmouth is an old steelmill town near the Kentucky border. Her father was formerly a steelworker, but the mill is now closed and the area is economically depressed.

YOUTH

Battle's earliest experiences of music were connected to family—her father was a tenor in a gospel quartet—and to her church, the African Methodist Episcopal Church, where her clear and lyrical soprano voice was first recognized and where she first performed. "They'd put me on a table and I'd sing at civic functions, banquets, church affairs," she recalls.

She was the only child in the Battle family to ask for music lessons, and she began taking piano, which she still plays, at the age of 12. Battle is a musician who is known for appearing for rehearsals perfectly prepared, and that trait may come from an early experience with the piano. When her mother paid for her lessons each week, "she'd say 'I hope you practiced,'" recalls Battle. "Once I was playing in a recital and I forgot the piece. I kept playing the first four measures over and over. I vowed never to let that happen again."

Many of Battle's fans in the music world are suprised but delighted that someone from her background became a reigning star of opera—a predominately white, Western European art form. Her first exposure to classical music came from a high school music teacher who gave her scores to learn, and she remembers not ever having heard a symphony orchestra when she began to study music in college. Yet she considers all of her musical background important in making her what she is today. "The culture I come from is just as rich as any Western European culture, therefore I believe what I'm bringing to it only enriches opera. Many times I'm asked, 'How can you be from a small town in the Midwest and sing Mozart?' Mozart was a human being with emotions and a sense of humor . . . we all share these qualities as human beings. As a black performer in opera . . . I grew up on the music of the sixties, the Motown sound, and I was touched and moved and formed in some way by that."

EDUCATION

Battle was educated at the local public schools in Portsmouth, and she graduated from Portsmouth High School in 1966. Although she always excelled in music and was encouraged to study voice in college, she also did well in math and science, and she almost chose math as her major. Instead, she entered the College Conservatory at the University of Cincinnati in 1966. Battle is known for her practical, straightforward approach to life and work, and, after deciding on music, she chose to pursue a degree in music education rather than music performance so that she "could have something to fall back on."

After receiving both her bachelor's degree and master's degree from Cincinnati, Battle taught music to eleven- and twelve-year-old students in Cincinnati's predominately black inner city schools for two years. She continued to study music, movement, and acting, and in 1972, she received her first big break. The late Thomas Schippers, then the conductor of the Cincinnati Symphony, chose Battle to sing the soprano lead in Johannes

Brahms's *German Requiem* for a performance he was directing at the Spoleto Festival of Two Worlds. The Spoleto Festival, founded by Schippers and composer Gian Carlo Menotti, takes place yearly in Spoleto, Italy, and Charleston, South Carolina. Battle's professional debut took place in Spoleto, Italy, and the experience gave her career its focus.

CHOOSING A CAREER

"That night was very magical for me," Battle said of her Spoleto debut. "After that experience I knew I wanted to be a singer and that somehow I would find a way to pursue music as a career."

CAREER HIGHLIGHTS

Her professional path was also helped by the important friendship and encouragement of a fellow musician from Cincinnati, James Levine, the director of the Metropolitan Opera in New York City. He first heard Battle in performance with the Cincinnati Symphony, and he was immediately taken with her talent. "I was blown away by that first audition," he recalls. "Some singers have little instinct but do have the intellect to balance technical and musical issues. Some have instinct and a beautiful voice but less intellect. I had never come across a more complete talent than hers." He became a trusted colleague and advisor, and when she moved to New York City in 1975, he continued to guide her career.

Battle arrived with $5,000 and the dream of becoming a star; with hard work and talent she realized those dreams. She came to New York City as an understudy in Scott Joplin's *Tremonisha*, and took over the title role in 1975. Her opera debut came in 1976 with the New York City Opera in the role of Susanna in Wolfgang Amadeus Mozart's *The Marriage of Figaro*, one of the many roles with which she has become closely identified. Her Met debut came in 1977, when Levine cast her as the Shepard in Richard Wagner's *Tannhauser*. Both of these performances received widespread praise, and her career blossomed.

Battle is known as a "coloratura," or lyric soprano, which means that her voice is light and agile. She has a range of two-and-a half octaves, from a low A to a high E. Critics have used every superlative to describe her voice, calling it "like Devonshire cream from a pitcher," having a "special silver purity," with "a shimmer, a gleam, above all, a heart." Yet the roles that have made her famous are not the starring roles of opera. She does not perform the leading roles of Tosca in the famous opera of that name, or Mimi in *La Boheme*; rather, she has won fame for her roles as the *soubrette*, or female servant, light and playful parts requiring a high, light, flexible voice. Throughout the mid-1970s and 1980s, she won fame for what are called the "-ina" and "-etta" roles, including Rosina in *The Barber of*

Seville, Despina in *Cosi fan tutte,* Zerlina in *Don Giovanni,* Pamina in *The Magic Flute,* Adina in *The Elixir of Love,* and Zerbinetta in *Ariadne auf Naxos.* For many listeners, she brings something special to these roles. In the words of her manager, Samuel M. Niefeld: "Historically, the girls with her repertory are pretty little things. They come in. The conductor pats them on the head and tells them to chirp. Kathy has a sensuality her colleagues do not. Her Zerbinetta is a thinking-man's Zerbinetta, not a tweety bird."

As her reputation has grown, she has worked with the leading conductors and artists of the time, including Sir Georg Solti and Herbert von Karajan, two European masters of symphony and opera performance; she also has continued to appear with James Levine and the Met in New York. Several of her most important performances occurred in the mid-1980s, including her work in George Friedrich Handel's *Semele* and in his *Solomon.* Andrew Porter of *The New Yorker* described her singing in *Solomon* as "the most ravishing performance of a Handel air I have ever heard." In 1985 she sang the role of Zerbinetta in *Ariadne auf Naxos* in her Covent Garden debut in England. Her performance was a triumph and won her the prestigious Laurence Olivier award. She was the first American to receive the honor.

Battle has gained the reputation as the leading soprano of her generation, and also the reputation as someone who comes to each rehearsal and performance thoroughly prepared. In her pursuit of perfection in what she does, she has sometimes been described as "difficult." Yet most admirers, including the *New York Times's* Bernard Holland, believe that what she demands of herself and her colleagues is done "in the name of the music" rather than for personal gain. For Battle, ego and artistry are linked: "In the arts, ego must play a part. I defy any performers to say they were selfless in making their way in the opera world." She claims that she has not faced racial discrimination in her rise to fame, saying that she has "no axe to grind" on the issue.

Battle is a singer who knows her voice: its strengths and weaknesses, and its suitability for different roles. Many singers damage their voices by trying to sing beyond their range and strength, and Battle is determined not to do that. She sings some 60 recitals a year and schedules her performances three years in advance. She trains constantly, not just with singing coaches, but also to perfect her ability to sing each language, whether French, Italian, German, or other foreign language, accurately and with the correct feeling. Yet she is always careful not to damage her voice with oversinging: "I won't stretch or pull my voice beyond its capacity and capability," she says. "In this business you have to be careful about scheduling or you pay an awful price—your voice." Her repertoire is broad, for in addition to her famous opera roles, Battle has also chosen to perform a number of recitals each year, where she sings songs of Handel and Mozart (a true favorite), as well as those of George Gershwin, Duke Ellington, and other modern composers.

She has always included spirituals in her recitals, and one of her most famous recordings was done in 1991 with soprano star Jessye Norman, in a performance that was also recorded for television. Her work with Jessye Norman is part of a series of successful collaborations she has done with other stars of the classical music world, including guitarist Chrisopher Parkening, flutist Jean-Pierre Rampal, violinist Itzhak Perlman, and, most recently, trumpeter Wynton Marsalis. In addition to the televised recital with Norman, she appeared in late 1992 in a televised performance of the opera *Un Ballo en Maschera* with renowned Italian tenor Luciano Pavorotti, and in a solo recital filmed in the Metropolitan Museum of Art. All of these recent performances continue to add to her reputation as an artist of range and talent, a singer at the height of her powers whose ability to delight and inspire audiences has not diminished.

Battle did not debut in New York City's famous Carnegie Hall until 1991. When she did, another famous singer was in the audience. "I'm grateful this evening for the presence of the great Miss Marian Anderson," said Battle, and sang Rachmaninoff's *In the Silence of the Secret Night* as a tribute to the singer.

MEMORABLE EXPERIENCES

Her career has contained many milestones, including a performance for the Pope. "We were in the apse of St. Peter's," she remembers. "The altar is off to our right and a little in front of us. After everyone is in place, the procession begins, and John Paul II is at the end, in full vestments. It's hard to speak of it as a musical occasion. It was a moment in life that one treasures. Oh, it was great to be there."

MARRIAGE AND FAMILY

Battle is single, and she is fiercely protective of her private life. "My personal life

is just that," she told one interviewer. She has an apartment on the Upper West Side of Manhattan and a home in Quogue, Long Island.

HOBBIES AND OTHER INTERESTS

Battle enjoys gardening and playing tennis for relaxation. She also loves clothes, and told *Vogue* magazine that they are her "most important hobby." Her many beautiful gowns for her recitals are created by costume designer Rouben Ter-Artununian. Battle is a strikingly attractive woman, called by *Time* magazine "the undisputed best-dressed concert performer in the business." The effect onstage is ravishing, and her audiences enjoy the spectacle: "In a live performance, who doesn't listen with their eyes as well?" says Battle.

HONORS AND AWARDS

Grammy Award: 1986, for *Mozart Arias*; 1987 (2 awards), for *Ariadne auf Naxos* and for *Salzburg Recital*

RECORDINGS

Mozart: *Mozart Arias*, Andre Previn conducting, 1985
Mozart: *Cosi fan tutte*, Ricardo Muti conducting, 1986
Strauss: *Ariadne auf Naxos*, James Levine conducting, 1986
Mozart: *Don Giovanni*, Herbert von Karajan conducting, 1986
Salzburg Recital [with James Levine], 1986
Mozart: *The Abduction of the Seraglio*, Georg Solti conducting, 1984
Handel: *Messiah*, Andrew Davis conducting, 1988
Kathleen Battle and Placido Domingo: Live in Tokyo 1988, 1989
Kathleen Battle and Jessye Norman: Spirituals in Concert, 1991
The Bach Album [with Itzhak Perlman], 1992
Baroque Duet [with Wynton Marsalis], 1992

FURTHER READING

BOOKS

Story, Rosalyn M. *And So I Sing: African-American Divas of Opera and Concert*, 1990
Who's Who among Black Americans, 1992-1993
Who's Who in America, 1992-1993

PERIODICALS

Chicago Tribune, Apr. 21, 1985, p.C12; June 26, 1986, p.C13; Oct. 5, 1989, p.C7
Connoisseur, Feb. 1985, p.108
Current Biography Yearbook 1984
Miami Herald, Dec. 31, 1989, p.K1

New York, Sept. 16, 1985, p.66; Oct. 5, 1992, p.107
New York Times Biographical Service, Nov. 1985, p.1364
Stereo Review, July 1992, p.81; Sept. 1992, p.76
Time, Nov. 11, 1985, p.93

ADDRESS

Columbia Artists Management Inc.
165 W. 57th Street
New York, NY 10019

Candice Bergen   1946-
American Actress, Photojournalist,
and Author
Star of "Murphy Brown"

BIRTH

Candice Bergen was born May 9, 1946, in Beverly Hills, California, to Edgar and Frances (Westerman) Bergen. Her mother was
a former model, and her father was a famous ventriloquist, whose
wooden dummy, Charlie McCarthy, had been delighting
audiences for decades at the time of Candy's birth. Candice Bergen
was a child of Hollywood, and many members of the press, who
scrutinized every aspect of her life from childhood on, made much
of the idea that she was Charlie's "sister"—at least until her brother,
Kris, was born when she was fifteen.

YOUTH

Candy Bergen grew up in wealth and privilege among Hollywood's richest and brightest stars. She was raised in the Beverly Hills suburb of Bel Air, with neighbors and family friends that included Ronald Reagan, Dick Powell, Jimmy Stewart, Arthur Rubinstein, and David O. Selznick. She remembers riding the toy train at "Uncle Walt" Disney's estate, and playing with the children of other stars. At Christmas time, "tinseltown" made up for the lack of snow by draping the trees with white flock to mimic the mythical "White Christmases" celebrated in the movies. Candy's own Christmas memories include attending parties where Santa was played by David Niven or Charlton Heston, stars of Hollywood's Golden Age and close family friends. Her private life was so public that when her pet turtle died, the "funeral" was attended by the press and the photographs ran in the *Saturday Evening Post*.

Birthday parties were ambitious extravaganzas, "lavish competitions in professional skill, loving displays of parental pride," Bergen recalls in her autobiography *Knock Wood*. "Most seemed to agree that the Oscar for Best Birthday Given by a Parent went to Vincent Minnelli for Liza's sixth given at Ira Gershwin's house in Beverly Hills. The Gershwin lawn rolled on forever, and in the center, children spun slowly on a many-colored carousel, while others clustered round the Magic Lady—a woman in a long blue gown sprinkled with stars who pulled doves from her sleeves and rabbits from hats. There were hot-dog stands and ice-cream cones and clouds of cotton candy. Clowns clowned and jugglers juggled and sleek, shining ponies circled the lawn at a tiny, clipped canter for any child who wanted a ride. It was a fairy-tale gift to a daughter from a father who was a master at making fairy tales come true."

Despite the sensational aspects of a Hollywood childhood, the Bergens tried hard to give their daughter direction in her world. "My parents made every effort to give me a sense of values so that I was ultimately much less spoiled than other kids with whom I grew up. I mean, I was the kid who had to earn her allowance and make her bed and didn't get a Corvette and all that stuff."

EARLY MEMORIES

Candice Bergen remembers spending a good deal of her young life trying to win her father's affection. This withdrawn man had a hard time showing emotion and letting those around him know that he loved them. He had created a hugely successful career as the "straight man" to his dummy, Charlie McCarthy, who was all wit and bluster, able to say the kinds of things Edgar Bergen could, or would, not. One of Candy's earliest memories is of spending Sundays with her father, when he would put

Charlie on one knee and her on the other, squeeze her neck, and speak for both of them. She cherished the Sunday afternoons they would spend flying to remote areas of California in her father's private plane, and riding the horses he bought for her. When she was six, she made her first appearance on her father's famous radio show, performing alongside Charlie and learning to play for the laughs.

EDUCATION

Candy was educated at the exclusive Westlake School for Girls in Bel Air. She was a good student, but she also remembers "clowning, wisecracking, and throwing my voice in class." When she was fourteen, she spent a year at a Swiss school, Montesano, where, she convinced her parents, she would learn about European culture. Instead, she learned to smoke and drink, and she bleached her hair. When her parents arrived for Christmas, they were appalled at the changes in Candy; after a long talk, they all decided that California was where she belonged. She graduated from Westlake, and in her last year was elected May Queen of the senior class.

In the fall of 1964, Bergen left California for the Ivy League world of the University of Pennsylvania in Philadelphia, where she was elected Homecoming Queen in her freshman year. The *Philadelphia Enquirer* ran a picture with the caption: "Charlie's Sister Homecoming Queen—No Dummy She." That spring, she began a modeling career in New York.

Bergen has always been a stunningly attractive woman, which she has considered more of a handicap than a virtue. Her father had told her that she would have to work harder at whatever she did to make people think she was smart and accomplished. "Something about the way I looked seemed to matter so much to other people; in fact, for a time, it seemed to be the *only* thing that mattered, leaving me to feel beside the point, practically an intruder on my looks." But without question, both her looks and her status as the daughter of a famous star opened doors for her throughout her career, doors that might have otherwise been closed. "I've had a lot of things handed to me and I'm still working through some of the guilt that involves," she admits.

Returning to Penn, she continued her studies, but only half-heartedly. She began her acting career, landing the role of Alma in Tennessee Williams's *Summer and Smoke,* for which she received the Best Actress and Most Creative Student Award. But she grew less interested in school than in the money she could make modeling. She rented an apartment in Manhattan and spent less and less time in Philadelphia. At the end of her sophomore year, she was kicked out, after flunking opera and art.

CHOOSING A CAREER

While at Penn, Bergen had met Mary Ellen Mark, who later became a celebrated photographer and who taught Bergen about the craft. Studying the works of the masters of photography, Bergen was particularly impressed with Margaret Bourke-White, an outstanding photojournalist who had been a pioneer for women in the field. After leaving Penn, Bergen thought about a career in photography, continued to model, and also began to make films. She made her film debut in *The Group* in 1966, playing the lesbian Lakey. Bergen was the only actress in the movie who was totally untrained, and it showed. For her performance, she received the types of reviews that would plague her work for years. The film critic Pauline Kael claimed Bergen "doesn't know how to move, she cannot say her lines so that one sounds different from the one before. As an actress her only flair is in her nostrils."

The criticism hurt, and so did the response of readers when she wrote of her film experiences in *Esquire*. Bergen had written a candid, humorous piece about life on the set of the movie, and people simply wouldn't believe she had the talent to have written it.

CAREER HIGHLIGHTS

Despite her success today, Bergen's acting career got off to a shaky start. Over the next several years, she made a number of movies, most of them forgettable. She claims she took the roles more for their locale than for their substance, because they offered her a chance to see the world. She played opposite Steve McQueen in *The Sand Pebbles* (1966), filmed in the Far East, and *The Day the Fish Came Out* (1967), filmed in Greece. Her next movie, made in Paris, was Claude Lelouche's *Live for Life* (1967). She also began to travel with the "jet set," dancing in discos till dawn and staying on ancestral estates in Europe for the hunting season, but she grew weary of the lifestyle and returned to California to family and old friends.

Now in her early twenties, Bergen still seemed to want to straddle several careers. She made several more notably bad movies, including *The Magus* (1969), *Getting Straight* (1970), and *The Adventurers* (1970). Reviewers routinely panned her performances, as in this comment on the last-named film: "Miss Bergen performs as though clubbed over the head." Still keeping a hand in photojournalism, she produced articles for *Esquire* and *Cosmopolitan*. In 1968, she hit the campaign trail, traveling with the press who covered the presidential contest that year, despite the fact that until then she really wasn't clear just what a "primary" was. That same year, a twelve-page play she had written in college, *The Freezer*, was selected as a Best Short Play, and when it was performed, she received a whopping $6.75 as a royalty.

At this time, she was living with Terry Melcher, a record producer who was the son of actress Doris Day. Melcher introduced her to political activism, which came as a shock to the daughter of conservative Republicans. Melcher was being hounded by a strange, counterculture type named Charles Manson, who wanted Melcher to make a recording of him and his group. When Melcher and Bergen moved out of their California house, they leased it to Sharon Tate and Roman Polanski. Weeks later, Tate and several friends were brutally murdered by Manson and his gang; Bergen and Melcher had narrowly escaped being Manson's victims.

More forgettable films, such as the witless sex-and-violence piece *Soldier Blue* (1970) followed. But she was given a chance to truly show her talents in Mike Nichols's *Carnal Knowledge* (1971), where she costarred with Jack Nicholson and Art Garfunkel and which she described as "dreamlike, idyllic—like working in a state of grace."

Bergen continued to be involved in political activism throughout the early 1970s, taking part in a sleep-in at Alcatraz prison and getting arrested in Washington, D.C., during a protest against the Vietnam War. Photojournalism assignments also came her way, including exclusive photo rights to Charlie Chaplin's return to the U.S. after years in self-imposed exile in Europe. She also traveled to China on assignment for *Playboy*, which resulted in the article, "Can a Cultural Worker from Beverly Hills Find Happiness in the People's Republic of China?" During a trip to Africa, she met and interviewed Emperor Haile Selassie, photographed members of the Masai tribe in Nairobi, and visited Jane Goodall in Tanzania, where she chronicled the work of the legendary animal behaviorist. Her photojournalism won her an offer from NBC to present occasional pieces on the "Today" show, and she was considered for a position on "60 Minutes."

Turning 30 in 1976, Bergen went through a brief period of deep depression. She just couldn't seem to get her life together. "I just think I had always set it up for myself that 30 was a milestone by which time I wanted to have certain things—a husband, a family—but I didn't feel I would have them. I knew it was my last gasp . . . that if I didn't get myself in hand, if I didn't fix stuff in myself that was dopey and self-destructive *now*, then I wasn't going to fix it, and it would be too late."

Two years later she was devastated by the death of her father. This was a period of a great deal of soul-searching for Bergen. She began to collect notes for the autobiography she would publish in 1984 as *Knock Wood*, driven by the need to understand her life and particularly her father's place in it. This heartfelt, poignant, and funny memoir spent several weeks on the best-seller list.

In the late 1970s, she finally began to hit her stride, starring in a comedy for the first time, *Starting Over* (1979), with Burt Reynolds. She played a singer with a terrible voice who leaves her husband to start a singing career. She was a hit and received an Oscar nomination for Best Supporting Actress for her work. Next came another comedic role opposite Jacqueline Bisset in *Rich and Famous* (1981). She continued to make a comic name for herself through several guest hosting stints on NBC's "Saturday Night Live." After her marriage to French filmmaker Louis Malle in 1980 and the birth of her daughter, Chloe, in 1985, Bergen was content to stay at the family's home in the south of France for several years and devote herself to motherhood. But in 1987, she returned to Hollywood and television to star in "Mayflower Madame," happy to be back to work.

"MURPHY BROWN"

It was while aboard an airplane that Bergen found the role for which she is best known today. She first read the script for "Murphy Brown," the CBS hit focussing on the outspoken, wisecracking television journalist, while on a flight to the U.S. in 1987. She loved the role and was determined to get it. She made her first phone call from an airplane to her agent, asking her to call Diane English, the show's producer.

English wasn't sure at first that Bergen, who had the reputation for being cool and self-contained, could handle the role of the rough and cantankerous Murphy. But "as I've gotten to know her," English claims, "she is more like the character than I ever expected. Although the public

Candice is very tactful, cool, and patrician, the private Candice, which she reveals to those she knows is somebody who'll put a whoopee cushion on your chair. She's wickedly funny. She can be very impatient. She'll say exactly what's on her mind, which always takes you by surprise. It's real Murphy."

Set in Washington, D.C., "Murphy Brown" chronicles the lives of the news team of "FYI," a television news magazine loosely based on "60 Minutes," ironically the show that once considered Bergen for a correspondent's position. In the company of Grant Shaud as Miles Silverberg, Joe Regalbuto as Frank Fontane, Charles Kimbrough as Jim Dyle, and Faith Ford as Corky Sherwood Forest, Bergen is part of a terrific acting ensemble that has brought the show top ratings in the four seasons since its debut in the fall of 1988. In that time, the show has dealt with topics as different as Murphy's trip to the Betty Ford Clinic for alcohol addiction to her discovery that, at forty, she is pregnant without a husband.

Bergen and English found themselves involved in the political fray in the 1992 presidential election when then-Vice President Dan Quayle criticized the show for glorifying Murphy Brown's single motherhood. The accusations made headlines across the country, much to everyone's surprise. "I don't know what goes on inside Dan Quayle's mind," said Bergen. "and I'm very happy for that mystery to stay intact. It's a landscape I don't especially want to explore." Husband Louis Malle had this to say: "Tell Dan Quayle from us that a woman working is good. In fact, Marilyn should go back to work." When the brouhaha became part of the election, Bergen commented: "It's been a surrealistic episode in this country's political life. As Ross Perot said, only in America could this become a campaign issue."

MARRIAGE AND FAMILY

Bergen married French filmmaker Louis Malle at his home in France on September 27, 1980. Their daughter, Chloe, was born November 8, 1985. As a mother trying to raise a child in Hollywood, Bergen is unhappy with the modern-day spirit of her old home town. "I find all of that very offensive, the way people want to display their wealth rather than put it to use in something creative and productive. I find the oblivion and narcissism and self-involvement and lack of information about everything except the film business really appalling. People's preoccupation with their looks and their clothes at a time when there's so much suffering in the country—I find it grotesque."

Bergen is making every effort to avoid the pitfalls of a celebrity childhood: "I'm raising her very similarly to the way I was raised. She has much less expensive clothes and fewer toys, less expensive toys, than a lot of kids she knows."

Malle has two children from previous relationships, Cuote, now 21, and Justine, 18. Bergen is a devoted stepmother to them both. Bergen and Malle currently have homes in California, New York, and France, and they spend a good deal of the year apart, due to their working schedules and Malle's professed dislike for L.A.

HOBBIES AND OTHER INTERESTS

Bergen is active in a number of charities, including the Starlight Foundation, which grants the wishes of children with terminal diseases.

HONORS AND AWARDS

Hasty Pudding Woman of the Year (Harvard College Hasty Pudding Theatricals): 1979
Emmy Award: 1989, 1990
Golden Globe Award: 1989

WRITINGS

Knock Wood, 1984

PERFORMANCES

FILMS

The Group, 1966
The Sand Pebbles, 1966
Carnal Knowledge, 1971
The Wind and the Lion, 1975
Starting Over, 1979
Rich and Famous, 1981

TELEVISION

"Hollywood Wives," 1985
"Mayflower Madame," 1987
"Murphy Brown," 1988-

FURTHER READING

BOOKS

Bergen, Candice. *Knock Wood,* 1984
Contemporary Theatre, Film, and Television, Vol. 3
Who's Who of American Women, 1991-92

PERIODICALS

Cosmopolitan, Nov. 1989, p.223
Current Biography 1976
Good Housekeeping, Mar. 1989, p.72; Feb. 1990, p.158
Harper's Bazaar, Aug. 1989, p.139; Mar. 1991, p.153
Ladies' Home Journal, June 1990, p.128
McCall's, Oct. 1991, p.109
Newsweek, Mar. 13, 1989, p.55
People, Dec. 12, 1991, p.159
Redbook, Apr. 1989, p.44
Rolling Stone, Jan. 26, 1989, p.18
Saturday Evening Post, May 1992, p.39
Time, Sep. 21, 1992, p.48
TV Guide, Dec. 23, 1989, p.4
Us, Oct. 30, 1989, p.85
Vanity Fair, Dec. 1992, p.224

ADDRESS

PMK
955 S. Carillo Dr., #200
Los Angeles, CA 90048

Boutros Boutros-Ghali   1922-
Egyptian Diplomat, Politician, and
Legal Scholar
Secretary General of the United Nations

BIRTH

Boutros Boutros-Ghali (BOO-trohs BOO-trohs GAH-lee), the first
Arab and first man from the African continent to serve as secretary
general of the United Nations, was born November 14, 1922, in
Cairo. His family was one of the most distinguished and politically
active clans in Egypt: his father was once that nation's minister
of finance, and his grandfather, Boutros Pasha-Ghali, served for
more than a year as prime minister until his assassination in
February 1910 by a radical Muslim student.

YOUTH

Boutros Boutros-Ghali was reared in affluence in the formal traditions of Egypt's Coptic-Christian society. Little has been published in English of his early years, but it is known that, even as a youth, he was scholarly and articulate and had a fine sense of humor that is still recognized as one of his most appealing characteristics. He was exposed to Western culture early in life and became fluent in French and English, as well as Arabic. In spite of his English proficiency, though, he speaks the language with a slight French accent, reflecting the influence of his student years in Paris.

EDUCATION

The young man who was to rise through academic and diplomatic circles to the most prestigious post in international service earned a bachelor of laws degree from Cairo University in 1946. Three years later, he received a Ph.D. in international law from the University of Paris, the institution more commonly known as the Sorbonne. Boutros-Ghali also has separate diplomas in higher studies in political science, economics, and public law, all earned at the Sorbonne. He later was a Fulbright research scholar at Columbia University in New York in 1954-55.

CAREER HIGHLIGHTS

In preparing for his eventual diplomatic career, Boutros-Ghali spent years in professional and academic activities. For 30 years, from 1949 to 1979, he was a professor of international law and chairman of the Department of Political Sciences at Cairo University. He was also, in 1963-64, director of the Center of Research of The Hague Academy of International Law, in the Netherlands. In 1960, Boutros-Ghali founded the publication *Al Ahram Iktiaadi*, which he edited for 15 years.

A no-nonsense man with a reputation for fairness, Boutros-Ghali accompanied the late Anwar Sadat on his historic mission to Jerusalem in 1977. His role in the Mideast peace process was pivotal. According to *Current Biography*, Boutros-Ghali "was an architect of the Camp David accords the following year, making possible the Egyptian-Israeli peace treaty of 1979."

Yet he had other political roles as well. Boutros-Ghali was a member of the Central Committee of the Arab Socialist Union in the mid-1970s, acting foreign minister under Sadat Briefly during 1977, and Egypt's Minister of State from 1977 to 1991. He has also been a member of the Egyptian parliament since 1987 and president of the Center of Political and Strategic Studies at Al-Ahram (Egypt) since 1975. He helped to forge the American-led coalition during the Gulf War in 1990 and was also instrumental in gaining the release of Nelson Mandela from prison in 1990. His activities on behalf of the UN include heading the Egyptian delegation to the UN General Assembly in 1979, 1982, and 1990.

THE UNITED NATIONS

In taking over the influential and demanding position of secretary general of the United Nations on January 1, 1992, Boutros-Ghali brought with him a lifetime of experience in international politics and diplomacy. As the first Arab and the first African to head the giant organization whose purpose is the promotion of international cooperation, Boutros-Ghali succeeds only five other secretaries general: Trygve Lie of Norway (1946- 53), Dag Hammarskjold of Sweden (1953-61), U Thant of Burma (1961- 71), Kurt Waldheim of Austria (1972-81) and, most recently, Javier Pérez de Cuéllar of Peru (1981-91).

It is the role of the secretary general to present problems and situations warranting their concern to the different bodies and agencies within the UN, such as UNESCO, the World Health Organization, and the Food and Agricultural Organization. The secretary's duties include the administration of a large staff, which is made up of a diverse group of individuals from around the world whose job is to work exclusively in the interests of the UN.

The secretary general of the United Nations is elected by the 166-member General Assembly, after being recommended by the 15-member Security Council, and in the case of Boutros-Ghali the recommendation was unanimous. Boutros-Ghali campaigned hard for his appointment, and his election impressed such specialists as former Carter official William B. Quandt, who called him "as international-minded as they come," praising him as "a walking UN in his own personal experience, and very fair-minded." Boutros-Ghali conceded, however, in an interview soon after his selection, that five years [before that time] he "would not have sought the position. The UN was not in good shape then, but I think that today it can fulfill its promise."

PLANS FOR THE FUTURE

The secretary general's concerns for the UN are many. He sees the need for down-scaling the huge and cumbersome organizational structure and is pressing for financial stability in order to meet obligations. "Every day we receive new demands, " he says. He is anxious, also, to maintain a permanent peacekeeping force, insisting that "the United Nations must never again be crippled as it was in the cold-war era that has now passed." His current concerns include its peacekeeping missions in Bosnia, the continued Arab-Israel conflict in the Middle East, the plight of millions in danger of starvation in Somalia and other parts of sub-Saharan Africa, and the continued investigation into human rights abuses around the world.

MARRIAGE AND FAMILY

Boutros-Ghali is married to the former Leah Nadler, a member of a prominent Egyptian-Jewish family from Alexandria. They have no children. Their home is in Cairo, on the west bank of the Nile and near the Great Sphinx and the pyramids.

An interesting note to Boutros-Ghali's background is that he, as a Copt, is a descendant of the world's oldest Christian community, and that the Coptic language (now used only for church ritual) is a variant of ancient Egyptian.

HOBBIES AND OTHER INTERESTS

Although he is slightly built and does not project an image of vigor, the seventy-year-old Boutros-Ghali remains active, swimming whenever his busy schedule permits. He is an early riser and spends the first hours of his day reading, writing in his diary, or working on literary projects. Currently, he is in the process of translating African literature into Arabic. One of Boutros-Ghali's avid interests is collecting Greek antiquities.

WRITINGS

The more than 100 publications and numerous articles that Boutros-Ghali has authored, mostly in French, deal with regional and international affairs, law and diplomacy, and political science. *Foreign Policies in World Change*, a 1963 publication, is among the few available in English.

HONORS AND AWARDS

Order of the Republic, First Class, Egypt
Grand Croix de l'Ordre de la Couvonne, Belgium
Cavaliere de Gran Crice, Italy
Gran Cruz de la Orden de Boyaca, Colombia
Gran Cruz de la Orden de Antonio José de la Irisarri, Guatemala
Grand Officier de la Légion d'Honneur, France
Gran Cruz de la Orden Nacional Al Merito, Ecuador
Gran Cruz de la Orden del Liberacion San Martin, Argentina
Trishakti Patta, Nepal
Grand Croix de l'Ordre du Mérite du Grand Duché de Luxembourg
Great Cross of the Order of Infante Dom Henrique, Portugal
Grand Officier de l'Ordre du Mérite du Niger
Grand Officier de l'Ordre du Mérite du Mali
La Condecoracion de Aguila Azteca, Mexico
Ordre Phoenix-Grand Cordon (premier ordre), Greece
Grand Cordon du Mérite, Chile
Order of the Crown, Brunei
Grand Cross of the Order of Merit, Federal Republic of Germany

Gran Cruz del Sol, Peru
Commandeur de l'Ordre du Mérite National, Ivory Coast
Grand Croix de l'Ordre du Danebrog, Denmark
Grand Officier de l'Ordre du Mérite Centraficain, Central African
   Republic
Commander Grand Cross of the Order of the Polar Star, Sweden
Order of Diplomatic Service Merit, Korea

In addition, Boutros-Ghali holds the prestigious decoration conferred by
the Order of the Knights of Malta, the most celebrated religious military
order of the Middle Ages. The award is titled Grand Croix de l'Ordre Pro
Merito Melitensi de l'Ordre Souverain Militaire et Hospitalier de St. Jean
de Jerusalem de Rhodes de Malta.

FURTHER READING

BOOKS

International Who's Who, 1992-93

PERIODICALS

Current Biography Yearbook 1992
Economist, Feb. 15, 1992, p.47; Aug. 8, 1992, p.31
New Statesman & Society, July 10, 1992, p.10
New York Times, Nov. 22, 1991, p.A1; Dec. 30, 1991, p.A1; May 3, 1992, p.A10
Time, Feb. 3, 1992, p.28
U.S. News & World Report, Dec. 2, 1991, p.13

ADDRESS

Office of the Secretary General
United Nations
New York, NY 10017

Chris Burke 1965-
American Actor
Played Corky Thatcher on "Life Goes On"
First Actor with Down's Syndrome to Star
in a Television Series

BIRTH

Christopher Burke was born August 26, 1965, in New York City
to Francis D. and Marian Brady Burke. Francis was a policeman
and Marian was a trade show manager. Chris was their fourth child;
sisters Ellen and Anne and brother J.R. are older. Several hours
after Chris's birth, his parents were told that he had Down's syndrome. "They said that it was likely that Chris might never be
able to feed and dress himself, or read and write, and they recommended that we institutionalize him," his mother remembers.

DOWN'S SYNDROME

Down's syndrome affects 250,000 Americans, and 5,000 babies each year are born with the condition. It is a congenital disorder, which is caused by an extra chromosome received at conception. People with Down's syndrome suffer mild to moderate mental retardation and share common facial features. Until recently, many children born with Down's were often raised away from their families. They were called "mongoloids," a term coined by Dr. J.L.H Down, who discovered the syndrome. Dr. Down believed that the white race was superior and that Asian, or "mongoloid" peoples, with the type of slant eyes characteristic of Down's syndrome, were inferior. For years people with Down's syndrome were condemned to a life of prejudice based on false perceptions of their true abilities. As recently as 15 years ago, parents like the Burkes were encouraged to institutionalize their kids with Down's syndrome, to accept that they were severely handicapped, and to be prepared for their early death. But now attitudes are different. People with Down's are doing things that no one a generation ago thought possible, and Chris Burke's success as an actor is both a tribute to this new thinking and an inspiration to others.

YOUTH

The Burkes ignored their doctor's advice and took Chris home, where the entire family took part in his upbringing. "It was like having five parents," they say. His development was delayed—he didn't speak until he was 18 months old, whereas most children begin to speak when they are around 12 months old, and he didn't walk until he was two years old, unlike most children who take their first steps between 12 and 15 months. But the family was determined to give him every chance and to provide him the additional love and encouragement he needed. "We showed him how to feed himself and, using flash cards, we taught him how to read. By the time he was five, he could even write his name," recalls his mother.

Now parents of Down's kids are taught methods of infant stimulation and exercise to prompt their children's growth; the Burkes just did it as part of raising Chris. His sisters would sit with him in front of the mirror, teaching him the words for eyes, ears, and nose while they pointed his hand to his features. He would try to repeat the words, and when he got them right, they would cheer him on. Most people who meet the adult Chris Burke talk about his warm, good-natured personality, and even as a toddler, he strove to do the best he could, with smiles and humor for his teachers. His brother taught him how to swim and play ball with endless patience. His siblings also helped their brother deal with the prejudice he encountered. Sometimes, when his mother would take Chris to a park, the mothers of the other children playing would take their kids away. Once J.R. heard other kids making fun of Chris. He didn't threaten them, he just said: "He can hear what you're saying. You could be more considerate." They got the message.

Even so, Chris has memories of being taken advantage of, sometimes cruelly. When he was eight, a local bully shoved pine needles down his throat. He almost died of the infection that resulted from the brutal attack. He also remembers when his class would be asked to sit in a separate area of a public place while on field trips.

EDUCATION

Unlike many Down's kids today, and unlike Corky Thatcher, the character he played on ABC's "Life Goes On," Chris Burke was not "mainstreamed," that is, he did not attend regular public schools. He went first to the Kennedy Child Study Center in New York City, a special education facility where he got his first taste of theater. His older siblings had been in commercials as kids, and Chris wanted to work in front of the camera, too. He often told his family that he was going to Hollywood. At the Kennedy school, he had one line in the school production of *The Emperor's New Clothes*, and he was hooked. He then went to the Cardinal Cushing School in Hanover, Massachusetts. He later attended the Don Cuanella School in Springfield, Pennsylvania. He moved back to New York and lived with his parents, continuing his love of movies and theater by taking night classes in filmmaking and improvisation at the Young Adult Institute.

FIRST JOBS

Chris wanted to work with handicapped kids, and his first job after school was as an elevator operator at a school for the handicapped in New York City. He also worked as an aide at P.S. 138 in New York City, a facility for the severely handicapped, where his niece, Nora, was a pupil. In addition, he volunteered at a camp for the handicapped.

CHOOSING A CAREER

In 1987 Chris was watching an episode of "Fall Guy" on television and saw the performance of Jason Kingsley, a young actor with Down's syndrome. He sent off a letter to Kingsley, and the two began a pen-pal friendship. In 1989, Michael Braverman, a television producer, was casting a pilot for a show entitled "Desperate," for which he needed an actor with Down's syndrome. He called Jason's mother, Emily Kingsley, who has served as a consultant to "Sesame Street" and as a producer of the show "Kids Like These," to ask if she had any ideas. She thought immediately of Chris, and soon Chris and his father flew out to Hollywood to test for the part. He got it!

The pilot never resulted in a full-time series, but the executives for ABC who saw Chris's performance loved him. They asked Braver-

man to develop a show for him, and that's how "Life Goes On" came
to be.

CAREER HIGHLIGHTS

"LIFE GOES ON"

First broadcast in 1989, "Life Goes On" chronicled the lives of the
Thatcher family. Chris played Corky, the middle child of Libby and Drew
Thatcher. The show, praised by *New York Times* critic John J. O'Connor as
"sensitively written, wonderfully cast, and beautifully executed," was
noted for its poignant treatment of a middle-class family facing the
problems of modern life, as well as the challenges of raising a child with
Down's syndrome. The cast included Broadway star Patti LuPone as Libby,
TV veteran Bill Smitrovich as Drew, Monique Lanier as Paige, and Kellie
Martin as younger sister Becca. In the first episode, Corky, 18, is being
mainstreamed into regular public school, where he and Becca are
both freshman.

The show dealt with the continuing debate on how kids with Down's and
other disabilities deal with entering the "mainstream" world of other
students without handicaps. Early episodes showed Corky being used
by a cruel fellow student who
goads him into running for
class president as a joke.
Corky's sensitive response,
when he's made aware of
what's been done to him,
indicated the depth and
tenderness of both the actor
and the show. The realities of
life for disabled students were
dealt with throughout the
series, including the teasing,
the rejection, and even the
physical aggression the kids
encounter.

The writers, aware of Chris's
abilities, wrote dialogue
tailored to his needs. He has
a fifth-grade reading level, and
memorizing his lines was the
most difficult part of the show
for him. He worked with a
dialogue coach every day. "If

he gets nervous, he doesn't remember," said coach Kaley Goldberg. "Sometimes, we'll work on [his lines] for eight hours and we'll get to the set and he'll forget. Other times, his father will have him write out a particularly difficult line 10 times to remember it." Chris's dad, Francis Burke, retired from the police force and moved with Chris to California when "Life Goes On" began, and the two lived in a two-bedroom apartment. Chris's mom, Marian, remained in New York to continue her job as a trade show manager, visiting often.

The writers were also sensitive to Chris's capabilities when it came to having his character try a new task. "In terms of Corky, we ask, 'Could Chris do this?' and we translate that to Corky's character." For instance, there was an episode where Corky tries, and fails, to drive a car, an episode that mirrored Chris's own experience. But the writers did take dramatic license occasionally, as when Corky was first stumped and then solved a multiplication problem in math class that was beyond Chris's abilities.

The show received the highest praise from the families and friends of kids with Down's syndrome, as well as from the kids themselves. "Dear Chris," read a letter from a fan in Iowa, "I am 17 years old and I have Down's syndrome just like you. You are my hero. You have changed my world." However, some parents felt that Chris's portrayal of Corky offered unrealistic expectations for all Down's kids. Chris is referred to as "high functioning," meaning that the level of his disability is not as severe as some with Down's. Yet, as Chris's achievements prove, the full range of what a person with Down's can do is only now being explored. In the words of Donna Rosenthal, the executive director of the National Down's Syndrome Society, "Life Goes On" "really shows what a person with Down's syndrome can do—that they *can* be part of the community and grow and share. It shows how much people with Down's syndrome can give to others. And most importantly, [it shows] that they're *human*."

The producers formed an advisory board of Los Angeles teens with Down's, whose comments they used in evaluating the series. Prompted by the suggestion of one member, Andrea Freidman, that Corky should have a girlfriend, the producers chose Andrea herself to play the role of Corky's girlfriend, Amanda, in a series of episodes in the series' third season. In the fourth season, Corky and Amanda eloped, and one focus of the show became the concerns of a young couple with Down's syndrome coping with the problems of marriage.

In its last season, the series expanded to include more emphasis on the character of Becca, played by Kellie Martin, particularly her involvement with a character with AIDS.

After four years in one of the toughest spots in the television lineup—Sundays at 7:00 p.m., opposite CBS's "60 Minutes"—"Life Goes On" was canceled in the spring of 1993. Although the show had a small but loyal viewing audience, the ratings were never spectacular. And with co-star Patti Lupone's decision to leave the show to return to the stage, the producers decided to call it quits. Chris was always very close to his screen mother and knows that he will miss her. "Patti and I had a difficult time saying goodbye. We were like mother and son. But I'm glad for her," he said.

Now Chris Burke is reviewing scripts and hoping to continue his career in acting. In the meantime, he has written and recorded a collection of songs for children, and he continues to be an active spokesperson and supporter for disabilities' groups. He has taken on the job of editor of the newsletter of the National Down's Syndrome Society. "It's good that I have a job, says Chris. "To work for a living is important."

ON DOWN'S SYNDROME

"I call it 'Up' syndrome," is Burke's description of his condition. "We can do the same things normal people do, although it may take a little longer. What we need the most is for people to give us a chance to show what we can do. Normal people can just say they can do something and everyone believes them. We must *show* people. When we can do that, and [a show like "Life Goes On"] gives us that chance, it works."

HOBBIES AND OTHER INTERESTS

Chris loves old comedies, particularly the films of the Marx Brothers and Charlie Chaplin, and has always loved music. He is spokesperson for the National Down's Syndrome Congress and also works with the Ronald McDonald McJobs program, which encourages employers to hire people with disabilities.

PERFORMANCES

"Life Goes On," 1989-1993

WRITINGS

A Special Kind of Hero: Chris Burke's Own Story, with Jo Beth McDaniel, 1991

FURTHER READING

BOOKS

Burke, Chris, with Jo Beth McDaniel. *A Special Kind of Hero: Chris Burke's Own Story*, 1991
Contemporary Theatre, Film, and Television, Vol. 8

PERIODICALS

Boston Herald, Oct. 20, 1989, p.E14
Dallas Morning News, Sep. 9, 1989, p.B7
Exceptional Parent, Oct./Nov. 1989, p.22; Oct./Nov. 1991, p.31
Ladies' Home Journal, Dec. 1990, p.104
Life, Nov. 1989, p.70
Los Angeles Times, Sep. 12, 1989, p.B5; May 22, 1993, p. F10
New York Daily News, Nov. 4, 1991, p.A5
New York Times, Oct. 12, 1989, p.C1; Oct. 22, 1989, p.B37
People, Oct. 16, 1989, p.61; Apr. 6, 1992, p.64
Reader's Digest, Feb. 1991, p.155
Redbook, Nov. 1989, p.48
Washington Post, Oct. 3, 1989, p.F10

ADDRESS

Cynthia Katz
Abrams Artists and Associates
420 Madison Ave.
New York, NY 10017

Dana Carvey 1955-
American Comedian and Actor
Former Star of NBC's "Saturday Night Live"

BIRTH

Dana Carvey was born April 2, 1955, in Missoula, Montana, where his parents, William and Billie Carvey, both worked as school-teachers. The family, which included Dana's three older brothers and a younger sister, soon moved to San Carlos, California, a southeastern suburb of San Francisco. Carvey jokes that, when he was born, his parents "wanted a girl so badly they named me Dana."

YOUTH

Carvey was a shy child who retreated into imitation and fantasy to bolster his self-esteem. He taped his impressions of Rich Little and Jonathan Winters, and created a character for his strict father, fashioning him as the commander of a submarine in a war movie, with the family "ever on alert." On Sunday mornings, the Carvey children would be extra quiet, hoping that their parents would oversleep and miss taking the family to services at the local Lutheran church. Carvey says now that his famous "Church Lady" character seen on "Saturday Night Live" is a combination of some of the parishioners in the front pews, saying with their disapproving stares, "Well, apparently the Carveys show up at the Lord's congregation when it's conveeeenient. Some of us don't care too much about our Savior, the Lord *Jee*sus. Who helps with our church scheduling? *Saaa*tan?"

In adolescence, Dana was a self-described "nerd." He claims not to have dated at all in high school—in retrospect, he sees advantages in this and other aspects of shyness. "I hope I'm still a nerd in some way, or a geek," he told an interviewer. "There's nothing more uncool than someone trying hard to be cool, so it's pretty good to keep some nerdiness about you."

EARLY MEMORIES

There were few outlets for a shy traditionalist in the world of high school drama. Carvey remembers his halting attempt at a serious drama class. He found a method actor in a black turtleneck repeating, "You are sandpaper. Become sandpaper." Neither this weighty approach nor the high school musical was the proper forum for Carvey's talents. It would be many years before he found his niche.

EDUCATION

Carvey attended San Francisco State University after his graduation from high school, majoring in radio and television broadcasting. Too shy to display his talents publicly, he holed up in his dorm room, practicing his impersonations while Neil Young and Todd Rundgren blasted on the stereo. Despite his reclusiveness, though, he was a "maniac" in the company of close friends, who have long celebrated his sense of humor.

In both high school and college, Carvey lettered in cross-country running, and he was a particular fan of the late Steve Prefontaine, the counterculture track idol of the early 1970s. He and his friends would make up such fictitious Prefontaine sayings as "I will destroy you and everything you believe in" and "I ran until I heard no footsteps." Carvey ran a 4:29 mile in high school, and posted a time of three hours and four minutes for the difficult, mostly uphill Ocean-to-Bay Marathon.

CHOOSING A CAREER

Reinforcing his resolve with numerous drinks (he says he has been drunk only twice in his life), Carvey finally climbed on stage for an open-mike night at a San Francisco comedy club in 1978. He did a Howard Cosell imitation and told obscene "Star Trek" jokes, routines popular enough at the time to garner him an invitation to return. He has made his living at comedy ever since.

MAJOR INFLUENCES

Rejecting "cool" comedians like Lenny Bruce and Richard Pryor, Carvey admired and patterned himself on Jackie Gleason and Carol Burnett. These preferences give his characters an edge, a mixture of eccentricity and innocence that provide them with a life of their own. "I try to invent characters who have humor and pathos going for them at the same time," he says. "That really excites me." An example of this type, from hero Gleason, is Ralph Kramden of "The Honeymooners." "Timeless," Carvey asserts. "The sad saps who never quite live up to it."

CAREER HIGHLIGHTS

Dana Carvey's career began inauspiciously, with a move to Hollywood in 1981. He was given small movie parts (including a cameo as a mime waiter in Rob Reiner's 1984 hit, *This is Spinal Tap*), but was typecast against his natural talent. Producers wanted him to be a clean-cut straight man. "I went through a lot of pain," he remembers. "I went through five years of frustration and hell, having this huge secret of all this stuff I could do and never being able to show it." Carvey was cast opposite Mickey Rooney in a failed 1982 television situation comedy, "One of the Boys." He claims to have been almost too nervous to perform.

His next TV role was an even bigger disaster—a part with James Farentino in 1984's "Blue Thunder," an action series based on the movie of the same name. "We were stuck in this mock helicopter with toy missiles strung on the end of fishing poles," he remembers. "There were bad guys and we would shoot them. It was a very original idea for a show." Compared to the critical reaction, Carvey's assessment was charitable. "If it's still possible for a show to be bad beyond all imaginings," wrote critic Tom Shales in the *Washington Post*, "this one is." Shales went on to call the show "absolutely stupefyingly appalling."

Compounding these failures was the poor advice of Carvey's management firm, Rollins and Joffe, who encouraged him to wear a jacket and tie and to drop the Church Lady from his stand-up routine because it was "too gay." A friend told *Rolling Stone* that these head games intimidated Carvey so much that "he wasn't the same comic." Salvation came in 1986 in the form of Lorne Michaels, who was looking to boost sagging ratings by hiring an all-new "Saturday Night Live" cast. Michaels caught Carvey's act, including an impersonation of rock star Sting telling his friends that he's going to be called a verb. Carvey, in the routine, then becomes one of the pals: "And my name's Bite, and this is my buddy Scratch." Michaels was so taken that he signed Carvey immediately, later telling Norman Atkins of *Rolling Stone* that Dana had the range and sensibility "SNL" needed. "He's tremendously centered, gentle, and one of those comedians who leaves no fingerprints."

SATURDAY NIGHT LIVE

Carvey was an instant hit on the show, largely because of the running sketch "Church Chat," hosted by his character Enid Strict, known as the Church Lady. Mocking both the church matrons of his youth and popular televangelist programs, the Church Lady scored with viewers because of her outrageousness, particularly her willingness to shoot down anyone with the condescending sneer, "Now, isn't that special?" Also popular was the near-spastic, hip-shaking, "superior dance" with which she closed each segment. Her put-down of fallen evangelist Jim Bakker ("apparently some of us do our thinking *below* the Bible Belt") won particular acclaim.

Worried that his popular character might pigeonhole him, Carvey quickly went to work creating others. Among the better known was Ching Change, the Chinese pet-chicken store owner who has become so attached to his birds that he tries to discourage people from buying them. "Chick-ens make lousy house peeehts," he whines desperately. "You don't want him." Carvey and Kevin Nealon also scored with Hans and Franz, the fanatical bodybuilders who deride all those who have not achieved their degree of "pumpitude" as "girlie men."

After George Bush became president in 1988, Carvey served up running political comedy in the form of impersonation. His staccato, syntactically fractured impersonation of President Bush would often open SNL with such gems as "New Hampshire. Voters. Mad as hell. Message. Fed up with the status quo thing. Message. Got it!" The caricature was so dead-on that many other comics shied away from imitating the president, fearing the inevitable negative comparisons. Fortunately, Bush himself had a sense of humor about it: one of Carvey's most prized possessions is a note from the former president to his nephew, which reads, "John, have now seen both 'Saturday Night Live' tapes. The guy is improving on his entertainment 'thing'. G.B." During the recent election campaign, Carvey played both Bush and independent candidate Ross Perot to Phil Hartman's Bill Clinton in mock debates on "SNL."

After rejecting countless movie scripts, Carvey finally said yes to *Opportunity Knocks* (1990), a feature in which he plays a con man who convinces an industrialist that he is an Ivy-League financial whiz and seduces the boss's daughter. The film featured several Carvey characters, but was poorly received by moviegoers and critics. One reviewer was unkind enough to call it "a poor excuse for popcorn consumption."

Carvey graced the big screen much more successfully in 1992. He co-starred in *Wayne's World* with "SNL" cohort Mike Myers in a film based on the TV sketch created by Myers. Carvey plays Garth, a wigged-out youth with stringy blond hair and thick glasses who is sidekick to Myers's Wayne. The two are teenagers from Aurora, Illinois, hosting a public-access show from Wayne's basement. They are proudly ignorant and inspired only by heavy-metal music, beer, and "babes." *Wayne's World* was a smash at the box office and, for a movie so purposefully silly, got surprisingly good reviews. Even co-star and rock idol Alice Cooper verfied the authenticity of such characters, claiming "I meet people like that every day." Wayne and Garth, like the Church Lady before them, have enshrined themselves in popular culture through language: their exclamation "Not!" has entered everyday speech.

Dana Carvey recently signed a five-year extension of his contract with NBC, and the terms are being kept secret. It is widely rumored that, now that David Letterman has gone to CBS, Carvey will leave "Saturday Night Live" to star in a new Lorne Michael's comedy show to run in the time slot formerly held by Letterman's "Late Night."

MARRIAGE AND FAMILY

Dana and his wife, Paula, were married in 1985. Paula, says Carvey, "met me ten, eleven years ago [when] I was a busboy. She's probably a little more attracted to me now, but she would be with me even if I were still a busboy." Dana claims that clean underwear is important in preserving a marriage: "That really, really fresh clean cotton smell helps us to relate to each other better."

The Carveys, who have an apartment on Manhattan's upper west side and keep a house in California's San Fernando Valley, recently had a son.

HOBBIES AND OTHER INTERESTS

Carvey still enjoys running and covers six to eight miles per day. He also is an avid fan of music and movies, claiming to have several hundred films on laser disc and to have a car stereo system as valuable as the Volvo that houses it. After each week's show, he plays pool downtown, unwinding until the wee hours.

CREDITS

FILMS

This is Spinal Tap, 1984

Tough Guys, 1986
Opportunity Knocks, 1990
Wayne's World, 1992

TELEVISION

"One of the Boys," 1982
"Blue Thunder," 1984
"Saturday Night Live," 1986-

HONORS AND AWARDS

American Comedy Awards: 1990-91, as Television's Funniest Supporting
   Male

FURTHER READING

PERIODICALS

Current Biography Yearbook 1992
Los Angeles Times, Mar. 31, 1990, p.F1
Newsweek, Apr. 13, 1987, p.70
Rolling Stone, Oct. 22, 1987, p.29; Mar. 19, 1992, p.37
TV Guide, July 2, 1988, p.9
Washington Post, Mar. 30, 1990, p. B1

ADDRESS

Brillstein-Grey Entertainment
9200 Sunset Blvd.
Suite 428
Los Angeles, CA 90069

OBITUARY

Cesar Chavez   1927-1993
American Political Activist and Labor Leader
President of the United Farm Workers

BIRTH

Cesar Estrada Chavez (SHAH-vehz), a migrant worker who founded the first successful farm workers' union, was born on March 31, 1927, near Yuma, Arizona. His parents, Librado and Juana (Estrada) Chavez, owned a store and worked on a family farm there. Cesar had one older sister, Rita, and four younger siblings, Richard (Rookie), Helena (who died when very young), Eduvigis (Vickie), and Librado, Jr. (Lenny). In addition, their cousin Manuel lived with the family.

72

YOUTH

Reading about Cesar Chavez provides an instant glimpse of the social history of farm workers in the United States. His life spanned the Great Depression, the great drought in the Southwest and the subsequent migration by many farm families to California, the hard life of migrant workers, the early efforts to organize workers, the political activism of the 1960s and early 1970s, and the conservative retrenchment that followed.

The Chavez family farm near Yuma, on the Arizona-California-Mexico border, was founded by Cesario Chavez, Cesar's grandfather and namesake. Papa Chayo, as the family called him, came to the United States from Mexico in the 1880s. He had escaped from a farm where he had been virtually enslaved, traveling across the Rio Grande River to El Paso, Texas. By 1888 he had saved enough money to send for his wife and 14 children. Eventually they settled in Arizona, in the Gila Valley along the Colorado River. It was desert there, but they dug irrigation ditches and homesteaded over 100 acres of land. Growing up, Chavez often heard his grandfather's stories of oppression and escape.

When Cesar was born, his father owned a store and helped out on the family farm. The family didn't have much, but they always had everything they needed. Cesar had a happy early childhood helping out on the farm and playing with his brothers, sisters, and cousins, swimming in the river, fishing, flying kites, and enjoying family picnics. His only real complaint was about school—he didn't like the clean clothes and new shoes, the long walk in the winter cold, and the teachers. They were mean to him, Chavez thought, because he spoke English poorly, after learning only Spanish at home. His greatest influence from that time was his mother. She believed strongly in charity and nonviolence, and she passed these beliefs, as well as her strong Roman Catholic faith, on to Cesar. Throughout these years, Juana Chavez would always share her family's meager rations with the hobos who would stop, hoping for a meal.

The Great Depression of the 1930s changed all that. Like many Americans, Librado soon lost his job and his home. A number of factors conspired together to uproot the Chavez family. Librado was cheated out of some land in a bad business deal, and he had to borrow money to buy it back. At the same time, they were earning little money, because few people could afford to buy goods from the Chavez farm or store. In addition, a great drought struck the Southwest, turning their land into desert and destroying their crops. Soon, Librado Chavez was unable to pay the taxes, and in 1937 the state seized their property. There were no jobs in Arizona, so Librado left for California, where he had heard there was work on the big farms. He found a job picking beans in southern California, and sent for his family to join him.

LIFE AS A MIGRANT WORKER

Like many others, the Chavez family packed up all their belongings in their car and headed west to California. As Chavez recalled in Jacques Levy's *Cesar Chavez: Autobiography of La Causa*, a biography based on his recollections, "I realized something was happening because my mother was crying, but I didn't really realize the import of it at the time. When we left the farm, our whole life was upset, turned upside down. We had been part of a very stable community, and we were about to become migratory workers. We had been uprooted." Still, they believed they could earn enough money to pay off the back taxes and reclaim their land. They were wrong. Instead, they discovered the hardships of life as migrant workers.

Migrant workers move from farm to farm as the season progresses, planting or harvesting each crop when ready and then moving on to the next. Often, whole families would move together, following the crops. The working conditions for migrant laborers, as the Chavez family soon discovered, were appalling. It was backbreaking work—for many crops, the workers would spend the whole day bent over double, low to the ground. They were paid on a per piece basis, which forced them to work faster and faster. They were continually exposed to dangerous pesticides sprayed on the crops. And there was often no drinking water available in the fields, despite the searing heat, and no bathrooms—workers were expected to simply squat down between the rows.

The living conditions were equally degrading. Farm owners often provided migrant workers with a place to live. Workers were crammed together, even sleeping ten to a room, or housed in tin shacks that would bake mercilessly in the summer sun. Some even slept outdoors, under bridges and in makeshift tents that let in all the winter damp and cold. And the pay was also horrendous. Unscrupulous owners would promise workers one rate and then underpay them, or even disappear before the workers received their wages. Migrant workers earned a mere pittance, not enough to feed, clothe, and house their families, and certainly not enough to save for those times when there was no work to be found.

What Cesar Chavez soon learned was that migrant workers were powerless. With the devastating economic conditions in the United States at that time, people were desperate. There was a constant stream of newly poor Americans and Mexican immigrants willing to endure any hardships just to earn enough money to feed their families.

Cesar and his family soon joined that stream of migrant workers, traveling up and down the rich agricultural region of California's Central Valley. They often stayed in San Jose, in a crowded *barrio*, or slum, called Sal

Si Puedes—Get Out If You Can. Cesar and his siblings worked alongside their parents in the fields. Life was unbearably difficult for the whole family, and they often didn't have enough to eat or a place to sleep. Despite their poverty, Librado Chavez taught his children to respect themselves and to stand up for themselves. As Cesar recalls, "I don't want to suggest we were that radical, but I know we were probably one of the strikingest families in California, the first ones to leave the fields if anybody shouted 'Huelga!'—which is Spanish for 'Strike!'" His father always joined in any attempts to protest the pay or the working conditions and to organize the farm workers, and it was from him that Cesar first learned about unions.

In addition to working in the fields, Cesar attended school for part of the day. He soon grew to hate school. The other children made fun of his dirty, worn clothes and his bare feet—he had no money for shoes. And the "Anglo" students and teachers clearly showed their contempt for Hispanics.

EDUCATION

Like most children of migrant workers, Chavez had an erratic education. He once estimated that he and his siblings had attended between 40 and 60 schools, some for only a few days at a time. In 1942, he left school for good when his father was injured in a car accident. By age 15, Cesar had completed only the seventh grade, and he was barely able to read and write. Years later, Chavez worked hard to educate himself. He read about many subjects but particularly labor history and people who had worked to help the less fortunate. He enjoyed biographies of labor leaders, but he was particularly inspired by the lives of St. Francis of Assisi, the thirteenth-century monk who helped the poor, and Mahatma K. Gandhi, the Indian leader who advocated non-violence in his country's struggle to gain independence from Britain. Nonviolence became a hallmark of the farm workers' movement.

FIRST JOBS

By 1942 Cesar was working full time in the fields, only 15 but carrying the responsibilities of a grown man. That same year he and his friends stopped in a snow-cone parlor, where he met a girl, about his age, wearing flowers in her hair. That was Helen Fabela, his future wife. She worked at a grocery store in Delano, where he visited each time his family passed through. Soon, they started to date. In 1944, during World War II, he enlisted in the U.S. Navy for two years, serving primarily as a deckhand. After his discharge, he returned to migrant labor in California, working also for a short time in the lumber industry in the north. In 1948, he and Helen were married, and they eventually had eight children.

COMMUNITY ORGANIZING

In 1952, Chavez's life changed. While living in Sal Si Puedes, he was approached by Fred Ross, who had formed the Community Service Organization (CSO) to help Mexican Americans use group power to improve conditions in their lives. Ross came to Chavez's home, hoping to enlist his help. For Chavez, it opened his eyes. To improve the lives of farm workers, he had tried to help them on an individual basis. Until Fred Ross came, he didn't know how to help the community as a whole. As Chavez later said, "He did such a good job of explaining how poor people could build power that I could even taste it, I could *feel* it. I thought, Gee, it's like digging a hole, there's nothing complicated about it." For Ross, the feeling was mutual. That evening, he wrote in his diary, "I think I've found the guy I'm looking for."

The CSO was conducting a voter registration drive, and Chavez began working immediately. He went out to workers' homes, explaining how important it was to vote. As a Hispanic and a farm worker, he had immediate credibility with community members. He started helping people in other areas of their lives, too, translating, writing letters, and intervening with government agencies. And in the process, people became very loyal to him. He did this type of community organizing with the CSO for about 10 years. At first he worked as a volunteer, and then he was hired by the CSO in 1953. In 1958 he was named National Director.

After a few years, though, Chavez decided to leave the CSO. While the group continued to focus on those living in the cities, he wanted to organize a union for farm workers. After convincing Helen, and with only $1200 in the bank, Chavez quit his job with the CSO. With his experience of poverty and a growing family to support, it took a lot of courage and commitment to leave a secure, paying job to dedicate himself to helping others.

Chavez and his family returned to Delano, where Helen's family still lived. He formed a new union, the National Farm Workers Association (or NFWA, later the United Farm Workers, or UFW). While Helen worked in the fields, Cesar and his two-year-old son, Anthony, would drive throughout the region, talking to workers, distributing leaflets, and trying to recruit union members. By late 1962, enough workers had joined to hold their first convention and to showcase the union flag—a black eagle against a white circle on a red flag, a symbol of their cause.

LA HUELGA AND LA CAUSA

Chavez's organizing efforts were put to the test in 1965. Another union representing grape pickers decided to go on strike and asked Chavez's union to support them. The membership agreed unanimously. From the start, Chavez was determined that the strike would remain nonviolent, no matter what provocation the growers offered. At first, they set up picket lines, shouting "Huelga" (Strike) to discourage workers from going into the fields. The growers, and sometimes the police, would harass and even beat them. But gradually the union began to broaden its base of support. Chavez spoke at local universities and convinced students to donate their lunch money to La causa (the cause). He recruited volunteers from outside the union, particularly civil rights workers who were accustomed to nonviolent protest. He enlisted the support of other unions, asking their workers not to load or ship any grapes. He led striking workers on a grueling 250-mile march, from Delano to the state capital in Sacramento, to call attention to their demands. He also began his first fast during this time, refusing all food to focus attention on the strike and to reinforce its nonviolent means.

The most far-reaching tactic, though, was to enlist the support of the American people. Chavez asked people to boycott, or refuse to buy, all grapes that didn't display the union label, knowing that the loss of earnings was the most powerful weapon against the growers. Their cause enlisted the support of many prominent people, including Robert Kennedy, Jr., Ethel Kennedy, Coretta Scott King, and Jesse Jackson. The strike and boycott continued for five years, but eventually the grape growers acceded to their demands and signed a union contract, increasing the workers' wages, protecting them against pesticides, and guaranteeing their right to representation and collective bargaining. It was the first time in U.S. history that farm workers were protected by a union contract.

Chavez continued to lead union activities throughout the 1970s, organizing other farm workers and fighting off rival unions. The Teamsters, who also wanted to represent farm workers, were believed to be in league with the growers, and they waged a long-standing campaign against the UFW, often resorting to violence against union members. Yet the UFW went on to other successes, in California lettuce fields, in Florida citrus groves, and in Arizona politics, where the union's voter registration drive sent many new Mexican Americans and Navajo Indians to the polls. The greatest achievement of this era was the passage in California of the Agricultural Labor Relations Act, the first bill of rights for farm workers in U.S. history. In retrospect, many experts agree that this bill, along with the grape boycott, was the high point of Cesar Chavez's work with the UFW.

RECENT ACTIVITIES

The 1980s and early 1990s saw the erosion of many of the gains that Chavez and the union had achieved. The right to be represented by a union and engage in collective bargaining; the increase in wages; the great improvements in working conditions, like eliminating the short-handled hoe and requiring drinking water and portable toilets in the fields; the fight against pesticides; the addition of unemployment, workers' compensation, and medical insurance—these and other benefits, which Chavez dedicated his life to securing and which many workers in other industries take for granted, are nonexistent for most farm workers. "There were many extraordinary accomplishments on behalf of farm workers in the 1960s and '70s," according to the labor historian Clete Daniel. "Yet today you still have people living in bridges, in lean-tos, in ditches. There is still an inexcusable level of misery."

What caused the decline in the union's influence is a question for historians to debate, but many experts agree on several contributing factors. Some have criticized Chavez's leadership, claiming that his authoritarian style alienated longtime supporters. They also criticize his high tech methods, claiming that his switch from organizing workers to organizing consumers via computerized mailing lists was ineffective. But observers point to other factors as well, including the difficulty of organizing a seasonal industry and the flow of illegal immigrants from Mexico. In addition, the change in political climate in California and throughout the U.S. brought to power conservative Republican administrations that favored the agricultural businesses while fighting or ignoring the union. The results, for the UFW, were fewer contracts, fewer members, and the return of some abusive practices.

The struggle was not yet over when Cesar Chavez died in his sleep on April 23, 1993, at the home of a supporter near Yuma, Arizona, his birthplace.

Chavez's legacy to the movement is two-fold, for the UFW has been both a labor union and a civil rights movement. In defining his importance to recent social history, many point to his ability to inspire people, and his work to empower them. According to Herman Gallegos, who joined up with Chavez in the 1950s, "He gave us a sense of pride, a sense of identity. Don't get caught up in the numbers game, or this business of how many union contracts he had. He provided such pride to our community. That's intangible—but priceless."

MAJOR INFLUENCES

Cesar Chavez's greatest influences were his parents, who taught him to honor all people, including himself, with dignity, respect, and charity. These early beliefs were reinforced by his study of the lives of St. Francis and Gandhi, and their teachings on charity and nonviolence.

HONORS AND AWARDS

Social Justice Award (United Auto Workers): 1972
Jefferson Awards (American Institute for Public Service): 1973, Greatest Public Service Benefitting the Disadvantaged
Martin Luther King, Jr., Nonviolent Peace Prize (Martin Luther King, Jr., Center for Nonviolent Social Change): 1974

FURTHER READING

BOOKS

Cedeño, Maria E. *Cesar Chavez: Labor Leader,* 1993 (juvenile)
Conord, Bruce. *Cesar Chavez: Union Leader,* 1992 (juvenile)
Dunne, John Gregory. *Delano,* 1971
Encyclopedia Britannica 1993
Franchere, Ruth. *Cesar Chavez,* 1988 (juvenile)
Levy, Jacques. *Cesar Chavez: Autobiography of La Causa,* 1975
Matthiessen, Peter. *Sal Si Puedes: Cesar Chavez and the New American Revolution,* 1973
Roberts, Naurice. *Cesar Chavez and La Causa,* 1986 (juvenile)
Rodriguez, Consuelo. *Cesar Chavez,* 1991 (juvenile)
Ross, Fred. *Conquering Goliath: Cesar Chavez at the Beginning,* 1989
Who's Who in America, 1992-1993
Who's Who among Hispanic Americans, 1991-1992
World Book 1992

PERIODICALS

Current Biography 1969
Economist, Mar. 28, 1993, p.C6
Los Angeles Times, Apr. 24, 1993, pp.A1, B7; Apr. 29, 1993, p.A1
New Republic, Nov. 25, 1985, p.20
New York Times, Apr. 24, 1993, p.A1
New York Times Magazine, Nov. 17, 1968, p.52; May 23, 1993, p.16
New Yorker, May 17, 1993, p.82

Henry Cisneros 1947-
American Civic Leader and Politician
U.S. Secretary of Housing and Urban
Development

BIRTH

Henry Gabriel Cisneros, the nation's best-known Hispanic public official, was born July 11, 1947, in San Antonio, Texas, where he would later serve as mayor. He was the first child of Elvira (Munguia) Cisneros and George Cisneros, who was in the military. Both the Cisneros and Munguia families had left a lasting mark on the American Southwest. George's ancestors were early Spanish settlers in the region, and Elvira's father, Romulo

Munguia—an intellectual, journalist and printer—was prominent in the encouragement and development of Mexican-American interests. He had brought his family to San Antonio in the mid-1920s to escape an oppressive political regime in his own country.

The four Cisneros siblings who quickly joined the family after Henry's birth are Pauline, George, Jr., Tim, and Tina.

YOUTH

Henry grew up in the midst of a devoted family, learning by example from an industrious father and a purposeful mother who, according to *Current Biography*, "imposed on her children a summertime regimen of chores, reading, spirited family debates, and creative projects, in the firm belief that [they] would fulfill a special destiny." All of the sisters and brothers eventually made their mother's dream a reality by their successes in a variety of professional careers.

The neighborhood where Henry spent his early years has been described by him as a "Norman Rockwell" kind of place—rural, small-town America—although, he adds, "the faces were all brown." It was San Antonio's West End, where Mexican-Americans had settled in a mixed section of middle-class, well-maintained houses and tiny, run-down shacks. The Cisneros children joined in the usual neighborhood activities, took trips with their father, and were absorbed into the happy, extended Roman Catholic family created by their grandparents. Later, as mayor of San Antonio, and with his wife and children, Henry would make Grandfather Munguia's modest home his own.

Young Cisneros felt great pride in his family, as described by writer John Gillies, author of *Senor Alcalde: A Biography of Henry Cisneros*. "His relatives," he writes in the book whose title translates as Mister Mayor, "were hard-working people who believed in freedom and democracy, as well as in education and self-discipline. Over the years, Henry would learn to apply these values to his own life."

EARLY MEMORIES

One particular day stands out in the memories of his youth, says Cisneros. It was November 21, 1963, when he walked over to Broadway Street from his high school to watch with excitement the motorcade carrying President John F. Kennedy and wife, Jacqueline. The next day, Kennedy was assassinated in Dallas, and a troubled and deeply moved Cisneros penned a touching poem to his lost hero.

EDUCATION

Young Henry spoke little English until he started kindergarten, since Spanish was the language heard at home and in his West Side neighborhood. He was highly motivated, though, and sailed through the curriculum at his parish elementary school, even skipping a grade. Graduating from San Antonio's Catholic Central High School at the age of sixteen, he was under age for the military career he had yearned for. He hoped to become a pilot but was too young to enter the Air Force. Instead, he began a course in aeronautical engineering at Texas A&M (Agricultural and Mechanical) University, but soon switched to a major in urban and regional planning—a good choice for the remarkable career that lay ahead. Cisneros earned a B.A. in 1968 and an M.A. two years later. During his university years, he was involved in a broad range of extracurricular activities, some of which foreshadowed his eventual leap into politics.

Over the next few years, Cisneros alternated periods of work and study, earning additional advanced degrees. With the help of a Ford Foundation grant, he earned a second master's degree in 1973, this time in public administration from Harvard's John F. Kennedy School of Government. While living in the Boston area, he performed doctoral research at MIT (Massachusetts Institute of Technology) and worked there as a teaching assistant. His Ph.D. in public administration was awarded by George Washington University in 1975. Ambitious and energetic, Cisneros accumulated scholastic credentials to pursue a career in public service.

FIRST JOBS

After earning his Bachelor's degree, Cisneros started his working career in 1968 in the San Antonio city manager's office. He was inspired by a personal vision for the future of his culturally and economically divided city. He gained practical experience there and in a similar position in nearby Bryan, Texas. In 1969, he was made assistant director of the federally promoted Model Cities program in San Antonio.

Cisneros's growing passion for involvement in community policy issues led him to a stint in Washington, D.C., as assistant to the executive vice president of the National League of Cities. In 1971, he applied for and won a White House fellowship, which placed him in an enviable political position as assistant to Elliot L. Richardson, secretary of what was then called HEW (Health, Education and Welfare). The agency is now restructured as HHS (Health and Human Services). It was after his prestigious internship under Richardson that Cisneros spent two years in Boston earning degrees at Harvard and MIT. He was offered a full-time faculty post at MIT, but turned it down to return home and teach labor economics and urban studies at the San Antonio campus of the University of Texas. His credentials were rapidly matching his career ambitions, and he was ready to enter the political arena.

CAREER HIGHLIGHTS

Public service may have begun with Cisneros's early jobs after college, but his career took off in earnest in 1975 when he was elected to the first of three terms on the San Antonio city council. The Hispanic community was looking for strong representation on the council, and according to a local news writer at the time, "They found it in the 27-year-old Cisneros. He is a man with impressive credentials and steady loyalty to his ethnic roots." During his first council term, Cisneros gained immediate popularity for his advocacy of economic development and his efforts toward cooperation between the Hispanic and Anglo factions of the city. When he ran for a second term in 1977, he garnered an incredible 92 percent of the vote.

Cisneros's final two years on the council had some rough spots—among them rejection by voters of a bond issue that he had supported and dissention within the council itself over his refusal to endorse construction sanctions. It was time, he felt, to try for the city's top administrative post—mayor. Setting out on an aggressive campaign that focused on economic development rather than ethnic elements, he was rewarded with more than 60 percent of the vote.

MAYOR OF SAN ANTONIO

In April 1981, 33-year-old Henry Cisneros became the first Mexican-American in 140 years to lead San Antonio. His inauguration also marked him as the first Hispanic mayor of a major U.S. city—San Antonio is the nation's ninth largest municipality. "We have managed to transcend the ethnic factor," he said when his election was certain, "and there's a great sense of anticipation that we're going to be able to work together, and that the coalition we built can be put to work for San Antonio."

Cisneros's vitality and effectiveness in building on his city's strengths brought him such popularity that he received 94 percent of the vote to gain a second mayoral term in 1983. He was reelected twice more during the '80s. As a four-term mayor, Cisneros rebuilt the city's economic base by attracting high-tech industries, expanding housing opportunities, recruiting convention business, increasing tourism, and creating jobs in downtown San Antonio. He quickly rose to national prominence and in 1985 was elected president of the National League of Cities.

A dynamic leader and an eloquent speaker, Cisneros was considered as a vice-presidential running mate for Walter Mondale in 1984. He was "viewed by many," said Peter Applebome in a 1988 *New York Times* article, "as the most promising Hispanic politician in the country and perhaps the most intriguing politician in Texas." However, he decided the following year against a bid for a fifth term as mayor of San Antonio, citing personal reasons. In 1990, Cisneros also ruled out the possibility of running for governor of Texas because of the fragile health of his youngest child. He left public service to become chairman of his own newly organized asset management firm for tax-exempt institutions. During this time in private business, he also hosted "Texans," a television show produced quarterly in his home state, and "Adelante" ("Onward"), a national daily Spanish-language radio commentary. Although out of office, the former mayor continued to maintain a prominent role in civic activities on local, state, and national levels.

A CABINET POST

Cisneros is often described as a man who understands the needs of the future and talks in terms of global relationships, and he soon returned to public life, as was widely predicted. This time he would make his mark as a federal official. His nomination by (then) President-elect Clinton to serve as secretary of the Department of Housing and Urban Development (HUD) was confirmed unanimously by the U.S. Senate on January 21, 1993, and he was sworn into office the next day. As secretary of HUD, Cisneros is now America's foremost federal housing and economic development official. HUD is one of the departments in the executive branch of government. It is charged with developing housing and community programs throughout the U.S. It fulfills this task in a wide variety of ways: by providing federal funds to local officials to build public housing, by creating community development programs, by paying part of the cost of housing for poor people, and by insuring mortgages and home improvement loans. The energetic public servant from San Antonio has come full circle from his youthful appointment to a White House fellowship scarcely more than two decades ago.

MARRIAGE AND FAMILY

Henry Cisneros married Mary Alice Perez, whom he had known since high-school days, on June 1, 1969, the year after his college graduation. They have three children—Teresa Angelica, 22; Mercedes Christina, 18; and John Paul Anthony, who was born six years ago with a life-threatening condition called asplenia syndrome. John Paul has no spleen, and his heart lacks two of the normal four separate chambers. A newly developed surgical procedure was performed in mid-July 1993 to reshape the openings in his malformed heart. According to *Time*, in late July, John Paul "now has a good chance of living a full life, beginning with his return home this week and his first day of kindergarten in September."

Over the past several years, Cisneros's marriage and family life have been sorely tested by personal troubles including his acknowledged involvement in 1988 with another woman. The dynamic Hispanic leader, then thought to be ready to seek a fifth term as San Antonio's mayor, put his political career on hold and entered private business. Mrs. Cisneros eventually filed for divorce, but quickly withdrew the petition, and friends reveal that the couple's problems have been resolved.

MAJOR INFLUENCES

Cisneros's childhood in a principled and supportive family set a positive example for his later accomplishments. It is generally agreed, however, that the motivating force in his public career was Elliot Richardson, under whom he served at HEW in the early 1970s. It was Richardson, says *Current Biography*, "who became his intellectual and political mentor" and who convinced him "that returning to San Antonio on completion of the [White House fellowship] program was a vital first step in climbing the political ladder."

HOBBIES AND OTHER INTERESTS

These days, since his little son still needs so much of his time and attention, Cisneros confines most of his nonofficial hours to family activities. He and his wife and grown daughters agree that "each moment with John Paul is precious." In addition, Cisneros is an avid reader and physically active man, who stays fit by jogging.

WRITINGS

The Entrepreneurial City, 1986

HONORS AND AWARDS

One of Ten Outstanding Young Men in America, Jaycees (U.S. Junior Chamber of Commerce): 1982
Distinguished Leadership Award (American Institute of Planners): 1985
President's Award (National League of Cities): 1989
Outstanding Mayor (*City and State* magazine): 1986
Local Government Leader of the Year Award (*American City and County* magazine): 1988
Hispanic Man of the Year (*VISTA* magazine): 1991
Hispanic Heritage Education Award: 1992, for founding San Antonio Education Partnership, an incentive program to prevent student dropouts

FURTHER READING

BOOKS

Diehl, Kemper and Jan Jarboe. *Cisneros: Portrait of a New American,* 1985 (juvenile)
Gillies, John. *Senor Alcalde: A Biography of Henry Cisneros,* 1988

Hispanic American Almanac, 1993
Who's Who Among Hispanic Americans, 1991-92
World Book Encyclopedia, 1992

PERIODICALS

Business Week, Feb. 20, 1989, p.40
Current Biography Yearbook 1987
Houston Post, June 9, 1988, p.A2; Oct. 15, 1988, p.A1; Nov. 20,
    1991, p.A17; Sept. 2, 1992, p.A2; Dec. 20, 1992, p.A22
Mother Jones, Mar./Apr. 1993, p.11
New York Times Biographical Service, Feb. 1988, p.226; Oct. 1988, p.1129
Newsweek, Oct. 24, 1988, p.25
Time, Oct. 24, 1988, p.43; Nov. 9, 1991, p.95
Wall Street Journal, Jan. 12, 1993, p.A14

ADDRESS

Office of the Secretary of HUD
Department of Housing and Urban Development
451 Seventh Street, S.W.
Washington, DC 20410

Hillary Rodham Clinton 1947-
American First Lady of the United States
Lawyer and Activist

BIRTH

Hillary Diane Rodham was born on October 26, 1947, in Chicago, Illinois. Her father, Hugh Rodham, Sr., was a salesman and later the owner of a small textile business; her mother, Dorothy Rodham, was a homemaker. Hillary has two younger brothers, Hugh and Tony, both of whom now live in Florida.

YOUTH

When Hillary was quite young, the family moved to the conservative, upper-middle class community of Park Ridge, Illinois, a suburb of Chicago. In addition to school, Hillary's many activities included ballet, piano lessons, swimming, ice skating, and Girl Scouts, where she earned every badge. She also played competitive sports. While not a great athlete, Hillary says that she still appreciates the lessons she learned: "You win one day, you lose the next day, you don't take it personally. You get up every day and go on." Like many kids, she did chores around the house and babysat for the neighbors—despite the Rodhams' comfortable financial position, Hillary's parents were determined that the children would develop a strong sense of responsibility and a willingness to work hard.

The Rodhams valued education highly. Both parents set very high expectations for Hillary and encouraged her to succeed. "I was fortunate because as a girl growing up I never felt anything but support from my family," she later acknowledged. "There was no distinction between me and my brothers or any barriers thrown up to me that I couldn't think about doing something because I was a girl. It was just: if you work hard enough and you really apply yourself, then you should be able to do whatever you choose to do." Her mother, who had never had the opportunity to go to college, was especially supportive: "I was determined that no daughter of mine was going to have to go through the agony of being afraid to speak her mind," Dorothy Rodham recalls. "Just because she was a girl didn't mean she should be limited."

EARLY MEMORIES

While her parents encouraged this attitude, much of society did not. In the early 1960s, the U.S. was in a race to catch up with the Soviet Union, which had recently launched the first manned rocket into space. At age 14, Hillary wrote to NASA, describing her academic strengths and asking how to become an astronaut. NASA replied that girls could not apply. This first experience with sexism was infuriating, but she didn't let it hold her back.

MAJOR INFLUENCES

In addition to her parents, Hillary calls her minister one of her strongest influences. When she started high school, the Reverend Don Jones took a position as youth minister at her church, First United Methodist. Fresh out of theological school, Rev. Jones took Hillary and the rest of the youth group into the inner city to meet with underprivileged black and Hispanic kids. This first brush with poverty was deeply affecting. Hillary participated in the church group throughout her school years, reading religious philosophy with Rev. Jones and organizing babysitting services for the children of migrant workers and the urban poor. Since this time, according to Jones, her Methodist faith continues to be a source of inspiration and support for her: "the key to understanding Hillary is her spiritual center. . . . Her social concern and her political thought rest on a spiritual foundation." To this day, Hillary is a devout Methodist who attends church regularly.

EDUCATION

Rodham attended Maine East High and then, after redistricting, was sent to Maine South for her senior year. Even then she was a leader—active in student government, a member of the debate team and the National Honor Society, the chair of the Organizational Committee, and, as a senior, voted Most Likely to Succeed. Encouraged by her teachers, she applied to Wellesley College, a prestigious women's college near Boston, and was accepted. Hillary graduated from Maine Township High School-South in 1965.

WELLESLEY COLLEGE

Arriving at Wellesley, Hillary was a product of her community—a conservative Republican, but one concerned about issues of social justice from her experiences with the youth ministry. She was soon affected, though, by the social upheaval of the era. Studying political science, she discussed the civil rights movement, the assassinations of Martin Luther King, Jr., Bobby Kennedy, and Malcolm X, the Black Panthers, the Weathermen, and the Vietnam War. She and her friends engaged in long political debates, where she developed a reputation as intelligent, articulate, confident, open-minded, forceful, insightful, and fun. As her political views evolved, she became more outspoken and active at school, taking on a leadership role. She organized student protests, but often served as a mediator, working with both the school administration and student groups to reach a consensus. She also taught reading to children from a poor neighborhood in Boston. In her senior thesis, which incorporates many of the issues she has addressed for 20 years, she evaluated community action programs for the poor, trying to determine which programs worked, and why.

In her senior year she was selected by her peers to be class speaker at graduation—the first time the college had ever allowed a student to speak. And as it turned out, the school administration was not pleased with her non-traditional approach: "We feel that our prevailing, acquisitive and competitive corporate life . . . is not the way of life for us. We're searching for more immediate, ecstatic, and penetrating modes of living." Excerpts from her speech appeared in *Life* magazine, her first brush with the national press. Hillary Rodham graduated from Wellesley in 1969 with high honors.

YALE UNIVERSITY LAW SCHOOL

Hillary then attended Yale Law School, not with the intent of becoming a highly paid corporate attorney, but instead to develop the credentials for public service and social activism. During the summers, instead of clerking for a law firm, she worked on social issues. She met Marian Wright Edelman, the founder of the Children's Defense Fund, who sent her to study the conditions of migrant labor camps; Hillary also explored the issue of tax-exempt status for segregated schools. In addition, she spent an extra year at Yale, studying child development and family law. As at Wellesley, she also played an active role in student movements and in mediating conflicts, becoming a well-known figure at the law school in the process. Hillary received her law degree from Yale University in 1973.

While at Yale, she met her future husband, Bill Clinton. Although they had seen each other around campus, they first met at the library one night when they were studying at opposite ends of the room. Bill was talking to someone, but watching Hillary the whole time. Finally, she got up and marched the full length of the room, coming up face-to-face. As he recalls, "She came up to me and she said, 'Look, if you're going to keep staring at me, and I'm going to keep staring back, I think we should at least know each other. I'm Hillary Rodham. What's your name?'" According to Clinton, "I was dumbstruck. I couldn't think of my name." They soon became involved, staying together throughout law school. But the end of law school created a seemingly unresolvable problem, and they went their separate ways: Hillary stayed on the East Coast to work in public policy areas, while Bill returned to Arkansas to eventually run for public office, as he had always planned.

FIRST JOBS

After leaving Yale, she worked in Cambridge, Massachusetts, for about six months as an attorney for Edelman's organization, the Children's Defense Fund, working on the problems of poor families. In January 1974 she was appointed to what most young attorneys considered a dream job: she was asked to work on the legal staff of the House Judiciary Committee, which was investigating the possible impeachment of President Richard Nixon after the Watergate scandal. The job came to an abrupt end in August, when Nixon resigned.

Exhausted and eager to leave Washington—and to be close to Bill—Hillary got a job at the University of Arkansas, teaching criminal law and setting up a legal aid clinic. Many of her friends objected to the move and were worried that she was sacrificing her dreams and her own chance at a career; some had hoped that she would ultimately serve in public office herself. But Hillary has never voiced any regrets: "I had no choice but to follow my heart there. Following your heart is never wrong."

In August 1974, Hillary moved to Fayetteville, Arkansas, where Bill also was teaching at the law school. She soon discovered that she enjoyed small-town life: "I liked people tapping me on the shoulder at the grocery store and saying, 'Aren't you that lady professor at the law school?'" After about a year Hillary took a trip, first to visit her parents near Chicago, then to friends in Boston, New York, and Washington, to see what she would be missing if she stayed in Arkansas. She realized that nothing meant as much to her as the time she had spent with Bill. She returned to Arkansas.

MARRIAGE AND FAMILY

Hillary Rodham and Bill Clinton were married on October 11, 1975, in Fayetteville. The bride kept her name, a decision that has often been an issue throughout her husband's political career. Their daughter Chelsea was born in 1980; both parents are said to dote on her and to fiercely protect her right to privacy.

CAREER HIGHLIGHTS

Since her marriage, Hillary has managed to juggle a number of roles. In addition to being a wife and mother, she has worked as the First Lady of Arkansas, a tireless political campaigner, an attorney in private practice, and an advocate for children on the national stage. These different roles have often overlapped—sometimes leading to conflict. For Hillary, the balancing act described by many working women began early.

In 1976, when Bill was elected attorney general of Arkansas, he and Hillary moved to Little Rock, where they lived until their move to the White House. Hillary was asked to join the Rose Law Firm, one of the top legal firms in Arkansas. She worked there throughout her husband's successful campaign for governor in 1978 and the birth of her daughter in 1980, and she soon became a partner in the firm. But after his first term as governor, Bill lost his reelection campaign. Although there were many reasons that he was rejected by the voters, most observers agree that Hillary's image was one of those reasons. She simply didn't fit the image Arkansans expected of their First Lady—she was an accomplished professional in her own right, paid little attention to her appearance, wore thick glasses and long frizzy hair, and, perhaps most importantly, didn't change her name when she got married. After Bill's defeat, both partners made concessions. For Hillary, this meant updating her wardrobe and hairstyle, trying once again, and successfully this time, to wear contact lenses, and taking her husband's name. Bill was reelected governor in 1982, and Hillary Rodham *Clinton* served as First Lady of Arkansas until December 1992.

Throughout her years in Arkansas, Hillary continued to work on behalf of children. In the late 1970s, she helped to found the Arkansas Advocates for Children and Families, which monitors state government's services to children. In 1983, she was appointed by her husband to chair the newly formed Arkansas Education Standards Committee, which was charged with improving the quality of education in the state's public schools. Hillary traveled around the state, meeting with school officials, teachers, and parents in each county. The committee eventually pioneered such reforms as school accreditation standards, smaller class sizes, and teacher testing. The latter, in particular, proved especially controversial. In 1985 she helped start HIPPY—the Home Instruction Program for Preschool Youngsters, a nationally recognized program that provides parent education to help poor women prepare their young children to start school. She also helped establish the state's first neonatal nursery and worked for the Southern Governors' Association Task Force on Infant Mortality.

In her legal work, she was a partner at Rose Law Firm until the 1992 presidential campaign. There she had a successful practice as a litigator, arguing cases in the courtroom. She has long been the main family breadwinner—she has recently earned about $180,000 a year, while Bill, as governor, earned $35,000 annually. From 1978 to 1981 she also served on the board of the Legal Services Corporation, a federal agency that funds legal aid clinics for poor people. In 1987 she was selected to chair the American Bar Association's first Commission on Women in the Legal Profession, and she was twice selected as one of the "100 Most Influential Lawyers in America" by *The National Law Journal*. She has also served on the boards of dozens of corporations and nonprofit organizations, including Wal-Mart, TCBY Yogurt, Arkansas Children's Hospital, the Children's Television Workshop, the Franklin and Eleanor Roosevelt Institute, and the Children's Defense Fund (CDF).

In addition to her efforts on behalf of families in Arkansas, her work as an advocate for children also includes her commitment to the Children's Defense Fund and her legal writings. She became involved with the CDF when she first met Edelman while in law school. She joined the board of directors at CDF in 1976, and served as chair of the board from 1986 until she resigned in 1992. With the CDF, Hillary worked to help children and their families, fighting for programs like prenatal care, day care, Head Start, parental leave policies, and new welfare policies. She has also written law articles on children's rights in which she argued that children should be able to speak in their own behalf in a court of law before their eighteenth birthday, an unusual idea at that time. In cases of such serious family trouble as abuse or neglect, older children deserve the right to have some input into crucial decisions in their own lives, she argued. These writings proved to be controversial during the campaign: while some political observers argued that Hillary wanted to undermine family unity and parental authority over their children, legal scholars claimed that her views had been misrepresented by her husband's opponents.

THE 1992 PRESIDENTIAL CAMPAIGN

The presidential campaign proved to be a wrenching experience for

Hillary. Several events pushed her into the media glare. She first came to national attention with her appearance on the TV news show "60 Minutes," in which she and Bill publicly discussed charges that he had had affairs during their marriage. Eventually, an anti-Hillary backlash ensued—"the Hillary problem," one commentator called it—and she came under the most intense scrutiny. Her hairstyle, makeup, clothes, legal and political views, and every remark became fair game. A wisecrack that "I'm not some little woman standing by her man like Tammy Wynette" angered many; another comment, which she thought was taken out of context, that "I suppose I could have stayed home and baked cookies and had teas," instead of pursuing a career offended women who have chosen the traditional role of homemaker.

Indeed, it is her nontraditional choices that proved to be the crux of the issue for many. "To a large extent," writes Margaret Carlson in *Time* magazine, "the controversy swirling around Hillary Clinton today reflects a profound ambivalence toward the changing role of women in American society over the past few decades." She is often described as a lightening rod for hostile attitudes about accomplished women. Of the choices and conflicts confronting women today, Hillary Clinton has this to say: "The rules [for women] that prevail all too often in our society go something like this: If you grow up and you don't get married and you don't have children, you're an oddball. If you get married and you don't have children, you're a selfish yuppie. If you get married, have children and go out into the work world as well, you're a bad mother. And if you get married, have children and stay home, you've wasted your education."

HER ROLE AS FIRST LADY

Despite "the Hillary problem," Bill Clinton won the presidential campaign and Hillary Rodham Clinton became First Lady of the United States in January 1993. A political wife who has her own career, Hillary represents a transition in the role of First Lady; as such, she is a pioneer in re-defining this role. She will continue to fulfill the traditional domestic and social duties of running the White House and being hostess at state functions. But she will also take on major policy roles. In an unprecedented step, President Clinton appointed her to chair the President's Task Force on National Health Care Reform. Reforming the $840 billion health-care system is believed to be one of the most complex and important domestic issue facing this country—a task that will require all the intellectual acumen, leadership ability, and consensus-building skills that Hillary Rodham Clinton can command.

HOBBIES AND OTHER INTERESTS

Hillary's various activities keep her extremely busy. She reserves her free time for her daughter and husband, and has often remarked that she has had to sacrifice her social life and time with friends in order to accomplish all that she wants to do.

WRITINGS

"Children Under the Law," *Harvard Educational Review*, Vol. 43, 1973, pp. 487-514; reprinted in *The Rights of Children*, ed. by Rochelle Beck and Heather Bastow Weiss, 1982
"Children's Policies: Abandonment and Neglect," *Yale Law Journal*, Vol. 86, No. 7, 1977, pp. 1522-1531
"Children's Rights: A Legal Perspective," in *Children's Rights: Contemporary Perspectives*, ed. by Patricia A. Vardin and Ilene N. Brody, 1979
"Teacher Education," in *Beyond the Looking Glass: Papers from a National Symposium on Teacher Education Policies, Practices, and Research*, ed. by Shirley M. Hord et al., 1985

HONORS AND AWARDS

Arkansas Woman of the Year: 1983
Arkansas Young Mother of the Year: 1984
Public Citizen of the Year (National Association of Social Workers, Arkansas Chapter): 1984
National Humanitarian Award (National Conference of Christians and Jews): 1988, jointly with Bill Clinton
One of the "100 Most Influential Lawyers in America" (*National Law Journal*): 1988 and 1991
One of *Glamour* magazine's Women of the Year: 1992
Lewis Hine Award (National Child Labor Committee): 1993, for distinguished service to children and youth
Arkansas Citizen of the Year (March of Dimes Birth Defects Foundation, Arkansas Chapter): 1993, jointly with Bill Clinton

FURTHER READING

BOOKS

Allen, Charles F., and Jonathan Portis. *The Comeback Kid: The Life and Career of Bill Clinton*, 1992
Warner, Judith. *Hillary Clinton: The Inside Story*, 1993

PERIODICALS

Arkansas Times, Oct. 1989, p.33
Glamour, Aug. 1992, p.208
Good Housekeeping, Jan. 1993, p.96
Harper's Magazine, Oct. 1992, p.74
New Republic, Dec. 14, 1992, p.12

New York Review of Books, Mar. 5, 1992, p.3
New York Times, Jan. 26, 1993, p.A1
Newsweek, Nov.-Dec. 1992, p.11; Feb. 15, 1993, pp.18, 24
People, Feb. 17, 1992, p.42; Jan. 25, 1993, pp. 52, 56
Time, Jan. 27, 1992, p.19; Nov. 16, 1992, p.40
U.S. News & World Report, Apr. 27, 1992, p.30
Vanity Fair, May 1992, p.140

ADDRESS

Office of the First Lady
The White House
1600 Pennsylvania Avenue
Washington, DC 20500

Jacques Cousteau 1910-
French Marine Explorer
Film Producer, Writer, and Inventor

BIRTH

Jacques-Yves Cousteau (ZHAHK-eev koos-TOE), the legendary undersea explorer, was born June 11, 1910, in St. Andre-de-Cubzac, near the port city of Bordeaux in southwestern France. His parents, Daniel P. and Elizabeth (Duranthon) Cousteau, were residents of Paris, but had returned to their native town for the birth of their second son. The Cousteaus' other child, Pierre-Antoine, was three-and-a-half years older than Jacques. Both father and mother had come from prominent St. André families; Daniel, a lawyer, was the son of a leading businessman, and Elizabeth's family had been wealthy wine merchants for generations.

YOUTH

Tales of Cousteau's childhood read like an exciting story. Home was a Paris apartment, but the family spent most of its time traveling with wealthy American businessman James Hazen Hyde, for whom Daniel was legal adviser, companion, and business analyst. Jacques Cousteau, eighty-three this year, still remembers being lulled to sleep by the motion of trains as they sped across Europe. As the years passed, it was a continuous round of holidays on the continent, winter terms at boarding school in Paris, and summers at glamorous seaside resorts. At about the time World War I ended (1914-1918), Daniel changed employers, this time working for Eugene Higgins of New York, richer still than Hyde—a yachtsman, golfer, equestrian, and social lion who stepped up the family's already hectic activities. For two years, beginning in 1920, Higgins moved the Cousteaus to New York, a vastly different environment that turned out to be a stimulating experience for Jacques and Pierre. From their new friends on 95th Street, they learned to play stickball (an American street game using a broomstick and a lightweight ball) and, in turn, they introduced young New Yorkers to two-wheeled European roller skates. Jacques was dubbed "Jack" by the kids in the neighborhood, although the family nickname for him (adopted later in life) comes from his initials, JYC, and sounds more like "Zheek."

The Cousteau boys were sent to Camp Harvey in Vermont that first summer. Jacques was unhappy with one of the instructors, Mr. Boetz, who insisted that he learn to ride horseback. "He didn't like me very much," Cousteau says, "and I didn't like him at all. He made me ride horses, and I fell a lot. I still hate horses."

But the future marine explorer, already a competent swimmer from months spent by the sea, had his first diving experience that summer. Forced by Boetz, as punishment for pranks, to clear fallen branches and other debris from the bottom of the lake, he found what came to be his favorite camp activity. "Like all kids," he remembers, "I tried to see how long I could stay under water. I worked very hard . . . in that murk without goggles, without a mask, and that's where I learned to dive."

Jacques's interests and talents were diverse, even at an early age. He built a four-foot working model of a marine crane when he was only eleven and, two years later, designed a battery-driven car. At fifteen he bought, from his allowance, a Pathé home movie camera that he used for making surprisingly good amateur melodramas. The home productions he wrote, filmed, and acted in were the first of a "lifetime of activities," says Richard Munson in *Cousteau: The Captain and His World*, "to be recorded by his camera and set down by his pen."

EARLY MEMORIES

Among the few memories that Cousteau shares about his childhood is one that shows his lifelong preoccupation with water. He was a frail child, too weak from anemia and enteritis (intestinal inflammation) to participate in robust sports, but his father's athletic employer pushed him to learn how to swim. "When I was four or five years old, I loved touching water. Physically. Sensually. Water fascinated me—first floating ships, then me floating and stones not floating. The touch of water fascinated me all the time." Later he would say that pondering the ships he watched from the seashore "triggered my mind to become a naval officer, and from then on, I wondered what was underneath my keel. It's a very simple story."

EDUCATION

During the two years the Cousteaus lived in New York, young Jacques attended Holy Name School in Manhattan. It was here in the classroom, as well as in streets with his American playmates, that he learned and perfected his English. Understandably, however, he speaks with a heavy accent to this day. Jacques was bright and inventive, but indifferent about his formal studies. Home again in France, he was expelled from his *lycée* (high school) for misbehavior. His studies improved, though, when his exasperated parents shipped him off to a rigorous and challenging institution in the Alsace region, on the German border.

From secondary school, he went on to Collège Stanislas (St. Stanislaus Academy), and from there to the Ecole Navale, the naval academy at Brest. He graduated in 1933, second highest in a class of 1,000, and was commissioned a second lieutenant in the French navy. Later he would attend the fleet aviation school at Hourtin, near Bordeaux, but disabling injuries from an auto accident prevented him from completing the course. A few weeks before graduation, he borrowed his father's car to go to a wedding. That night, on a lonely, curving mountain road, his headlights failed, he spun out of control, and crashed into the darkness. With crushed ribs, perforated lungs, a severely fractured left arm, and a paralyzed right arm, he was fortunate to be found alive. Remembering the horror of the night, he says, "I thought I was going to die. I was losing my blood. . . .Trying to lie down on my back, which hurt a lot, looking at the sky and the stars, I said 'my God, how lucky I was to have seen so many things in my life.'"

Strange as it may seem, the accident probably saved Cousteau's life. He was reassigned to a different section of the navy after long months of therapy and recuperation. Says author Alex Madsen in *Cousteau: An Unauthorized Biography*, "With one exception, all his clasmates at the aviation school were killed in the opening weeks of the war that was only three short years away."

CHOOSING A CAREER

Even as a boy, Jacques Cousteau knew that he wanted to spend his life at sea, so his efforts to be accepted at the naval academy were a natural progression of his dreams. As a midshipman he sailed with his class on a round-the-world cruise and used his ever-present camera to make a documentary. "In many ways," says Susan Sinott in her 1992 book, *Jacques-Yves Cousteau*, "this first full-scale expedition whetted his appetite for future seafaring expeditions."

CAREER HIGHLIGHTS

Cousteau's first assignment after graduation from the naval academy was at the French base in Shanghai. He returned to France to train as a navy flier and after his accident was reassigned to a base at Toulon, and then to carrier duty in the Mediterranean. When France fell to Nazi Germany in World War II (1939-1945), Cousteau worked for the underground resistance movement. The underground fought against the Nazis and the Vichy government, which the Germans had set up to control France. For his services, which he has never discussed in detail, but which made use of his skills at photography, he was given France's highest military award, the Légion d'Honneur, as well as the Croix de Guerre (War Cross) with palm.

Cousteau was also concentrating on his most compelling interest during the war years. He continued to dive and make underwater films and to work on the problems of breathing beneath the surface. From his experimentation on the latter, he and a Paris engineer, Emile Gagnan, developed equipment that is now used throughout the world by divers—self-contained underwater breathing apparatus, or SCUBA. After the war, a French company manufactured Cousteau's Aqua-lung, the frogman breathing unit that revolutionized undersea exploration.

In 1946, Cousteau organized and led the French navy's Undersea Research Group in clearing German mines from Mediterranean ports. The team also used the Aqua-lung to perfect diving techniques and underwater photography and to observe sea life in its own habitat. Cousteau's postwar service to the French government was in direct contrast to what was happening in his brother's life. Pierre, a controversial journalist, had been convicted of collaborating with, or supporting, the Germans. He was sentenced to death. The sentence was commuted, however, and Pierre spent ten years in prison. "Jacques's display of loyalty to his collaborationist brother," writes Richard Munson in his biography, "haunted him throughout his naval career . . . . Cousteau would be given responsibilities, but he remained a captain while [others] earned further advancements."

THE OCEANOGRAPHIC VESSEL

Eager to further his exploration of the deep, Cousteau formed a nonprofit organization in 1946 to buy a converted British minesweeper. He christened the vessel the *Calypso*, after the sea maiden in Homer's ancient epic *The Odyssey*. With friends Philippe Taillez and Frédéric Dumas, the naval officer and champion spearfisherman who would remain his partners in adventure, he outfitted the ship with a diving platform and underwater observation chamber and readied it for its first expedition to the Red Sea. His crew searched through the remains of shipwrecks, looked for oil, and made underwater films. In 1952, Cousteau came to the United States to find additional funds for his explorations on the *Calypso*. The National Geographic Society responded, making it possible for the French adventurer to continue his work and to record his expeditions on film. Although much of the new equipment and many techniques developed on the *Calypso* have found their way into commercial use, Cousteau's primary aim has remained exploring the wonder and enjoyment of the adventures themselves. One of his oft-quoted remarks on the subject explains: "In the beginning . . . I was investigating an unknown world—not unknown scientifically, but unknown visually. Naturally, I was fascinated by it. It was like giving a child an inexhaustible new toy. It was the same with inventions. It is fun to play with toys."

In 1957, Cousteau retired from the navy and turned his energies full-time to his marine explorations. He invented a submarine unit called the "Diving Saucer" in 1959 and three years later developed the first of three underwater research colonies. In Conshelf I (Continental Shelf Station), two aquanauts (people who explore the sea) spent a week under water. Conshelf II in 1963 was a similar success with a staff of five who were able to make dives as deep as 360 feet. From this latter experiment came the 1964 Oscar-winning film, *World Without Sun*. Cousteau's marine explorations continued in 1965 with Conshelf III, during which six men spent a month beneath the water. Their experience became a television special, shown in the United States as "The World of Jacques Cousteau."

Books, lectures, films, and TV specials followed as Cousteau and his team journeyed the oceans, seas, rivers, and large lakes of the world, capturing their adventures on film. In 1985, a still-vigorous Cousteau, seventy-five years old, set out on his refurbished *Calypso* for a round-the-world voyage called Rediscovery of the World.

Jacques Cousteau is deeply committed to environmental issues. His Cousteau Society was founded in 1974 as a nonprofit organization dedicated "to the protection and improvement of life" on this planet. "The aim of our society is to make waves," he says. He has met that aim through wide media coverage and has also inspired considerable controversy over his outspoken efforts. "Those of us who love the sea," he pleads, "who recognize the blood relationship of all Earth's beings, who see on this water planet a growing threat to our most fundamental biological machinery . . . can wield the formidable power of our numbers."

Cousteau's vigorous efforts continue despite his increasing age. In the summer of 1992, a month past his eighty-second birthday, Cousteau presented a new environmental film at the international Earth Summit in Rio de Janeiro, Brazil.

MARRIAGE AND FAMILY

On July 12, 1937, Jacques Cousteau was married to Simone Melchior, a descendant of three generations of French admirals. They were natural for one another—he with a promising navy career, she with a young life influenced by a family dedicated to service at sea. Simone had spent part of her childhood in Japan, where her father was stationed before retiring to become an executive with Air Liquide, France's major producer of industrial gases.

Two children were born to Jacques and Simone Cousteau: Jean-Michel in March 1938, and Philippe in December 1939. Both boys were introduced early to the sea and became expert divers when they were little more than toddlers. The youngest son, a dashing adventurer, cinematographer, and aquanaut who worked with his father on expeditions and productions, was killed in a seaplane accident near Alverca, Portugal, on June 28, 1979, leaving a pregnant wife (an American, Janice Sullivan) and a young daughter; a son was born a few months later. Jean-Michel, trained as an architect, became more involved with his father's activities and businesses after his brother's death. In addition to Philippe's children, there are two other grandchildren in the Cousteau family.

The senior Cousteaus spent most of their time for decades aboard the *Calypso,* but also kept an apartment in Paris and another in Monaco, overlooking the Mediterranean. Simone died in Paris on January 2, 1990, at the age of seventy-two. Today, Jacques is often at the Monaco apartment, where he continues to summon friends and acquaintances for a meal or for conversation about new ideas and new technologies. Even at his advanced age, Cousteau declines to work on his memoirs. Perhaps, as Richard Munson writes, "they hold the terrors of a life coming to an end."

MAJOR INFLUENCES

The internationally celebrated Cousteau, who numbers heads of state, prominent scientists, giants of industry, and celebrities from all walks of life among his friends and associates, credits his mother with having the most profound influence on his life. Her death in the early 1950s came as a crushing blow to him and to the entire family, which had looked to

Elizabeth for strength in the difficult days during and immediately following World War II. She had withstood her eldest son's disgrace as a Nazi collaborator, and in fact was in Paris to visit him in prison when she was felled by a stroke.

"On Jacques's seventy-fifth birthday," writes biographer Richard Munson, "he declared that of all the people he ever met, his mother had the greatest influence on his life. 'She was a sincere, hardworking woman who never committed a sin, never hurt another human being. She demanded performance and quality. She promoted the arts. She provided stability.'"

MEMORABLE EXPERIENCES

In a lifetime filled with experiences far beyond what most people can imagine, Jacques Cousteau recalls one special day, when he was only twenty-six, that changed the focus of his life forever. Wearing aviator's goggles as he combed the waters of the shoreline near Toulon for fish, he slipped beneath the surface and felt a new thrill at being able to see so clearly under water. Cousteau later recounted that moment in *The Silent World*, his 1953 book written with Frédéric Dumas. "I was astounded by what I saw," he said. "Rocks covered with green, brown and silver forests of algae and fishes unknown to me swimming in crystalline water. Standing up to breathe I saw a trolley car, people, electric light poles. I put my eyes under again and civilization vanished with one last bow. I was in a jungle never seen by those who floated on the opaque roof."

HOBBIES AND OTHER INTERESTS

So much of Cousteau's life has been spent on his career that little has been said about his many other interests. He is known to write poetry—which he discards—to paint landscapes, and to play the piano, for which he had classical training as a child. At times, he sits alone to listen to music from his extensive record collection.

SELECTED WORKS

BOOKS

The Silent World (with Frédéric Dumas), 1953
Captain Cousteau's Underwater Treasury (editor, with James Dugan), 1963
The Living Sea (with James Dugan), 1963
World Without Sun (English-language edition edited by James Dugan), 1965
The Shark: Splendid Savage of the Sea (with Philippe Cousteau), part of the "Undersea Discovery" series that included *The Whale: Mighty Monarch of the Sea*, 1972; *Diving for Sunken Treasure* (with Philippe Diolé), 1972; and *Dolphins*, 1975
Calypso (part of the "Ocean World" 22-volume encyclopedia series), 1984

FILMS

The Silent World, 1956
The Golden Fish, 1959
World Without Sun, 1964
Voyage to the Edge of the World, 1975

Cousteau also produced 20 short documentaries between 1942 and 1956.

TELEVISION SERIES

"The World of Jacques-Yves Cousteau", 1966-68
"The Undersea World of Jacques-Yves Cousteau", 1968-76
"Oasis in Space", 1977
"The Cousteau Odyssey Series", 1977-81
"The Cousteau Amazon Series", 1984-85

TV SPECIALS

"The Silent World", 1966
"Cries From the Deep", 1982
"St. Lawrence: Stairway to the Sea", 1982
"The Reluctant Ally", 1985
"The Friendly Foe", 1985

HONORS AND AWARDS

SELECTED LIST

Légion d'Honneur and the Croix de Guerre, with palm (after World War II)
Berthault Prize (Academy of Sciences): 1958
Gold Medal (National Geographic Society): 1961
Gold Medal (Royal Geographic Society of London): 1963
Washburn Medal (Boston Museum of Science): 1965
Potts Medal (Franklin Institute): 1970
International Environmental Prize (United Nations): 1977 (co- recipient)
Founders Award (International Council of National Academy of Arts and Sciences): 1987
Presidential Medal of Freedom: 1985
TV Hall of Fame: 1987
Centennial Award (National Geographic Society): 1988
Induction into French Academy: 1989
Third International Catalan Prize: 1991

Also:

Oscar Awards (National Academy of Arts and Sciences): 1957, 1960, 1964
Emmy Awards (National Academy of Television Arts and Sciences): 1970, 1971, 1972, 1974

FURTHER READING

BOOKS

Contemporary Authors, Vol.15
Cousteau, Jacques-Yves. *The Silent World*, 1953
Madsen, Axel. *Cousteau: An Unauthorized Biography*, 1986
Munson, Richard. *Cousteau: The Captain and His World*, 1989
Sinnott, Susan. *Jacques-Yves Cousteau*, 1992
Something About the Author, Vol.38

PERIODICALS

Current Biography Yearbook 1976
New York Times Biographical Service, June 1979, p.753
UNESCO Courier, Nov. 1991, p.8

ADDRESS

Cousteau Society
870 Greenbrier Circle
Chesapeake, VA 23320

Cindy Crawford 1966-
American Fashion Model

BIRTH

Cynthia Crawford was born February 20, 1966, in De Kalb, Illinois, a rural community and also the home of Northern Illinois University. Her father, Dan, was an electrician and glazier, and her mother, Jennifer, was a homemaker. She has two sisters, Chris, who is older, and Danielle, who is younger. Another sibling, Jeff, died of leukemia when Crawford was eight. Her parents are now divorced.

EARLY MEMORIES

Her parents' marriage disintegrated several years after her brother's death. Crawford has bitter memories of that period of her life.

"The hardest thing in my life has been to see my parents step off a pedestal. I was angry because I grew up thinking they were perfect." Her father left, and her mother bore the brunt of Cindy's anger. She found her mother's acceptance of the traditional role of homemaker to be backward and unchallenging. "I was rebelling against what my mother was at the time. I loved her, but I didn't respect her. She didn't fight being a mom."

YOUTH

As teenagers, Cindy and her sisters used to ride around town in an old 1976 Impala, driving to a mall that was some 40 miles from home. During the summer, Cindy would babysit, clean houses, and work in the corn-fields, pollinating corn. She was pretty, and her friends often encouraged her to get into modeling, but it didn't appeal to her. At that time, she neither wore makeup nor read the fashion magazines for which she would later model.

EDUCATION

Cindy attended the local grade schools and did well academically. She was a straight-A student and graduated from De Kalb High School as valedictorian. "From the sixth grade on, Cindy never saw a grade under an A," a teacher from her high school remembers. She had aspirations at the time to become the first woman president, and she remembers wearing an ERA (Equal Rights Amendment) button on her senior class trip. She applied and was accepted into the chemical engineering program at Northwestern University. But modeling intervened, and she never finished her degree.

FIRST JOBS

Cindy began modeling at the age of 15, during her sophomore year in high school, first at a local department store, then in Chicago and surrounding areas. She was chosen to appear as "Co-Ed of the Week" for a local college newspaper, then she volunteered as a model for a Clairol demonstration in Chicago. Her parents wanted her to make it on her brains and not her face, so they were less than encouraging. But they lent her $500 to get started, and the money she made was so good that she was able to pay them back with her first paycheck. During her senior year, she would drive to Chicago, fly to shoots, and get back in time the next day for classes. The agency she was working with merged with the famed Elite Modeling Agency in New York, and Crawford entered the Elite Look of the Year contest. She didn't win, but she did make the finals. The summer after her senior year, she worked in Europe and hated it. She was forced to cut and dye her hair, and the hours and demands were too much. She returned home and entered Northwestern.

While in college, Crawford continued to model part-time. She began to work with legendary Chicago fashion photographer Victor Skrebneski, and doors started opening for her. She stayed with Skrebneski for two years, leaving college in the process and making $200,000 a year. After a falling out with Skrebneski over a dual booking, she left the Midwest and settled in New York in 1986, at the age of 20.

CAREER HIGHLIGHTS

Crawford was a surprise and instant hit in the modeling world. With her olive skin, brown eyes, and curvaceous figure, she was a distinct departure from the previous modeling ideal of a waif-like, blue-eyed, and painfully thin blonde. She also had a distinctive mole above her lip, one that early modeling coaches urged her to have removed, advice she refused to take.

This supermodel, whose face has graced more than 200 magazine covers, now earns $1 million a year from her Revlon contract alone, and makes $10,000 a day as a working model. She got to the pinnacle of her profession through hard work and determination. In a field where models are often notorious prima donnas, prone to outrageous behavior and a wild lifestyle, Crawford is admired as a smart, courteous professional. "A lot of models go to clubs after work and stay out until three in the morning, but I'm not one of them," she says. When she was getting started, she worried so much that she wound up getting an ulcer. She now has learned to take the demanding life of a model—the hectic scheduling and the travel—more in stride.

Crawford appeals to many age groups and types. The rock star Prince wrote a song for her, called "Cindy C," that appeared on his *Black Album*. Besides her Revlon ads, she is also seen in a well-known commercial for Pepsi that first aired during the 1993 Superbowl, in which two little boys, watching Cindy approach a Pepsi machine, are more impressed by the new Pepsi can than by her.

Crawford appears to have a realistic focus on her chosen field: "*Vogue* uses me. I have no delusions. They say they love me, but when I don't sell their magazine, they won't love me anymore. It's flattering, it's fun, some girls get caught up in it. What does it really matter, four covers for *Vogue* or five or ten? I plan to make bigger contributions than that in my lifetime." And she condemns the attitude that models are dumb: "It's not just outsiders who think we're dumb. People within the business talk down to you, use one-syllable words. I was valedictorian of my high school—a four-point average—and I don't think I should be treated like someone with an elementary school education."

In 1988, Crawford made the move into television, becoming the host of "House of Style," a very successful program on MTV that appears six times a year and features segments on the latest in the fashion industry. Her work on "House of Style" has been praised by New York Times critic Woody Hochswender, who finds her delivery "poised and articulate," and who notes her "gentle cynicism of an insider, one who would demystify fashion without debunking it."

Crawford likes the turn in her career. She feels that, because she is an insider, the models and photographers will be more open with her. She has no pretensions about the show's purpose: "It isn't hard news. It can be funny or goofy." But she does want to tackle more serious issues on the show and has included segments on bulimia and breast implants. She also plans a piece on the pitfalls of modeling. "We get so many letters from girls who want to find out how to become models. Every 15-year-old girl wants to be a model, but most of them don't have the look or the height or whatever. We'll expose some of the scam schools." In another career move outside the realm of modeling, Crawford released a best-selling exercise video in 1992.

Already planning for the post-modelling part of her life, Crawford hopes to be the "Barbara Walters of my generation," and also wants to eventually get into Hollywood films. She's been offered film roles she finds demeaning, and she has refused them. "Hollywood scares me," she admits. "It's really Boys Town out there . . . . Modeling is perhaps the only business in the world where women have more power than men. To go back to being

another girl isn't all that interesting." With her current schedule of commitments, she can take her time until the right offers come along.

MARRIAGE AND FAMILY

Crawford met her husband, actor Richard Gere, at a party photographer Herb Ritts threw for Elton John in 1988. They eloped to Las Vegas in December 1991, exchanging wedding rings made of tin foil. She acknowledges the difficulties of keeping up a relationship when both members have hectic schedules. "If anything's a priority, [the marriage] would be it." Crawford and Gere have three homes: a Manhattan apartment, a California beach house, and a country home in New York's Westchester county. Crawford would love to have children, and she is looking forward to that phase of her life. "I love kids and sort of feel that's the thing in my life I'm going to be best at, a mother."

HOBBIES AND OTHER INTERESTS

One-half of the proceeds from Crawford's successful pin-up calendar go to support the research efforts to fight leukemia, the disease that took her brother's life. Crawford is also an avid reader and mentions Lillian Hellman and Isabella Allende among her favorite authors.

CREDITS

House of Style, 1989-
Cindy Crawford: Shape Your Body Workout, 1992

FURTHER READING

BOOKS

Italia, Robert. *Cindy Crawford,* 1992 (juvenile)

PERIODICALS

Harper's Bazaar, July 1988, p.112; July 1989, p.58
Mademoiselle, Sep. 1992, p.162
New York, Oct. 30, 1989, p.33
New York Times, Dec. 19, 1991, p.C14; July 19, 1992, p. IX: 5
Parade, Jan. 31, 1993. p.12
People, Jan. 13, 1992, p.36; Apr. 27, 1992, p.117
Redbook, Sep. 1992, p.110
Seventeen, May 1990, p.165; Mar. 1992, p.182
Style, Spring 1992, p.41
Vogue, Aug. 1989, p.378; Nov. 1992, p.258

ADDRESS

Elite Model Management
111 E. 22nd St.
New York, NY 10010

Macaulay Culkin   1980-
American Actor
Star of *Home Alone* and *Home Alone 2: Lost in New York*

BIRTH

Macaulay Culkin was born in New York City on August 26, 1980. His father, Christopher (Kit), is a former actor, taxi driver, and Catholic church sacristan, while his mother, Pat, is a former homemaker and telephone answering service operator. Both quit their jobs to help manage his career. Mack, as he prefers to be called, has six brothers and sisters: Shane, Dakota, Kiernan, Quinn, Christian, and Rory. Performing seems to run in the family. In addition to his father, several of Macaulay's siblings also act, as does his aunt, Bonnie Bedelia, best known for her roles in *Heart Like a Wheel*, *Die Hard*, and *Presumed Innocent*.

YOUTH

Mack lives on the Upper East Side of Manhattan, in New York City. Until recently, his family was crammed into a four-room apartment, and Mack shared a bedroom with all of his siblings. The success of his movies has allowed the family to buy a five-bedroom brownstone, where Mack now has his own room—and, more importantly, his own TV. "I watch everything. My parents can't limit me," he claims, "because I have a TV in my room and a lock on my door." He particularly enjoys Bart Simpson and "Saturday Night Live," especially Wayne and Garth.

But he has other interests as well. Mack likes skateboarding, playing Nintendo, bowling, professional wrestling, listening to music, and hanging out at the Museum of Natural History. Despite his large income, he gets $10 a week as an allowance, although his parents will usually give him extra money if he asks. If all this sounds like just an average kid, he is also a friend of Michael Jackson's; the two like to play video games and go shopping at Toys R Us, and Culkin appeared in Jackson's "Black and White" video.

EDUCATION

Culkin first attended the private St. Joseph's School of Yorkvile, a parochial school on the Upper East Side of Manhattan, and more recently transferred to a school for professional children, also in New York. While filming, he spends at least three hours each day working with a tutor on the set, as mandated by law. School is definitely not his favorite pastime. His teachers say that he likes math and science, but hates English class. He is known for playing pranks on his tutors, like pretending to be dead on the floor of his trailer, stealing a walkie-talkie to order champagne and caviar for lunch, and, in one inspired bit, putting two-sided sticky tape on a toilet seat so the tutor got stuck there. According to the instructor who worked with him on the set of *My Girl* (the one who got stuck to the toilet seat), "He is a B student academically, but I give him an A for street smarts."

CAREER HIGHLIGHTS

For someone so young, Culkin has had quite a varied career. A talented actor and dancer, he has appeared in plays, films, and dance productions. He started acting at age four, appearing on stage with the rest of his siblings in 1984 in "Bach Babies." He was taking dance lessons already, and at a recital that year he first demonstrated an instinct for good theater.

"He did this little dance step," his father recalls. "He wasn't self-conscious, he wasn't looking for his parents, and the audience was immediately amused. He had that kind of joie de performance—like the stage was the only place to be." He appeared in several other theatrical productions before winning his first movie role, in *Rocket Gibraltar* (1988) with Burt Lancaster. In 1989 he appeared in *Uncle Buck,* and many reviewers credited him with stealing the show from the accomplished comic actor John Candy.

HOME ALONE

While he went on to appear in other films, it was *Home Alone* (1990) that made his fame. In this story he played Kevin McCallister, who is accidentally left at home when his family leaves on a Christmas trip to Paris without him. The movie depicts a great childhood fantasy: Kevin lives on junk food, bounces on the beds, slides down the bannister, and even defends his home and fends off a pair of inept burglars by devising a bunch of pranks. Mischievous, imaginative, and clever, Kevin is said to be much like Mack. Though the film was criticized as implausible and overly sentimental, it was a phenomenal success. While Culkin was only paid about $100,000 for his work on the film, *Home Alone* is the highest grossing comedy and the third-highest grossing movie of all time (after *E.T.* and *Star Wars*), earning almost $300 million in the U.S. and Canada and over $500 million worldwide.

Some of Culkin's success can surely be credited to his parents. As his managers, they read the scripts and decide which roles will best suit his talent and which films will best further his career. Mack himself often points to their role, saying "I don't read many scripts. My parents read them and tell me about it and say whether it's any good or not. It's not my opinion, it's not like I choose." In addition, his parents deal with the movie studios, negotiating salaries and contracts.

They have been criticized for some of their decisions. Mack followed up his leading role in *Home Alone* by next appearing in a supporting role in *My Girl* (1991), a dark comedy about a young girl dealing with growing up and the deaths of her mother and her friend. The Culkins soon came under fire in the media, as many objected to the film's handling of the issue of death. There were also reports that Mack's parents had begun to throw their weight around following the success of *Home Alone,* holding up production on a film for which many, including its director, believed Mack was unsuited. The Culkins describe it differently. They say that they look for films that will broaden their son's appeal and strengthen his career as an actor, and they also argue that he deserves to wield some clout, based on the phenomenal financial success of his movie and the fortune that he has made for the studio.

HOME ALONE 2

Culkin scored another hit with the sequel *Home Alone 2: Lost in New York* (1992). It's Christmastime again, and the McCallisters are getting ready for another holiday trip, this time to Florida. Problems arise, though, when Kevin gets on the wrong plane at busy Chicago O'Hare airport and ends up alone in New York. Kevin sets up camp at the posh Plaza Hotel while his parents frantically try to reach him. Once again he meets up with the creepy burglars (who have escaped from prison), is helped by strangers, successfully boobytraps a house, and is ultimately reunited with his family. The movie received mixed reviews: some considered the familiar storyline reassuring and enjoyable, while others considered it formulaic and predictable. Although the plot might be similar to the earlier movie, Culkin's salary changed dramatically: it's been reported that he received about $5 million. Like its predecessor, *Home Alone 2* was an immediate box office hit and is expected to gross about $400 million.

FUTURE PROSPECTS

Since finishing *Home Alone 2*, Culkin has worked on a couple of other projects, including dancing in a production of "The Nutcracker" with the New York City Ballet; the film version is due out in 1993. There has been much speculation on whether Culkin will be able to make the transition from child star to adult actor, when he is no longer so cute. Few child

stars do. As David Handelman wrote in the *New York Times Magazine*, "[It's] difficult to assess the long-term prospects of someone who hasn't yet gone through puberty. Mack has an ineffable charm and believability, but it's unclear how that will translate in deeper waters." Still, according to Chris Columbus, the director of the *Home Alone* movies, Culkin has the talent to make it: "He could certainly continue if he doesn't get bored with it. He was always really interested in the cameras and the storyboards, so, who knows, maybe he'll be a director one day." For now, Culkin just says, "I don't think that far ahead."

ACTING TECHNIQUE

Reviewers often note Culkin's captivating presence on screen. As explained by Howard Zieff, the director of *My Girl*, "When he's doing the scene live, it seems like a straight reading. So we were always surprised, when we looked at the dailies [film from that day's work], how much he was giving. He's just one of those lucky actors the camera loves. He has his own technique; what comes out of him is straight Mack." Acting is "simple," according to Culkin: "I just pretend I'm that person. I like pretending."

But director Chris Columbus disagrees with Culkin's assessment of his own talent: "He says he just pretends when he acts, but he has more technique than he's aware of. There's maybe a 30 percent intuition factor."

STAGE AND FILM CREDITS

AfterSchool Special, 1987 (stage performance)
Rocket Gibraltar, 1988
See You in the Morning, 1989
Uncle Buck, 1989
Home Alone, 1990
Jacob's Ladder, 1990
My Girl, 1991
Only the Lonely, 1991
Home Alone 2: Lost in New York, 1992

HONORS AND AWARDS

American Comedy Awards: 1991, Funniest Actor in a Motion Picture, for *Home Alone*

FURTHER READING

BOOKS
Reisfeld, Randi. *Young Stars*, 1992

PERIODICALS

Ladies' Home Journal, May 1991, p.112
New York Times Magazine, Dec. 29, 1991, p.10
People, Dec. 17, 1990, p.127; Nov. 23, 1992, p.58
Saturday Evening Post, Apr. 1991, p.82

ADDRESS

ICM
40 W. 57th St.
New York, NY 10019

Lois Duncan 1934-
American Writer for Children and Young Adults
Author of *Stranger with My Face* and
Don't Look Behind You

BIRTH

Lois Duncan Steinmetz Arquette, who writes under the name Lois
Duncan, was born in Philadelphia, Pennsylvania, on April 28,
1934. Her father and mother, Joseph Janney Steinmetz and Lois
(Foley) Steinmetz, both worked as magazine photographers. Duncan has one younger brother, Bill.

YOUTH

Duncan grew up in Sarasota, Florida, where the family moved
soon after brother Billy was born. They lived in a relatively isolated

spot near the beach. From there, her parents were able to take photo assignments throughout the South and in the Caribbean, too, usually during summer vacations so the children could accompany them. Her early home life was loving, secure, and completely devoid of the violence that often shows up in her books: "I was raised in a very loving, gentle home, we had rules and I obeyed them and all my friends obeyed them. I didn't know violence existed; we didn't even have television to let us know that."

Duncan was a bit of a loner, a solitary child who enjoyed riding bikes, playing in the woods, and exploring the beach by herself. This tendency was reinforced, in part, by her visual disability. Duncan has no visual memory, and she finds it extremely difficult to recognize people, even just after she has met them. Making new friends was a difficult process of trying to memorize their features. She found the whole experience so embarrassing, in fact, that she wouldn't even discuss it with her parents—this at a time when a number of disabilities were commonly undiagnosed that can be treated today. For years she simply used memory tricks in an attempt to make up for her disability. It wasn't until years later, when one of Duncan's children was diagnosed with a learning disability at school, that she learned that hers was a medical condition related to the shape of the brain. As she eventually discovered, though, two things helped to solidify her memory of a scene—to take a picture of it, or to describe it in writing. No wonder that photography and writing became her two favorite pastimes.

BECOMING A WRITER

As Duncan recalls, her love of writing began at an early age. "I can't remember a time when I didn't think of myself as a writer. When I was three years old I was dictating poems and stories to my parents, and as soon as I learned to print, I was writing them down for myself. At 10 I was submitting stories to magazines, and at 13 I started selling them. Throughout my teens I wrote regularly for youth publications, such as Seventeen, and I wrote my first young adult novel when I was 20.

"Obviously, I was not your everyday, well-adjusted kid. A shy, homely little girl, I was a bookworm and a dreamer."

Many of Duncan's early experiences are described in her autobiography, Chapters: My Growth as a Writer. This book includes Duncan's descriptions of the events from her youth and her stories from the same time, allowing the reader to trace the development of her skill. Above all, it documents her tenacity and determination to become a writer.

Although she began to submit stories at 10 to national magazines, for three years, she jokes, her hobby was collecting rejection slips. One factor in her success was some advice she received from family friend and Pulitzer-Prize winning writer MacKinley Kantor. Duncan, not quite a teenager, had been writing passionate stories about romance and violence. As Duncan recalls, Kantor said it was all trash. "Good writing comes from the heart, not off the top of the head," he advised. "Throw this stuff away, child, and go write a story about something you know. Write something that rings true."

Although Duncan was devastated, she followed his advice. Her next story was accepted by the teen magazine *Calling All Girls*, earning $25. And as her autobiography makes clear, this was the most exciting event of her youth. With that first published piece she chose "Lois Duncan" as her pen name, using her first and middle name and dropping her last name to avoid being confused with her mother, after whom she was named. Duncan continued to work hard, and her efforts soon paid off: at age 16 she won second prize in *Seventeen* magazine's annual short story contest, at age 17 she won third prize, and at age 18 she won first prize.

EDUCATION

By that time she had come out of her shell a bit, and was having more success both socially and academically. She worked on both the high school yearbook and newspaper, and by her senior year she was editor of the yearbook. As Duncan recalls, she had expected to be named to the top position at the newspaper as well, editor in chief. But the journalism teacher said that position was always given to a boy, so she resigned herself to being managing editor.

Education was a tradition for Duncan's family. Her mother and father (graduates of Smith and Princeton) expected her to attend college, and she willingly enrolled at Duke University in North Carolina. But as she says, "It was a total surprise to discover that I was out of place there." The lack of privacy drove her crazy, and the sea of new faces, coupled with her visual disability, made it impossible for her to identify people. She did well in her classes though, making the honor roll in her first semester. While she managed to complete all her term papers, she was frustrated by her inability to write stories and novels, a problem that continued for the next few years. By the end of her first semester she announced to her parents that she might quit after her first year. The choices, if she did so, were few. At that time, single women didn't typically live on their own; they lived either with their parents, at college, or got married. So she returned to school and started dating a senior pre-law student. In May 1953, at age 19, Duncan got married and dropped out of Duke.

Years later, Duncan returned to college and graduated cum laude from the University of New Mexico in 1977, with a B.A. in English.

FIRST MARRIAGE

Duncan was married to her first husband, whom she now identifies only as Buzz, for nine years. They had three children, Robin, Kerry, and Brett. Those were difficult years for Duncan. During the first two years of their marriage, Buzz was in the U.S. Air Force, and the family moved frequently as he was transferred around. After receiving his discharge, Buzz moved the family to St. Petersburg, Florida, where he enrolled in law school. Between attending classes, studying at the library, and socializing with other students, Buzz soon spent little time at home. That only got worse when he completed law school and began working long hours as an attorney.

Despite her busy life caring for her children, Duncan was finally motivated to return to her writing. She started out with magazine articles and soon moved on to teen romance novels. Her first success came with *Debutante Hill* (1958). Against the advice of her new agent, she submitted it to a national contest sponsored by the publishers Dodd, Mead and Company—and won! Prizes included $1000, publication of her story, and a contract for her next book. Duncan took great pride in publishing her first book. Finally, she felt, she could call herself an author. Over the next few years, she went on to publish several more teen romances.

Despite this success in her work life, Duncan's personal life was falling apart. When she was 27, Buzz fell in love with someone else. He and Lois were divorced shortly after the birth of their third child, and Duncan and her children moved to Albuquerque, New Mexico, to be near her brother, Bill.

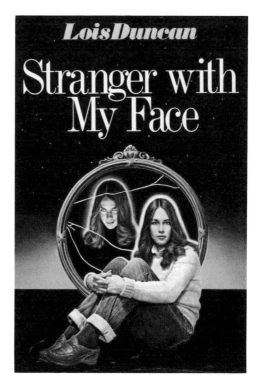

BUILDING A CAREER

With three small children to support, Duncan began working at a small advertising agency, doing general office work and writing some ad copy. On her lunch hours, she entered writing contests. When she won $500 for a short piece on the most frightening experience of her life, she quickly decided to quit her job. For the next few years Duncan supported her family by free-lance writing, sitting down to her typewriter each day to compose articles, short stories, and fictional "confessions"—purportedly true magazine stories in which the author confesses to some dreadful act.

SECOND MARRIAGE

Duncan continued writing confessions for several years, until the time of her second marriage. On July 15, 1965, she married Donald Wayne Arquette, an electrical engineer. He adopted her three children, and they had two of their own, Donald Jr. and Kaitlyn.

CAREER HIGHLIGHTS

Duncan's remarriage brought her the financial security to leave confessional writing behind. When she tried writing other types of stories, she was surprised and pleased to discover that those years of practice had paid off. At the time, Duncan was only trying to earn enough to support her children, but in retrospect, it is clear that she was also teaching herself the elements of good writing. As she later wrote, "Somehow, during those years of sitting down every day and forcing out words, I had learned the professional way of telling a story, and those story-telling techniques could evidently be transferred over into other forms of writing."

Since that time, Duncan's career as a writer has taken off in several different directions. She began publishing articles and stories for adults in such national magazines as *Good Housekeeping, Redbook, McCall's, Ladies' Home Journal, Reader's Digest,* and *Saturday Evening Post,* among others; she also became a contributing editor for *Woman's Day* magazine. In addition, she taught journalism classes at the University of New Mexico from 1970 to 1982. For a woman who had dropped out of college after only one year this required no small amount of courage, and her success as a college instructor motivated her to work toward her own bachelor's degree, which she received in 1977.

In addition to her work for magazines, Duncan began to write in a variety of genres, including humor books, romances, picture books, poetry, historical fiction, biography, and other nonfiction. But novels for teenagers proved to be her favorite. She quickly discovered that the world had changed a great deal since she published *Debutante Hill* in the late 1950s. As she explained, "One major change is the sophisticated subject matter that is now deemed appropriate for teenagers. The first book I wrote was returned for revision, because in it I had a 19-year-old drink a beer. Today, there are books for young people on every subject imaginable, from alcoholism to premarital sex to mental illness."

Duncan soon began to explore such serious issues in her own young adult writings, often in the context of a mystery or suspense story. *Ransom* (1966), a story about five teenagers who are kidnapped by their bus driver, was her first such young adult novel. In *A Gift of Magic* (1971), Duncan tells the story of three siblings and the special gift of extra-sensory perception (ESP) that one possesses. This was her first book to feature psychic and supernatural phenomena, a subject that proved immensely popular and that has distinguished many of her subsequent critically acclaimed and award-winning books, including *Summer of Fear* (1976), *Killing Mr. Griffin* (1978), *Stranger with My Face* (1981), *The Third Eye* (1984), *Locked in Time* (1985), and *The Twisted Window* (1987). Her last work of suspense was *Don't Look Behind You* (1989), a story about a family relocated under the FBI's Witness Protection Plan. In it, the character April Corrigan is chased by a gunman in a Camaro. When Duncan's youngest child, Kaitlyn Arquette, was killed in July 1989, the circumstances eerily paralleled those in *Don't Look Behind You*.

Kaitlyn Arquette, just 18, was chased and shot by a gunman in a Camaro while she was driving home from her girlfriend's house in Albuquerque, New Mexico. The police called it a random shooting, but Duncan has never believed it. Her own attempts to understand what happened motivated her to write a book about the experience, *Who Killed My Daughter?* (1992). This account details some of the events that led up to and followed Kaitlyn's death, including information about the police investigation and the family's use of psychic detectives. In an Author's Note preceding the story, Duncan explained her goal: "After spending two years investigating Kait's death, our family has managed to accumulate enough information to form a fragmented picture of what may have happened to her, but the jigsaw puzzle still lacks the few key pieces that could nail the identity of her killers. It is my hope that reading Kait's story will motivate potential informants to supply us with those pieces." The case is still unsolved.

While many have called *Who Killed My Daughter?* strangely reminiscent of Duncan's own fiction, her plans to return to such work are currently on hold. Instead, she plans to follow up her recent experiences with a book investigating psychic phenomena. She is currently collaborating with Dr. William Roll, the director of the Psychical Research Foundation, on a non-fiction book tentatively titled *The Psychic Connection*.

HOBBIES AND OTHER INTERESTS

Duncan's hobbies include riding horses, traveling, attending the theater, reading murder mysteries, and planning family events. She is also an avid fan of photography. As she writes in *Chapters*, "To broaden myself as a person, I took up photography, and found to my amazement that I enjoyed it tremendously. Growing up in a photographers' household, I had unconsciously absorbed a good deal of knowledge about technique and composition, and before long I was taking good enough pictures to use as illustrations for some of my articles. I also discovered that photography was one way of coping with my visual memory problem. If I lined a scene up in the viewfinder of a camera, I remembered it! Not the scene itself, but the camera image. And with the photographic print to reinforce my memory, I could actually absorb a person's features so well that I knew who he was the next time I saw him."

Since her daughter's death, though, Duncan has neglected such interests, and most of her energy has gone toward finding Kait's killers.

WRITINGS

FOR YOUNG ADULTS

Debutante Hill, 1958
Love Songs for Joyce, 1958 (as Lois Kerry)
A Promise for Joyce, 1959 (as Lois Kerry)
The Middle Sister, 1961
Game of Danger, 1962
Season of the Two-Heart, 1964
Ransom, 1966 (also published as *Five Were Missing,* 1972)
Major Andre, Brave Enemy, 1969
They Never Came Home, 1969
Peggy, 1970
A Gift of Magic, 1971
I Know What You Did Last Summer, 1973
Down a Dark Hall, 1974
Summer of Fear, 1976
Killing Mr. Griffin, 1978
Daughters of Eve, 1979
Stranger with My Face, 1981
Chapters: My Growth as a Writer, 1982 (autobiography)
The Third Eye, 1984 (also published as *The Eyes of Karen Connors,* 1985)
Locked in Time, 1985
The Twisted Window, 1987
Don't Look Behind You, 1989

FOR YOUNGER READERS

The Littlest One in the Family, 1960
Silly Mother, 1962
Giving Away Suzanne, 1963
Hotel for Dogs, 1971
From Spring to Spring: Poems and Photographs, 1982

The Terrible Tales of Happy Days School, 1983
Horses of Dreamland, 1985
Wonder Kid Meets the Evil Lunch Snatcher, 1988
The Birthday Moon, 1989
Songs from Dreamland, 1989

FOR ADULTS

Point of Violence, 1966
When the Bough Breaks, 1974
How to Write and Sell Your Personal Experiences, 1979
Who Killed My Daughter? 1992

HONORS AND AWARDS

Seventeen magazine's annual short story contest: 3 times
Seventeenth Summer Literary Award (Dodd, Mead & Co.): 1957, for
    Debutante Hill
Best Novel Award (National Press Women): 1966, for *Point of Violence*
Best Books for Young Adults (American Library Association): 1976, for
    Summer of Fear; 1978, for *Killing Mr. Griffin;* 1981, for *Stranger with My Face;*
    1982, for *Chapters: My Growth as a Writer;* 1990, for *Don't Look Behind You*
Library of Congress' Best Books: 1981, for *Stranger with My Face*
New York Times' Best Books for Children: 1981, for *Stranger with My Face;*
    1988, for *Killing Mr. Griffin*
New York Times' Outstanding Books of the Year: 1981, for *Stranger with
    My Face*
Notable Children's Trade Book in the Field of Social Studies (National
    Council for Social Studies and Children's Book Council): 1982, for
    Chapters: My Growth as a Writer
Children's Choice (International Reading Association and the Children's
    Book Council): 1985, for *Locked in Time*
Children's Books of the Year (Child Study Association of America): 1986
    (2 awards), for *The Third Eye* and *Locked in Time*
Parents' Choice Honor Book for Literature (Parents' Choice Foundation):
    1987, for *The Twisted Window*
Margaret A. Edwards Award (*School Library Journal*/Young Adult Library
    Services Association): 1992

FURTHER READING

BOOKS

Contemporary Authors New Revision Series, Vol. 36
Duncan, Lois. *Chapters: My Growth as a Writer,* 1982
———. *Who Killed My Daughter?* 1992

Something about the Author Autobiography Series, Vol. 2
The Writers' Directory, 1992-94

PERIODICALS

School Library Journal, June 1992, p.20
Woman's Day, June 2, 1992, p.34

ADDRESS

Bantam-Doubleday-Dell
1540 Broadway
New York, NY 10036

Marian Wright Edelman   1939-
American Advocate for Children
Founder and President of the Children's
Defense Fund

BIRTH

Marian Wright (later Marian Wright Edelman) was born on June 6, 1939, in Bennettsville, South Carolina, to Arthur Jerome Wright and Maggie Leola (Bowen) Wright. The youngest of five children, Edelman has one sister and three brothers. Over the years, a total of twelve foster children also lived with the family.

YOUTH

The abiding lesson of Marian Wright Edelman's youth, as she often testifies, was that "Service to others is the rent you pay for living on this planet." This was the credo by which the Wright family lived, and around which Marian has constructed her life. As a child, she recalls, "Service was as essential a part of my upbringing as eating and sleeping and going to school."

That lesson began with her parents. Her father was a minister, the pastor of Shiloh Baptist Church; her mother took care of the family and helped out with his ministry. Marian grew up in the small, rural, and segregated community of Bennettsville. Helping others was a part of her father's profession, of course, but it also meant building a playground behind the church for the local black children, who couldn't use the "white" facilities, and starting up a place for the elderly, run by her mother, that was the first home for black senior citizens in South Carolina. All the Wright children helped out, learning early what is meant by service to others. Today, the description she gives of her youth is of a community that worked together to care for all its members, young and old. Her community was so supportive that years later, when Marian attended college, people would send her shoe boxes stuffed with chicken and biscuits and the occasional greasy dollar bill.

EARLY MEMORIES

Despite the strength of her family and community, Wright was deeply aware of segregation, and often humiliated and angry by racial discrimination. She recalls being scolded when she was only five about using a whites-only drinking fountain, and being forced to sit in the blacks-only balcony of a movie theater. One of her earliest memories is of an accident that occurred on the highway in front of her home. Two vehicles were involved. An ambulance came, determined that the white truck driver was OK, and drove off—leaving the black family from the other car lying bleeding in the road. "I remember watching children like me bleeding," Edelman says. "I remember the ambulance driving off. You never, ever forget."

EDUCATION

There were certain values that Arthur and Maggie Leola Wright taught to their children: hard work, self-discipline, belief in oneself, and, above all, the importance of education. And Marian learned these values well. She participated in several activities, including the drum majorette corps and lessons in voice and piano, but she maintained a straight-A average all the while. The family held a study hour every evening for the children to do their homework. According to her brother, "If you said the teacher hadn't assigned you anything, Daddy would say 'Well, assign yourself.' It was just read, read, read." When Marian was 14, her father had a heart attack and died. In the ambulance, his last words to her before falling unconscious were "don't let anything get in the way of your education." Marian took this directive very seriously.

After graduating from Marlboro Training High School in 1956, Wright attended Spelman College in Atlanta, the nation's oldest private liberal-arts college for black women. She was an outstanding student. For her junior year, she won the Charles Merrill scholarship to study and travel in Europe. She spent the first summer at the Sorbonne in Paris, studying French civilization, then attended the University of Geneva in Switzerland during the academic year. That second summer she spent in Russia, exploring an interest that was kindled by reading Tolstoy in high school. As she later said, "That year gave me a sense of confidence that I could navigate in the world and do just about anything." She then returned to Spelman for her senior year, planning a career in the foreign service.

But history conspired to change that. Wright returned to college in Atlanta as the civil-rights movement was getting underway. She began doing volunteer work for the National Association for the Advancement of Colored People (NAACP) and joined civil-rights demonstrations. There was one massive sit-in at the segregated cafeteria at Atlanta City Hall, where a group of black students were determined to show their opposition to racial discrimination. Many were arrested, including Marian Wright, who spent a night in jail reading the book she had brought just in case. With this first taste of the civil-rights movement, she decided to forego graduate studies in Russian in preparation for the foreign service; instead, she chose law school. "I didn't think I had an aptitude for the law," she later recalled, "but I wanted to be able to help black people, and the law seemed like a tool I needed."

After becoming class valedictorian and graduating from Spelman with a bachelor's degree in 1960, Marian Wright entered Yale Law School as a John Hay Whitney Fellow. A pivotal experience came during spring break of her third year, when she traveled to Mississippi. She saw the police there attack a group of black people who were peacefully trying to register to vote. The police ordered their guard dogs to attack the group, and then arrested them and threw them in jail. When Wright tried to call a lawyer to get them released from prison, she discovered that there were only three black lawyers for 900,000 blacks in the whole state of Mississippi. As she recalls, "That's really when I decided to become a lawyer." She returned to Yale and received her law degree in 1963.

FIRST JOBS

Her mission then was clear. She joined a new program run by the NAACP Legal Defense and Education Fund (LDEF) to train young attorneys in civil-rights law, studying for a year in New York. She then returned to Mississippi as the director of the LDEF office there, planning to do legal work on civil-rights cases. She arrived during a massive voters' registration drive. It was extremely dangerous—three civil-rights workers were killed in Mississippi the summer of 1964. And almost all of the clients that she had released from jail had been severely beaten there.

She soon realized, though, that working for civil-rights and the right to vote, which black people were guaranteed with the Voting Rights Act of 1965, would not relieve the unspeakable poverty and hunger she found in Mississippi. She began to do community work as well. Despite strong opposition from the state's white leadership, she was instrumental in bringing in a large federal grant to set up the state's first Head Start program. Head Start is a federally funded preschool program designed to ensure that all children begin elementary school ready to learn. According to writer and educator Robert Coles, "It's almost impossible to convey to people what it meant for a black woman to do that in Jackson, Mississippi, in 1965. She has unwavering moral courage." Wright stayed in Mississippi for four years, becoming the first black woman to pass the bar there.

MARRIAGE AND FAMILY

It was in Mississippi that Wright met her future husband. At that time, Peter Edelman was a legislative assistant to Senator Robert F. Kennedy. Wright met Edelman, a graduate of Harvard Law School and a former law clerk on the Supreme Court, when she testified before a Senate subcommittee hearing in Mississippi on local poverty conditions. One year later, she moved to Washington, D.C., because she wanted to live near Edelman and also because she had come to realize that the people she worked with in Mississippi had no voice in the capital, no one to safeguard their interests. She was determined to become that voice.

Marian Wright and Peter Edelman were married in July 1968, and she took the name Marian Wright Edelman. They have three sons, now grown: Joshua, 24, a Harvard graduate and teacher; Jonah, 22, a Rhodes scholar at Oxford; and Ezra, 18, an undergraduate at Yale. The children have been raised in a home that combines their mother's Baptist beliefs with their father's Jewish heritage, including a "Baptist bar mitzvah" that each boy celebrated in the garden of their family home in Washington, D.C.

CAREER HIGHLIGHTS

Marian Wright Edelman has worked throughout her professional career as an advocate for those who are disadvantaged, for the poor, and for children.

With a Field Foundation grant to study how to make U.S. law work for poor people, Marian Wright Edelman started the Washington Research Project after her move to the capital in 1968. She and a small staff did research and advocacy on public policy issues. It was a wrenching time for the nation, the year both Martin Luther King, Jr., and Robert F. Kennedy were assassinated. Following her marriage that summer, she and

Peter took a five-month trip around the world, visiting Africa, India, Indonesia, and Vietnam, where American troops were fighting. With her return to the U.S., Edelman continued to direct the Washington Research Project. The family moved to Boston in 1971, when Peter became vice-president of the University of Massachusetts; Marian worked there as head of Harvard University's Center for Law and Education. Despite this new job, Marian continued her work in the capital, traveling there once a week. The Edelman family moved back to Washington in 1979.

FOUNDING THE CHILDREN'S DEFENSE FUND

Over time, though, the nature of her work changed. She was haunted by the words spoken by a young man the day after King was assassinated. She had tried to persuade him and other teens that looting and rioting would destroy their future. As she later reported, he replied, "Lady, why should I listen to you? Lady, I ain't got no future." His feeling of hopelessness, plus the political realities of the era, motivated her to change direction. The desire for social change, so prevalent in the 1960s, faded in the 1970s, as many people lost interest in helping blacks or the poor. A new strategy was needed. She thought that focusing on the needs of children would cut through the issues of race and class, cut through ideological lines, and bring together liberals and conservatives.

In 1973, Edelman founded the Children's Defense Fund (CDF), whose mission is "to educate the nation about the needs of children and encourage preventative investment in children before they get sick, drop out of school, suffer too-early pregnancy or family breakdown, or get into trouble." For the past twenty years, CDF has provided information to public policy makers on such topics as child health, education, youth employment, child welfare and mental health, and family support systems. Quality affordable day care and pregnancy prevention for teens have been the focus of intensive long-term campaigns, with particular emphasis on breaking the cycle of poverty that recurs when teenagers have babies before they have such resources as an education or a job. A 1992 campaign summarized the Fund's overall goal: a healthy start (basic health care), a head start (quality preschools), and a fair start (economic security for all families). One of the CDF's earliest and strongest supporters is First Lady Hillary Clinton. She first worked for Edelman while a law student in the early 1970s; later, she sat on the board of the CDF, serving for many years as chairperson.

The Children's Defense Fund is a private, nonprofit foundation with an annual budget of about $10 million and a staff of over 100. Their approach is to begin with well-documented research into social problems, then to publicize their findings in reports that detail problems and possible solutions—they publish about 2000 pages of research reports each year.

Here are some of the statistics they have compiled:

One in five (14 million) U.S. children live in poverty.
Every 32 seconds an infant is born into poverty.
Every 14 minutes a baby dies in the first year of life.
100,000 children are homeless.
Every 13 seconds child abuse and neglect are reported.
Every day 135,000 children bring a gun to school.
Every 26 seconds a child runs away from home.
Every 8 seconds a child drops out of school.
Every minute a teenager has a baby.

Edelman is widely acknowledged to be the foundation's best resource. She speaks out in interviews, speeches, and commencement addresses, to keep the work of the CDF constantly in the public eye. As Calvin Tomkins wrote in a lengthy profile in *The New Yorker*, Edelman has "gained an enviable reputation over the years for political astuteness and tactical skill in the hardheaded, highly competitive long-range process of influencing social policy and legislation." Her critics call her bullheaded and unable to compromise, a '60s liberal trying to solve '90s problems by throwing money at them. Yet others admire her intensity and her relentlessness on Capitol Hill, roaming the halls of Congress to lobby legislators. Lobbyists try to persuade lawmakers to support laws that favor the special interests they represent; but unlike some, she can't contribute to politicians' campaign funds, hoping to secure their attention. Edelman has only her statistics, her unbounding energy, and her commitment fueled by anger—anger that our nation, with such tremendous resources, would allow its children to suffer in poverty.

Recently, many political observers have wondered what influence Edelman will wield during the Clinton administration, because President Clinton has emphasized many of the same domestic issues and because Hillary Clinton values her as both friend and mentor. Whatever her influence, one thing remains clear—Edelman will continue to work for, in her words, "those who have no voice."

HOBBIES AND OTHER INTERESTS

Consistently working 12-hour days leaves Edelman little free time. She loves to read, consuming books on policy issues, religion, and philosophy, plus the occasional thriller, and she does so whenever possible—even in the bathtub. She also enjoys music, gardening, and looking at paintings. She attends church regularly, and her Baptist faith is a particular source of strength for her.

WRITINGS

Families in Peril: An Agenda for Social Change, 1987

The Measure of Our Success: A Letter to My Children and Yours, 1992

HONORS AND AWARDS

One of *Mademoiselle* magazine's Most Exciting Young Women in America: 1965
One of America's 200 Young Leaders (*Time* magazine): 1971
Presidential Citation (American Public Health Association): 1979
Leadership Award (National Women's Political Caucus): 1980
Rockefeller Public Service Award: 1981
Roy Wilkins Civil Rights Award (NAACP Image Awards): 1984
MacArthur Foundation Prize: 1985
Hubert Humphrey Civil-Rights Award (Leadership Council on Civil Rights): 1985
Public Service Achievement Award (Common Cause): 1985
William P. Dawson Award (Congressional Black Caucus): 1987
Albert Schweitzer Humanitarian Prize (Johns Hopkins University): 1988
Radcliffe Medal: 1989
Murray-Green-Meany Award for Community Service (AFL-CIO Award): 1989
Gandhi Peace Award: 1990
Perlman Award (B'nai B'rith Women): 1992

FURTHER READING

BOOKS

Otfinoski, Steve. *Marian Wright Edelman: Defender of Children's Rights,* 1991 (juvenile)
Who's Who of American Women, 1991-92
Who's Who among Black Americans, 1992-93

PERIODICALS

Current Biography Yearbook 1992
Harper's Bazaar, Feb. 1993, p.154
Lear's, Mar. 1993, p.88
Los Angeles Times, Oct. 11, 1990, p.E1
New Republic, Feb. 15, 1993, p.21
New Yorker, Mar. 27, 1989, p.48
Parade, Feb. 14, 1993, p.4
People, July 6, 1992, p.101
Rolling Stone, Dec. 10, 1992, p.126

ADDRESS

Children's Defense Fund
25 E Street, NW
Washington, DC 20001

Cecil Fielder 1963-
American Baseball Player with the
Detroit Tigers
Major-League Leader in Runs Batted-In,
1990-1992

BIRTH

Cecil (SESS-il) Grant Fielder was born in Los Angeles, California,
September 21, 1963, the eldest son of Edson Fielder, who ran a
janitorial service, and Tina Fielder, the manager of a Mazda dealer-
ship. He has one sister, Kaory, and a brother, Craig.

YOUTH

Fielder grew up in a close family that moved from Los Angeles
to nearby La Puente while Cecil was still a toddler. He was always

physically bigger than his peers, so much so that, as a Little League star, he brought protests from parents of his opponents. Some even passed around a petition demanding that he play against older kids who were more his size. His sister Kaory remembers that parents of his "victims" would sometimes demand to see his birth certificate. As a pitcher, he would regularly strike out as many as six batters in a row.

Despite the tough nature of his surroundings in La Puente, Cecil was not the bully that his size might have indicated. "His mother was very supportive," says his high-school coach John Romano, "and he never got involved in the gang things. Never." Fielder instead concentrated on developing his many and diverse athletic talents.

EARLY MEMORIES

Edson Fielder, himself a high school all-star ball player, began pitching balls to his son as soon as Cecil could walk. The future slugger connected for his first smash early—at the age of three—when he hit the ball over the roof of the family's two-story apartment building. "Look, Ma," Tina recalls him yelling, "Willie McCovey!" (the famous outfielder of that era). Cecil says that he still remembers the surprise and the thrill of the moment.

EDUCATION

Fielder graduated from Nogales High School in La Puente in 1981, having already proved his prowess in three sports. Surprisingly, he did not even play varsity baseball until his junior year, preferring football and especially basketball, games in which he was also an all-state player. Mark Salas, a former professional baseball player who was Fielder's teammate at Nogales, was surprised at Cecil's career choice. "I thought he was just going to stick with basketball," Salas says. "He was great. When he was there, they won just about everything." Indeed, Fielder was a four-year starter on a team that lost only ten games in four years and went 29-0 in his senior year before losing in the state semifinals. He was named MVP (Most Valuable Player) in the San Gabriel Valley, an area with nearly forty high schools. In the meantime, he doubled as a quarterback and free safety on the football team.

While basketball was Cecil's favorite game, scouts were not looking for a 6'3", 230-pound point guard. The scholarship offer came in baseball from the University of Nevada at Las Vegas. Fielder spent a year there before being drafted by the Kansas City Royals in June 1982.

CHOOSING A CAREER

"That was my game," Fielder says of basketball. "Shoot, pass, dunk, there was nothing I couldn't do. But I just didn't get that high tout. . . .If I had pursued basketball, it would have been a tough hustle." Thinking logically about his future, Cecil settled for a sport he didn't love. "I knew I could hit with power," he says of baseball, "so I figured that was the sport I could do something in." Baseball scouts concurred, despite his bulky build, which has proved to be a liability over the years as managers often preferred the sleek, athletic build of most ballplayers

In fact, Fielder's size has hurt him in the eyes of many. "I know what a great [baseball] player looks like growing up, and Cecil wasn't there when he played for me," reveals former coach Romano. "I figured maybe twenty homers and eighty RBIs (runs batted in) tops, if he even *made* the majors. . . . But he worked. He worked so hard. That's why he deserves everything he got." And, needless to say, he chose the right sport.

CAREER HIGHLIGHTS

FROM THE MINORS TO THE MAJORS TO JAPAN

After drafting him in the fourth round in 1982, the Kansas City Royals sent Fielder to Butte, Montana, where he led the Pioneer League with 20 home runs and 176 total base hits in his first year, and was named the circuit's all-star first baseman. Kansas City, however, had another prospect with a better physique, and traded Fielder to the Toronto Blue Jays for outfielder Leon Roberts. The bounce around the minors continued with the Jays, who sent him to single-A teams in Florence (South Carolina) and Kingston (North Carolina), and then to Knoxville (Tennessee). Fielder continued to bash minor-league pitching until his promotion to the majors on July 18, 1985. In 30 games in Toronto, the big man hit .311, including a double off the wall in his first major-league appearance.

The Blue Jays began 1986 with Fielder as their everyday designated hitter, but demoted him to Syracuse when he struggled early with the bat. The next year, back in Toronto, Fielder was platooned with Fred McGriff at first base and responded with 14 home runs in only 175 at-bats. While such a performance would normally earn a player more time, the Jays limited Fielder to only 174 at-bats in 1988, deciding to go with the left-hander McGriff. Only 25 years old, Fielder appeared destined to spend his career as a reserve. Then came his historic career move.

The Blue Jays told Fielder that they would accept $750,000 from the Hanshin Tigers of Japan's Central League if Fielder would take Hanshin's million-dollar-plus offer to play in Kobe, near Osaka. While most players would consider this an extraordinary gamble—few play in Japan and return to successful careers here—Fielder jumped at the chance to play every day and prove himself. In addition, his salary would be increasing more than nine-fold. After a brief period of culture shock, Cecil hit .302, smacked 38 homers (third in the league), and led the league with a batting average of .628. He was "such a free swinger," reported Ken Marantz in *Sports Illustrated*, "that he was dubbed *ogata senpuki*, 'the big electric fan.'" Fielder improved his conditioning through the more rigorous Japanese training regimen, while enjoying the well-equipped luxury apartment with an ocean view provided by the team.

The *Sacramento Bee* told amusing tales of how Cecil and his wife "rode the bullet train, toured shrines and, whenever they longed for American dishes, hit Disney World in Japan. Stacey took lessons in Japanese and learned just enough to get herself lost and back home again. Prince [their little son] went to an English school and frequently brought home an army of friends." Life as a *gaijin* (the term given to the two foreign players allowed to each Japanese team) suited Cecil Fielder so well that he was reluctant to return to the States.

The *gaijin*, though, have little job security. So, when the Detroit Tigers came calling, Fielder exercised the escape clause in his contract and grabbed the opportunity. The Tigers had finished last in 1989, and most baseball observers thought that their signing of Fielder to a seven-figure contract ($3 million, plus bonus, for two years) was a desperate gamble.

BACK HOME TO MAKE HISTORY

Cecil wasted little time in proving them wrong. After a slow start in the 1990 season, he exploded into the major leagues with a record-breaking performance and has not looked back since. He smashed three homers in a game on two separate occasions, became the first Tiger to hit a ball over Tiger Stadium's left-field roof, homered against every American League team, and awed players and fans alike with his consistency and tape-measure blasts. And, on the last day of the season, he thrilled the crowd at Yankee Stadium by becoming the first player since 1977 to hit 50 home runs in one season. The 1990 numbers gave pause to those who had underestimated Fielder's

chances in the majors: 51 home runs and 132 RBIs to lead the majors; American League titles in hitting, total bases, and extra base hits; and, perhaps most important, rescuing the Tigers from the cellar and bringing them to near the .500 mark.

The gentle giant still had to prove to doubters that 1990 was no fluke. He took care of that skepticism in 1991 when he became only the second Tiger to hit 40 or more home runs in two consecutive seasons. For the second straight year, he was selected to play in the All-Star game, and this time he managed to keep his team in the pennant race until autumn. Fielder's seasonal statistics were once again as astonishing as his blast over the bleachers at County Stadium in Milwaukee. He tied for the American League lead in home runs with 44, and once again led the majors with 133 RBIs, while cutting his strikeouts by 30. He also silenced critics of his weight by playing in all 162 games, one of only three major leaguers to do so. Surely, he thought, he would be recognized as the most valuable player that year, an award he was denied in 1990 purportedly because of his team's losing record. The usually soft-spoken Fielder did not hide his bitterness when he finished second in the MVP balloting to Cal Ripkin, Jr., of the Baltimore Orioles, a team that had suffered a dismal season. It seemed that the man who was now, without question, baseball's premier slugger was still being denied respect. However, after a brief outburst, Fielder set about the business of proving himself again in 1992.

He did not fail. While his batting average and home-run totals tailed off, he knocked in 124 runs, joining the most rarified company in the history books of the sport. Fielder became the third player ever to lead the majors in RBIs for three consecutive seasons—the others, writes Rob Parker in the *Detroit Free Press*, were the legendary Babe Ruth and Ty Cobb. Incredibly, Fielder was left off the 1992 All-Star team, causing many to wonder just what he had left to prove. But his Detroit fans knew he had it all: Fielder is the only Tiger ever to hit 35 home runs in three consecutive seasons, and the first to drive in 120 runs in three straight campaigns. At the corner of Michigan and Trumbull, the site of Tiger Stadium, his legion of avid followers demonstrate that Cecil Fielder suffers no lack of respect.

Fielder's consistency at the plate can be attributed to skills that few power players possess: he has no weak spot in the strike zone and he can hit the ball to all fields. Rather than swinging wildly for the fences, Fielder operates as a complete hitter, using his astonishing strength to make the ball travel farther. He is also a better-than-average first baseman despite his lack of speed. He fields the balls he gets to, and has "soft hands" that allow him to snare bad throws for putouts. Lastly, he has the respect of other players because of his gentlemanly demeanor on the field and off. Reporters say that in an age of "hot dogs," Fielder approaches the game in a businesslike manner and never taunts opponents.

As the 1993 season came to a close, Fielder tried but failed to become the first player ever to earn the major-league RBI title for four straight years. Signed to a multi-year contract by the Tigers in early 1993, Fielder and company tried to battle their way out of a slump to take part in the game's most exciting pennant race in years. Although 1993 won't find the Tigers in the World Series, Fielder's place in the record books is secure. One Chicago sportswriter puts it this way: "The big man has hit it big, Stateside."

MAJOR INFLUENCES

Fielder's resiliency in the face of criticism and underestimation go back to one source—his mother, Tina. "Mom was always telling him that if he wanted something he had to take it. Now. Today," says sister Kaory. "And that whatever people throw at you, you have to use it." Tina has few regrets in warning her son that talent would not be enough in facing a hostile world. "Maybe I was too cynical," she reflects, "but I think a lot of the things I've been saying are starting to ring some bells."

MARRIAGE AND FAMILY

Fielder is married to Stacey Granger, his sweetheart from high-school days. They have a son, Prince, who at nine years of age has already shown enough talent to make his parents believe that he could one day eclipse his father's accomplishments. A daughter, Ceclyn, was born in February 1992. Fielder is extremely devoted to his family. "If I can walk around this house and see these folks smiling," he says, "that's all I care about."

The Fielders recently purchased a home in suburban Detroit. Until the spring of 1993, their main residence had been in suburban Dallas, Texas, where they still have many friends and interests.

HOBBIES AND OTHER INTERESTS

Cecil Fielder's concern for children does not stop with his own family. Not only does he contribute significantly to several charitable foundations, he plans to privately finance his own after leaving baseball. "I never wanted to do anything conglomerate-wise when I got done playing," he said recently. "I've known for a while that I'd rather be in something where I can help somebody. . . .[If] we can catch some kids at a delicate age, get them into a learning program and some sports, that would be super."

HONORS AND AWARDS

American League All-Star Team: 1991-93
Associated Press Major League Player of the Year: 1990
Sporting News American League Player of the Year: 1990
AP (Associated Press) Major League All-Star Team: 1990-1991

UPI (United Press International) American League All-Star Team: 1990-91
Sporting News American League All-Star Team: 1990-91
Hillerich & Bradsby Silver Slugger Award: 1990-91

FURTHER READING

BOOKS

Contemporary Black Biography, Volume 2
Encyclopedia Brittanica, Book of the Year, 1990
Who's Who Among Black Americans, 1992-93

PERIODICALS

Detroit Free Press, Apr. 1, 1990, p.F1; Sep. 25, 1990, p.F1; Mar. 5, 1992,
   p.C1; Jan. 8, 1993, p.C1; July 3, 1993, p.C2
Detroit News, Jan. 29, 1993, p.C1
Los Angeles Times, June 5, 1990, p.C1
New York Times, July 14, 1992, p.B14
New York Times Magazine, Apr. 5, 1992, p.20
Sport, June 1991, p.32
Sporting News, Apr. 6, 1992, p.S4; Sep. 28, 1992, p.16
Sports Illustrated, Sep. 24, 1990, p.68; Mar. 21, 1991, p.61; Sept. 30, 1991, p.36
Toronto Globe and Mail, May 5, 1990, p.A13

ADDRESS

Detroit Tigers
2121 Trumbull Avenue
Detroit, MI 48216

Bill Gates 1955-
American Computer Software
Company Executive
Chairman and Chief Executive Officer of
Microsoft, the World's Leading Computer
Software Firm

BIRTH

William Henry Gates III, a pioneer in the personal computer revolution, was born in Seattle, Washington, on October 28, 1955. His father, William H. Gates, Jr., is a partner in one of Seattle's biggest law firms, which today represents his son's company; his mother, Mary (Maxwell) Gates, who has long been active in community service, is on the Board of Regents of the University of Washington and has served on the boards of many other corporations and public institutions, including the charitable organization the United Way. The second of three children, Bill Gates has two sisters, Kristianne, two years older, and Libby, nine years younger.

YOUTH

Bill, known to his family as "Trey" for the "III" following his name, grew up in a close-knit, upper-middle-class family in Seattle. Surrounded by bright people, his parents and their friends, Bill grew up listening to their discussions about their work. "It was," he now says, "a rich environment in which to learn."

As a child, Gates enjoyed some fairly typical activities: he rode bikes, had a paper route, joined the Cub Scouts and, later, the Boy Scouts, and played sports like tennis, rollerskating, skiing, and baseball. Summers were spent at the local beach club and at "Cheerio," a group of rustic cabins near Bremerton, where his father grew up. For several weeks each summer the Gates family and their friends would convene at Cheerio, where they would organize games, build bonfires, and play watersports.

The school year, though, was far less idyllic. Gates had problems at school. He was a troublemaker who encouraged other kids to create disturbances in class. His parents became worried about his self-discipline, his study habits, and his ability to get into a good college. As his father recalls, "It wasn't as if he was some kind of obvious super-bright kid. I think we recognize it better looking back than we did at the time. At the time we just thought he was trouble." Rather than continue in the public schools, Bill moved to the private Lakeside School.

EDUCATION

Lakeside School proved to be very different from his earlier experiences in education. It was structured, tradition-bound, and academically rigorous, and required a serious adjustment for Gates. It was also the place where he first learned about computers, setting his course for life.

When Gates was 13, the Lakeside Mothers Club used the money it raised from a rummage sale to pay for the use of a time-share computer. It is hard now to imagine that during the late 1960s only a select few owned or knew how to operate a computer. Of course there were no personal computers; the only ones available were huge, expensive, and typically owned by large businesses and universities. They were virtually inaccessible. So it was quite a coup for the kids at Lakeside to hook up their terminal to a computer operated elsewhere. Gates and a small band of math and science students, including Paul Allen, with whom he would later found Microsoft, began teaching themselves computer programming.

For the next few years, much of his energy was devoted to gaining access to computers, and finding ways to pay the expensive hourly rates. He devised several computer-related money-making schemes while still at Lakeside: he and a few others, including Allen, developed a program for class scheduling, earning $4200 (Gates later admitted that he had put himself in classes with all the prettiest girls). They managed to get jobs at a local time-share computer center, where they searched for bugs in the programs being run there. Gates also learned how to make an operating system crash, successfully trying out this new skill on Control Data Corporation's CYBERNET system, which earned Gates a serious reprimand. They created a new company, Traf-O-Data, to analyze traffic patterns around Seattle; the firm earned $20,000 by the time Gates was in tenth grade, but eventually lost business as their customers learned that they were only high-school students. In his senior year, Gates took a several-month leave from high school to work with Allen as a programmer at TRW, helping write the computer programs that would control a giant hydro-electric system for the Bonneville Power Administration in Vancouver, Washington.

HARVARD UNIVERSITY

After scoring 800 on his math SAT—a perfect score—Gates graduated from Lakeside in 1973 and left that fall to attend Harvard University. He studied pre-law, but he ended up staying at Harvard for only two years. What happened next has become one of the legendary stories in computer lore. In January 1975, Paul Allen showed Gates an article in *Popular Electronics* magazine that described a new microcomputer, the Altair 8600, manufactured by MITS, a company in Albuquerque, New Mexico. While simple by current standards—it boasted a memory of just 256 bytes, compared to 640,000 for most computers today—it was revolutionary for its time. But while MITS had developed the hardware, they had created no software—no system of commands that would enable the computer to *do* anything. Allen urged Gates to help write a program, and Gates essentially abandoned his courses. "We realized that the revolution might happen without us," Gates later explained. "After we saw that article, there was no question of where our life would focus."

Gates and Allen set up a partnership and then set out to adapt the programming language BASIC (Beginner's All-Purpose Symbolic Instruction Code), written for large computers. Their goal was to condense the language enough to fit into the memory of the smaller Altair. They called the president of MITS, lied and said that they had already written the program, and then spent several feverish weeks of day and night activity. And they succeeded, creating the first language for a personal computer (PC) and landing Microsoft's first customer. Despite his parents' objections, Gates dropped out of Harvard at the end of his sophomore year, in June 1975.

FIRST JOBS

Gates, like Allen before him, moved to Albuquerque. There they worked first with MITS and eventually won contracts from such other new hardware companies as Apple and Commodore. Their first big job came in 1977, when they were hired by Tandy Corporation to create software for the popular Radio Shack computers. In 1979, they moved the company headquarters to Washington. Even then, their goal was clear: "A computer on every desk and in every home, all running Microsoft software." Their big break came just one year later.

CAREER HIGHLIGHTS

A COMPUTER REVOLUTION: THE IBM PC AND MS-DOS

In 1980 the computer giant IBM, which then dominated the industry, approached Gates and Allen about creating an operating system for their new personal computer. PCs are comprised of several parts: the hardware, which is the actual physical equipment; the operating system, or the series of commands, written in a symbolic computer language, that controls the basic functions of the computer; and the applications software, which are the supplementary programs that allow the computer to perform such tasks as word-processing and financial analysis. Gates and Allen were uncertain whether they could develop a system for IBM by the deadline so they recommended a competitor, Digital Research. Unable to reach an agreement with Digital, IBM returned to Microsoft, and this time Gates and Allen agreed.

Microsoft bought an operating system created by another programmer, expanded and polished it, and sold it to IBM for their new personal computer. When it debuted in 1981, the IBM PC with MS-DOS (Microsoft Disk Operating System) revolutionized the industry and immediately pushed Microsoft into the big leagues. As a writer for *The Vancouver Sun* explained, "DOS has become to the personal computer what the internal combustion engine is to the car. It was as if Ford had cornered the exclusive right to manufacture a vehicle with gasoline-driven engines at the beginning of the century." Several factors came together to push Microsoft to the forefront of the industry: IBM's commanding role in the field obliged other companies to create compatible software; Microsoft shared information about its system with other software companies to encourage them to write programs that would fit with MS-DOS; and the resulting abundance of applications software made these systems even more appealing to consumers. Eventually, Microsoft's pioneering operating system would run on over 80% of personal computers, with the company collecting royalties on every one.

But the company didn't stop there. Those royalties funded the development of applications software for IBM and IBM-compatible PCs, as well as Apple and Macintosh computers. Successes continued despite the departure of Paul Allen in 1983, after he was diagnosed with cancer; later, with the cancer in remission, he went on to start a new software company. In 1986, Microsoft went public by selling stock on the New York Stock Exchange, and many employees who had received stock as part of their compensation package became millionaires. In 1988, Microsoft became the largest software company in the world. Much of its recent success derives from its user-friendly Windows software. Like the Macintosh system, the user can point a "mouse" at a graphic depiction of each computer function, rather than type in a lengthy command or press buttons for a specific function. After several less successful versions, Windows 3.1 was introduced in 1992 to unprecedented demand, becoming Microsoft's best-selling applications product to date. By 1992, the company had grown to almost 12,000 employees, with sales of $2.7 billion in the year ending June 1992.

RECENT PROBLEMS AND FUTURE PROSPECTS

Despite these successes, there have been problems as well. Microsoft currently faces several challenges to its products from competing software firms, notably a recent alliance between IBM and Apple. More importantly, though, the company faces legal problems. Microsoft is the target of a Federal Trade Commission (FTC) investigation into its business practices. The FTC has questioned whether the company's dominance of the software market may have resulted in anti-trust violations, whether the company used any unfair tactics to eliminate competition from other companies. The purpose of the investigation, according to the FTC, is to determine if Microsoft "has attempted to monopolize the market for operating systems, operating environments, computer software, and computer peripherals." The charge is extremely serious.

Looking to the future, Microsoft has several new projects in development. The company's biggest project is in the area of multimedia software, in which they have already invested over $40 million in research and development and which many see as the industry's next technological breakthrough. Multi-media software is an electronic data base that integrates art, music, photographs, literature, and historical information in a personal computer, with high-definition video screens for display.

GATES'S ROLE IN THE COMPANY

As the Chairman and Chief Executive Officer of Microsoft, Gates oversees both management issues and technical development. Known for his fierce devotion to his work, he arrives shortly after 8:00 A.M. and often works until midnight, sometimes continuing after he gets home; he takes only Sundays off. He is passionate about his work and his commitment to the company, and he expects such devotion from his employees as well.

In return, Microsoft employees have a lot of freedom; the company is known for its relaxed standards of conduct, casual dress, and parties. But Gates also has the reputation of being abrupt, argumentative, competitive, rude and sarcastic in disagreements (especially with his own employees), and unaccustomed to losing. For many, this is offset by his unique talent: his profound grasp of both technological issues and business principles sets him apart from many other software innovators. Today, with a personal fortune worth over $6 billion, Gates is believed to be the richest man in America.

All technological areas, and especially computer software, are highly volatile fields, where a leader today can quickly be pushed aside by the next big development. For Gates, this is especially crucial, as much of his fortune is tied up in Microsoft stock, whose value is closely linked to the company's position in the industry. Gates will have to use all his personal drive, visionary foresight, keen business sense, commanding intellect, competitive spirit, and good fortune to remain on top.

MARRIAGE AND FAMILY

After years of keeping his personal life strictly under wraps, Gates announced his engagement to Melinda French, a 28-year old mid-level executive at Microsoft, in March 1993. She and Gates have dated for about five years, and he was so concerned about their privacy that he persuaded the authors of a new biography on him not to mention her name. Rivals within the industry are delighted with Gates's news, hoping that domestic life will dull his fierce competitiveness. Willard "Pete" Peterson, former vice president of WordPerfect software, joked: "If the rest of the industry is lucky, he'll have a couple of kids soon." Gates says that they would like to have children someday, and has included five kids' rooms in the home that he is building outside Seattle. The house is said to be over 40,000 square feet—for contrast, 2,000 square feet would be considered fairly generous for a single-family home. Gates's new place, on the shore of Lake Washington, is said to contain a swimming pool, salmon run, racquetball court, 14,000-book library, pavilion with dinner seating for 100, and a large array of electronic equipment, including large-screen high-definition TV monitors to preview Microsoft's new multimedia technology.

FAVORITE BOOKS

Gates is a voracious reader who will exhaustively explore any area that excites his interest. He particularly enjoys books on scientific topics, notably biotechnology, but he has also read widely in such fields as law, business, and history, as well as biographies of individuals in those fields. Yet he also enjoys fiction: his favorite books are said to be *The Catcher in the Rye* by J.D. Salinger and *A Separate Peace* by John Knowles.

HOBBIES AND OTHER INTERESTS

Despite his heavy work schedule, Gates has managed to develop quite a few outside interests, in addition to reading. He doesn't watch TV, but he does enjoy watching videotapes of physics lectures, especially those by the Nobel Prize-winning theoretical physicist Richard Feynman. Gates also loves to drive fast cars and has owned, at different times, a Lexus, Porsche, Mercedes, Jaguar, and a classic Mustang. A decent athlete, he plays tennis and still enjoys the watersports he first played as a child.

Recently Gates has added philanthropy to his ongoing interests. He had long said that he planned to concentrate on business throughout his forties and later turn his energies and resources to charitable giving. He has recently made several large bequests, donating $12 million to the University of Washington to create a department of molecular biotechnology and $6 million to Stanford University to help fund a computer sciences building.

HONORS AND AWARDS

National Medal of Technology: 1992

FURTHER READING

BOOKS

Manes, Stephen, and Paul Andrews. *Gates: How Microsoft's Mogul Reinvented an Industry—and Made Himself the Richest Man in America,* 1993
Slater, Robert. *Portraits in Silicon,* 1987
Wallace, James, and Jim Erickson. *Hard Drive: Bill Gates and the Making of the Microsoft Empire,* 1992
Who's Who in America, 1990-91
Zickgraf, Ralph. *William Gates: From Whiz Kid to Software King,* 1992 (juvenile)

PERIODICALS

Business Week, Apr. 13, 1987, p.68; Feb. 24, 1992, p.60; Mar. 1, 1993, p.82
Current Biography Yearbook 1991
New York Times Magazine, Aug. 25, 1991, p.26
People, Dec. 26, 1983, p.36; Aug. 20, 1990, p.91
USA Today, Mar. 31, 1992, p.B1
U.S. News & World Report, Feb. 15, 1993, pp.64, 70
Washington Post, Dec. 30, 1990, p.H3

ADDRESS

Microsoft Corporation
1 Microsoft Way
Redmond, WA 98052-6399

Sara Gilbert 1975-
American Actress
Stars as Darlene Connor on "Roseanne"

BIRTH

Sara Gilbert was born on January 29, 1975, in Santa Monica, California. Her father, Harold Abeles, is a lawyer; her mother, Barbara (Crane) Gilbert, is a talent manager and producer. Her parents' marriage was the second for her mother, and Sara has two siblings from her mother's first marriage, Melissa Gilbert-Brinkman, now 28, and Jonathan Gilbert, 25. Harold Abeles and Barbara Gilbert divorced when Sara was a young child. Though she lived with her mother and siblings, she always kept in close touch with her father, and still sees him frequently to this day. Sara grew up in the family's five-bedroom home in Encino, just outside Los Angeles in southern California. Her mother has since remarried, to diamond manufacturer Manny Udko.

FAMILY BACKGROUND

Accounts of Sara Gilbert's childhood usually focus on her family's experiences in show business. Her grandfather, Harry Crane, was the creator of the legendary TV show, "The Honeymooners," starring Jackie Gleason; Crane continues to work on several TV shows. Her grandmother, Julia Crane, was a dancer and a former Miss Brooklyn. And her older sister and brother, Melissa and Jonathan, grew up on the long-running TV series "Little House on the Prairie." Her mother, Barbara, managed their careers when they were young, and now does the same for Sara.

EARLY MEMORIES

After watching the careers of her older siblings, Sara Gilbert decided that she, too, wanted to act. And by age six, she was adamant about it. "I was always jealous of my brother and sister being on TV when I was little, but what really got me involved was watching my sister get a star on the Hollywood Walk of Fame one day," Gilbert explains. "I don't remember if my mother was thrilled or not that I wanted to act, but she did warn me that it was going to be a very hard thing to do. When I convinced her that I really was serious, she found me an agent, and I started going on interviews and auditions. It was as simple as that." Her mother, who considers Sara more reserved than her sister and brother, was surprised at this choice, but has supported her decision.

YOUTH AND EDUCATION

After that, most of Gilbert's childhood combined acting and keeping up with school. She debuted on TV in the movie *The Apple Dumpling Gang Rides Again* in 1981, appeared in a Kool-Aid commercial, and then landed a role in the 1984 TV movie, *Calamity Jane*. She kept up with her schoolwork with the help of a tutor, eventually earning an A average at her private school. After just a few years she retired from acting to have more time for school and fun things like skiing, ice skating, and summer camp.

Out of retirement by age 11, Gilbert filmed more commercials and a couple of small parts. Her first professional disappointment came when, after five auditions, she was turned down for a role on the TV series "The Facts of Life." "I was pretty bummed," she admits, although she now says that rejection ultimately helped her. "Many child actors, I think, run into problems because all they've ever had in their life was a job, and the minute they don't have one, they fall apart. But I worked sporadically. And as a result, I went to school, had friends, and did regular things. I wasn't famous. I wasn't even recognized."

CAREER HIGHLIGHTS

Little did she know then, but her big break was just around the corner. Her mother heard about auditions for a young actress to play a smart and funny tomboy on the new series "Roseanne," based on the comedy routines of Roseanne Arnold. Gilbert showed up for the audition in her baseball uniform, Roseanne saw the audition tape, and Gilbert got the part. She says that she got the part because Roseanne thought that she was funny and that they look alike, but there was another reason, too: "Roseanne, who helped pick all the kids in the series, told me later that she wanted me because I reminded her of herself at that age. Professionally, she looks out for me on the set. Personally, I think of her as my second mom—someone I can go and tell my problems to."

"Roseanne" depicts the often-chaotic life of the Connors, a working-class family with three children. The show focuses on real-life family problems: lost jobs, failed businesses, financial hardship, teen sexuality and depression. Since the show's debut in 1988, it has become the top-rated situation comedy in the country. Gilbert plays Darlene Connor, the middle child, whose parents are played by the talented comedians Roseanne Arnold and Dan Goodman. Darlene, who has grown from a young girl to a teenager since the series began, is typically described as spunky, brash, sarcastic, headstrong, outspoken, and down-to-earth. Gilbert's true-to-life portrayal of Darlene has won raves from critics and viewers alike.

In addition to her ongoing work on the series, Gilbert has also taken on a few additional roles. She appeared in the cable TV movie *Sudie and Simpson* (1990), which dealt with the difficult subjects of racism and child molestation. She recently drew praise as the schoolgirl Cooper in the feature film *Poison Ivy* (1992), with Drew Barrymore. And she's also doing the voice this season for Bart Simpson's neighbor on "The Simpsons" TV show.

FUTURE PLANS

Gilbert has been accepted at Yale University, and says that she plans to begin there in the fall of 1993; it has been reported that she might leave the series. By selecting Yale, she is following in the footsteps of her idol Jody Foster, who took time out after her career as a child star to attend Yale and then successfully made the transition to adult roles and directing. Gilbert has said, at different times, that she will study psychology at Yale in case her acting career bombs, but she has also hinted that she might study theater to prepare her to become a director. Yet a recent report in *Variety* calls these plans into question: it was suggested that Gilbert may star in a spin-off series in which Darlene leaves home to attend college— at Yale! For now, Sara Gilbert's future plans remain uncertain.

MARRIAGE AND FAMILY

At only 18, Gilbert is unmarried. She lives at home with her mother, although she has recently been talking about moving out and getting her own place. Her bedroom is rumored to be as messy as Darlene's.

FAVORITE BOOKS

Gilbert's favorite book is *The Catcher in the Rye* by J.D. Salinger.

HOBBIES AND OTHER INTERESTS

Like Darlene, Gilbert loves sports. She enjoys snow skiing—both downhill racing and slalom—water skiing, sailboarding, and snowboarding. She also spends a lot of time hanging out with her friends, particularly in her backyard teepee. And music is very important to her, too. She likes composing music, playing guitar, and listening to The Beatles, Pink Floyd, David Bowie, Bob Marley, Sting, and Edie Brickell and the New Bohemians.

Gilbert has a serious side, too. She often appears as a spokesperson for environmental causes, particularly in her work for Earth Communications Office (ECO), for which she is youth director. She acted as co-host for the recent childrens' special "50 Simple Things Kids Can Do to Save the Earth." Her concern for the environment led her to become a vegetarian a few years ago. She has a special interest in the 1960s, in its movements for free speech and social change, and also in its music and culture.

PERFORMANCES

The Apple Dumpling Gang Rides Again, 1981 (TV movie)
Calamity Jane, 1984 (TV movie)
"Runaway Ralph," 1985 (TV special)
"Roseanne," 1988- (TV series)
Sudie and Simpson, 1990 (TV movie)
Poison Ivy, 1992 (feature film)

HONORS AND AWARDS

Youth in Film Award: 1990, for Best Actress in a Comedy ("Roseanne");
1991 (2 awards), for Best Actress in a Comedy ("Roseanne") and Best
Actress in a Cable Special (*Sudie and Simpson*); 1992, for Best Actress
in a Comedy ("Roseanne")

FURTHER READING

PERIODICALS

People, Mar. 20, 1989, p.111; June 8, 1992, p.105
Philadelphia Inquirer, Aug. 6, 1989, p.4 (TV section)
Seventeen, Sep. 1989, p.75
USA Today, May 30, 1989, p.D3
USA Weekend, Sep. 11-13, 1992, p.4

ADDRESS

Guttman and Pam Ltd., Public Relations
118 S. Beverly Drive
Beverly Hills, CA 90212

OBITUARY

Dizzy Gillespie   1917-1993
American Trumpeter and Composer
Co-Founder of Bebop Style of Jazz

BIRTH

John Birks Gillespie, known as "Dizzy" to jazz fans around the
world, was born in the small rural town of Cheraw, South
Carolina, on October 21, 1917. He was the ninth child born to
James and Lottie Powe Gillespie, although only seven of the
children survived childbirth: Edward, Mattie, James, Hattie Marie,
Eugenia, Wesley, and John Birks.

YOUTH

Cheraw was a poor town surrounded by cotton fields. Dizzy

grew up in a house where the only source of water was from the local well. The family was poor and struggled to make ends meet. In addition to his work as a brickmason, James Gillespie played piano in his own band on the weekends. Dizzy recalled how his father collected instruments: "We had a piano, a guitar, a set of drums, a mandolin, and a big red one-stringed bass fiddle laying around our front room." The little boy was fascinated by the way the instruments felt and sounded.

EARLY MEMORIES

James Gillespie was a hard man. He beat his sons every Sunday with a leather strap. "He was usually mean," Dizzy recalled in his autobiography, "and hated to hear about his children misbehaving . . . . He wanted us all to be tough, and he turned me into a tough little rebel, very early, against everyone but him." James Gillespie was so hard on his children that two of the boys ran away while still in their teens.

Dizzy's sisters and brothers remember the youngest Gillespie as a rugged little troublemaker, and Dizzy remembers getting pushed around in his large family.

EDUCATION

Dizzy's formal education began at Robert Smalls Public School in Cheraw where he recalled that he "spent alot of time getting into mischief." He skipped kindergarten because he already knew his alphabet, how to count, and a little bit about reading. He was smaller and younger than the rest of the kids in his classes, and he was rambunctious. He got into a lot of fights, but eventually developed a stronger interest in school. He especially liked English. In the third grade he had a teacher, Mrs. Alice Wilson, who, in his words, "became my mentor, and later, the greatest early influence in my development as a musician."

James Gillespie died when Dizzy was ten, and the family was thrown into wrenching poverty. Dizzy's way of coping with his father's death and the family's deprivation was to become angry. "Anger got control of me after Papa died, and instead of grieving I became real mean and used to do all kinds of devilish things." Alice Wilson came to his rescue, intro-ducing him to music and redirecting his energies. Wilson headed the annual minstrel shows at the school, and she got Dizzy involved. The school had just received a group of musical instruments, and Dizzy join-ed the band, beginning on the slide trombone, even though his arms were so short that he couldn't reach the extended positions. Dizzy surprised himself with how much he loved making music and how willing he was to spend hours practicing. He later started playing a neighbor's trumpet, which he loved, and then played the cornet, shaped like a small trumpet. He had an old horn, held together with tape.

While still an adolescent, Dizzy began playing with his own band, and he would also sit in on other bands when they came to Cheraw to play. He also got invited to play in some of the white clubs in the area. This was the time of the segregated South, where there were separate facilities—schools, restaurants, buses, clubs, etc.—for whites and blacks, and where blacks were neither welcome nor safe in the white part of town. Dizzy knew white folks in Cheraw—he was such a good trumpeter that he was asked to teach students at the local white high school while he was still in grade school. He knew that it was his talent that allowed him entrance to that world; but he also knew the hatred some whites felt for blacks, and the lengths they would go to show it. One member of his band, Bill McNeil, disappeared one day and never returned. A rumor came out that he had been killed by white men. His body was never found. "We all knew that it could just as easily have happened to any of us," Gillespie said. "Our band never sounded the same again, but it made us want to improve ourselves so we could get the hell out of Cheraw."

In 1933, a friend of Dizzy's who knew his talent recommended him to the head of the Laurinburg Institute, a private high school for blacks in North Carolina. They needed a trumpet player for the band and were willing to provide room, board, tuition, and an instrument to Gillespie. He spent the next several years at Laurinburg studying music, focusing on trumpet and piano, and also playing on the football team.

EARLY JOBS

After their father's death, the Gillespie kids did whatever kind of work they could find to help bring in money. Dizzy worked as a door guard at a movie theater in Cheraw, and he also played wherever he could, whether the job paid or not. In 1935 the family moved to Philadelphia to find work, and Dizzy dropped out of Laurinburg to join them. His siblings soon found jobs, and so did he: he started to play trumpet in a band at the Green Gate Inn for $8.00 a week. The entire Gillespie family was living in a three-room apartment at the time.

Gillespie's reputation began to get around Philadelphia, and he landed an audition with Frankie Fairfax's band. He wasn't nervous, but he couldn't read the hand-copied music, and so he didn't get the job.

CAREER HIGHLIGHTS

Dizzy auditioned again for Fairfax's band and made it, gaining a new job and a nickname. Trumpet player "Fats" Palmer Davis listened in as Gillespie warmed up one day, commenting, "listen to that dizzy cat." The name stuck. Fairfax's group was a "swing" band, which played a type of jazz music popular in the 1930s and 1940s that had a steady beat, a distinct melody, and simple harmonies. From the time he first began to play, Dizzy liked to take the melody apart, to rearrange chords, and to explore the harmonies and rhythms he heard in the music. This style of individual expression wasn't always appreciated in the swing bands Gillespie played with throughout the 1930s, because the band leaders wanted a more stylized, consistent sound from their players. But Dizzy was on his way to creating the type of jazz—bebop—with which his name became linked and which made him famous.

In 1936, Gillespie moved to New York City, where he played with Lucky Millender's band and sat in with small jazz groups. That same year, he took the place of one of his idols, Roy Eldridge, in the Teddy Hill Orchestra. Eldridge had joined Fletcher Henderson's band, and Dizzy got the job with Hill largely because he could emulate Eldridge's style. Hill asked Gillespie to tour Europe with the band, at a salary of $70 a week. "Europe . . . ? For $70 a week? Yeah! I was 20 years old, single, and insane!" was Dizzy's recollection. While in Paris, he bought his first beret, which later became his trademark and the symbol for a generation of jazz musicians. He continued his impish ways and became almost as well known for his comic personality and antics on stage as for his new approach to music.

After a terrific tour of Europe, Gillespie returned to New York, but couldn't get steady work because he hadn't joined the union. While he waited for his union card to come through, he had to bum change to eat. Around this time, he met his future wife, Lorraine Willis, who was a dancer at Harlem's famed Apollo club. He was interested in her, but she wasn't sure at that time how she felt about him. However, she did feel sorry for the hungry young musician and would bring him sandwiches and soup from home. They married in 1940, and Lorraine was his close confidant and friend until his death some 53 years later.

In 1938, with a union card in hand, Dizzy had offers coming in from several top-notch jazz bands. He played with the Savoy Sultans, with Teddy Hill's Orchestra again, and with Alberto Soccares, who headed a Latin band. In 1939, while playing with Teddy Hill, Gillespie met Kenny Clarke, who later became a renowned jazz drummer, and a major musical partnership was born. Like Dizzy, Clarke was anxious to explore the new innovations in jazz, and they would jam with other musicians in small clubs in New York, which for years provided the incubator for jazz.

In 1939, Gillespie joined Cab Calloway's big band and toured with the group. It was while on tour with Calloway in Kansas City that Gillespie met Charlie Parker, known as "Yardbird," the alto saxophonist whose name is also linked to the birth of bebop. Parker soon moved east and took part in the now-legendary jam sessions at Minton's Playhouse in Harlem, run by Teddy Hill, where Parker, Gillespie, Thelonius Monk, Kenny Clarke, Don Byas, and others met to continue the experimentation in harmonics and rhythms that led to bebop. Calloway was unimpressed: "I don't want you playing that Chinese music in my band," he told Dizzy. In his two years with Calloway, Dizzy recorded over 50 sides with the band, including one of his first important compositions, "Pickin' the Cabbage."

Dizzy and Calloway parted company in 1941 in the aftermath of an infamous incident. Calloway noticed someone throwing spitballs during a concert and accused the ever-mischievous Gillespie, who protested his innocence. The exchange became so heated that Gillespie took a knife to Calloway's backside; Calloway fired him from the orchestra.

THE BIRTH OF BEBOP

Gillespie was picked up right away by Ella Fitzgerald's band, then played with the groups of Benny Carter, Les Hite, and Earl "Fatha" Hines, whose band featured Charlie Parker on alto and debuted the talent of a young up-and-coming jazz vocalist and piano player, Sarah Vaughan. Throughout the early 1940s, Gillespie also played with groups headed by Coleman Hawkins and Duke Ellington and frequented the jazz clubs that were making 52nd Street in New York the hot spot for the latest in jazz. At the Onyx, he played with Oscar Pettiford, Don Byas, George Wallington, and Max Roach, creating music in which their new ideas began to come together. In one tune, he sang the words "salt peanuts, salt peanuts," instead of taking an octave jump on his horn, thus creating one of his most famous songs. On another tune, he substituted the words "bebop" to indicate a short two-note phrase, and the term stuck to this and the other music Gillespie and his band of innovators were formulating.

In 1944, Billy Eckstine put together what is considered the first bebop orchestra, with Gillespie as musical director and Sarah Vaughan and Charlie Parker as featured soloists. Neither Dizzy nor bebop were well-accepted wherever they went. Gillespie was considered too innovative by some, and the new bebop music was hard on the ears of audiences accustomed to the more melodious music of the big bands.

Unlike the swing style of jazz played by the big bands, bebop was music to listen to, not to dance to. Its complex chords were too unusual for some who were used to the easy harmonies of swing. Bebop was influenced in part by the musical theories of such classical composers as Igor Stravinsky and Paul Hindeminth, and the musicians who developed bebop had spent years talking, thinking, and playing out their own interpretations. Improvisation has always been a part of jazz, but even in this area bebop offered something new. Bebop explored the harmonic qualities, especially the chord progressions, rather than the melodic possibilities of a piece. This gives the music its distinctive and often dissonant flavor.

Dizzy's own style of the 1940s was described by *New Yorker* jazz critic Whitney Balliett this way: "He would start a twelve-bar blues chorus with a blaring single note, follow it with a split-second silence, go into a jolting descending run, drop in another tiny punctuating pause, and play a soft triplet and a hurrying ascending figure capped by a second shout."

This was the style Gillespie shared with his co-creator in the birth of bebop, Charlie Parker. Gillespie's collaboration with Parker is one of the most famous and innovative in the history of jazz. "Yard and I were like two peas," Gillespie said in his autobiography. "His contribution and mine just happened to go together, like putting salt on rice. Before I met Charlie Parker my style had already developed, but he was a great influence on my whole musical life. The same thing goes for him too because there was never anybody who played any closer than we did on those early sides like 'Groovin' High,' 'Shaw Nuff,' and 'Hothouse.' Sometimes I couldn't tell whether I was playing or not because the notes were so close together." But Parker, whom Gillespie called "the other side of my heart-beat," was hooked on heroin and, after a tragic, deteriorating slide into addiction, died in 1955.

In the 1940s, on recordings with Parker, Cootie Williams, Red Norvo, Sarah Vaughan, and others, Gillespie continued to play and write what became the standards of bebop: "Salt Peanuts," "Bebop," "Woody 'N You," "Groovin' High," and one of his most famous tunes, "Night in Tunisia." In the late 1940s, Gillespie took another innovative turn when he

encountered the Cuban jazz of Chano Pozo. Together, they created another new musical genre, Afro-Cuban jazz, characterized by the polyrhythmic beat of African percussion, as heard on Gillespie's "Manteca."

In the 1950s, Gillespie founded his own record label, Dee Gee, but the business was shortlived. In 1953, Gillespie, Parker, Bud Powell, Max Roach, and Charlie Mingus got together in Toronto's Massey Hall for what has become known as "The Greatest Jazz Concert Ever," and which featured Parker blowing a plastic sax borrowed from a local music store.

In 1954, at a birthday party for his wife in New York City, a comedian stepped on Dizzy's trumpet, causing the bell to stick up in the air. "I was angry at first, of course," he said. "It was cracked, which closed up the air current. But when I played it—boy that sound!" Thus, one of Gillespie's trademarks was born. Another famous trademark, his bulging cheeks, occurred over the years as his facial muscles collapsed. It is now a recognized medical condition known as "Gillespie's pouches."

In 1956, Gillespie formed a new band, and as representatives of the U.S. State Department, toured the Middle East and South America. One of the musicians who helped organize the tour was a young Quincy Jones, now one of the most important artists of American music. Gillespie was always involved in developing young talent, from his earliest days to the time of his death. In the forties and fifties, in addition to the giants of his own era, he gave a start to the careers of such artists as John Lewis, Milt Jackson, and Percy Heath, who, together with his old friend Kenny Clarke, formed the Modern Jazz Quartet, one of the most successful ensembles in jazz. Just years before his death, he recorded with Wynton and Branford Marsalis, Kenny Kirkland, and Marcus Miller, working with the newest and perhaps most promising young talents of the current generation. Nearly all the musicians who worked with Dizzy mention his unselfishness and his dedication to the best in music.

The 1960s and 1970s saw Gillespie touring constantly with his own ensembles and other jazz bands. He also ran for president in 1964, claiming that "anybody coulda made a better President than the ones we had in those times, dillydallying about protecting blacks in the exercise of their civil and human rights and carrying on secret wars against people around the world." He didn't remember how many votes he received, but knew it was in the thousands.

Around this time, in 1968, he embraced the Baha'i faith, drawn to its concepts of unity and seeing a parallel between religion and jazz: "In jazz, a messenger comes to the music and spreads his influence to a certain point, and then another comes and takes you further. In religion—in the spiritual sense—God picks certain individuals from this world to lead mankind up to a certain point of spiritual development."

In the 1980s, he was still touring 300 nights a year and forging new jazz alliances with such stars as Paquito de Rivera. In 1992, at the age of 75, Gillepsie was treated to a series of tributes from generations of adoring fans. He gave back in kind, playing for four weeks at New York City's Blue Note, accompanied by some of the brightest talents in jazz, young and old.

Reflecting on his life and what he hoped would be his legacy, Gillespie said this: "I would like to be remembered as a humanitarian, because it must be something besides music that has kept me here when all of my colleagues are dead. My main influence on whatever we'll have as a historical account must be something else because God has let me stay here this long, and most of my contemporaries . . . are gone. So maybe my role in music is just a stepping stone to a higher role. The highest role is the role in the service of humanity, and if I can make that, then I'll be happy. When I breathe the last time, it'll be a happy breath."

MARRIAGE AND FAMILY

Dizzy and Lorraine Gillespie were married for 52 years at the time of his death on January 6, 1993, in Englewood, New Jersey, of pancreatic cancer. They had no children.

HOBBIES AND OTHER INTERESTS

Gillespie was a talented photographer and also enjoyed swimming, playing pool, and, always, listening to music.

SELECTED RECORDINGS

Teddy Hill and His NBC Orchestra, 1937
Cab Calloway and His Orchestra, 1940
The Men from Minton's, 1941
Billy Eckstine with the Deluxe All-Stars, 1944
Dizzy Gillespie All-Star Quintet, 1945
Dizzy Gillespie and His Orchestra, 1947
Dizzy Gillespie Sextet, 1951
Quintet of the Year: Jazz at Massey Hall, 1953
Groovin' High, 1955
Dizziest, 1955
Dizzy Gillespie's All Stars, 1956
Dizzy Gillespie and his Orchestra, 1957
Manteca, 1958
Dizzy Gillespie Quintet, 1961
An Electrifying Evening with the Dizzy Gillespie Quintet, 1961
A Portrait of Jenny, 1971
Giants, 1971
Oscar Peterson and Dizzy Gillespie, 1975
Dizzy Gillespie Jam: Montreux '77, 1977

Dee Gee Days, 1985
Oo Pop A Da, 1985
Dizzy Gillespie and His Orchestra, 1988
To Bird with Love, 1992
To Diz with Love, 1993

WRITINGS

To Be or Not . . . to Bop: Memoirs, 1979

HONORS AND AWARDS

Handel Medallion (New York City): 1972
Grammy Awards: 1975, for *Oscar Peterson and Dizzy Gillespie*; 1980, Lifetime
  Achievement Award; 1991, for *Live at the Royal Festival Hall*
National Music Award (the Music Industry): 1976
Chevalier of the Legion of Honor (French Government): 1989
National Medal of the Arts (National Endowment for the Arts): 1989
Kennedy Center Honors: 1990

FURTHER READING

BOOKS

Feather, Leonard. *From Satchmo to Miles*, 1972
Gentry, Tony. *Dizzy Gillespie*, 1991 (juvenile)
Gillespie, Dizzy. *To Be or Not . . . to Bop: Memoirs*, 1979
Horricks, Raymond. *Dizzy Gillespie and the Be-Bop Revolution*, 1984
McRae, Barry. *Dizzy Gillespie: His Life and Times*, 1988
Terkel, Studs. *Giants of Jazz*, 1975
Who's Who among Black Americans 1992-93

PERIODICALS

Atlantic, Mar. 1992, p.114
Current Biography, Jan. 1993
Downbeat, Dec. 1985, p.19
Ebony, Sep. 1986, p.50; Dec. 1992, p.76
New York Times, Jan. 7, 1993, p.C19
New York Times Biographical Service, June 1978, p.735
New Yorker, Sep. 17, 1990, p.48; Jan. 25, 1993, p.92

Al Gore 1948-
American Political Leader
Vice President of the United States

BIRTH

Albert A. Gore, Jr., the newly inaugurated vice president of the United States, was born March 31, 1948, in Washington, D.C., to Albert Arnold Gore, Sr., and Pauline (LaFon) Gore. At the time of the child's birth, the elder Gore was serving a tenth year in the House of Representatives as a Democratic congressman from Tennessee; he would eventually serve four more years in the House before winning three consecutive terms in the Senate. The family's only other child, Nancy, ten years older than her brother, died in 1984.

160

YOUTH

Al Gore was reared in the heady atmosphere of government affairs. He spent half of each year with his parents in an apartment at the Fairfax, an exclusive residential hotel on Embassy Row in Washington, absorbing the passionate interest in politics that consumed their lives. The other half was spent on the family farm in Tennessee, where he was often left in the care of a tenant family while the senator and his wife tended to the duties of their electoral district. A revealing account of those young years appeared in a recent *New York Times Magazine* article, telling how young Al "lived in two worlds that could hardly have been more different." In Carthage, he "essentially adopted the Thompsons [the tenant farmers] as a second family . . . . Their home became a kind of emotional citadel, a refuge from the larger world, where great expectations awaited him."

Growing up in the public eye produced in Al Gore a sense of balance and caution that made him seem more adult than his peers. Shifting from school terms at St. Albans, in a setting of wealth and power, to less structured summer months in the cornfields of Tennessee, he became, says *Newsweek*, "a combination of St. Albans polish and down-home charm."

Gore lived in a family of super-achievers, and friends say now that the starchiness he often shows in public is the result of always trying too hard for perfection. He grew up in shadows cast by a famous father, an educated and politically savvy mother, and an older sister whose own intensity and accomplishments mirrored the family fervor. Expectations were high for young Al but, by all accounts, he lived up to them. In his high-school yearbook, he was called "the epitome of the all-American young man."

EDUCATION

Al Gore attended Washington's elite St. Albans Episcopal School, where he was an honor student and captain of the football team. He then attended Harvard University. His jobs during college were rather distinctive: his first paid employment was as a copyboy for the *New York Times*, and during his last summer before graduation, he worked on Eugene McCarthy's 1968 presidential campaign as chairman of Tennessee Youth for McCarthy. Gore graduated from Harvard *cum laude* (with distinction) in 1969, earning a bachelor's degree in government.

CHOOSING A CAREER

At that time, when Gore expected to be launching a professional career, he found himself in a painful situation. Like thousands of other young men of his generation, he opposed the war in Vietnam and seriously considered resisting the draft. But with his father in a tight race for reelection to the Senate, Gore chose to submit to the draft so his actions would not reflect on his father. There had been no pressure from his family—they urged him to follow his conscience, and his mother even offered to flee with him to Canada should he decide to avoid service. The decision was his own and one he made, say old friends, both as a point of personal honor and as a political sacrifice. From 1969 to 1971, Gore served in the U.S. Army in Vietnam, working as a reporter with the 20th Engineering Battalion outside Saigon. Despite this, Albert Gore senior lost his long-held Senate seat in 1970, presumably because of his outspoken opposition to the war and his support of civil rights.

Serving as an army reporter in Vietnam led the younger Gore into a career in journalism when he returned to the States. From 1971 to 1976, he worked for the *Tennessean* in Nashville, first as a reporter and later as an editorial writer. But he also enrolled in the School of Religion at Vanderbilt University. He decided to attend divinity school, he says, not with an eye toward ordination, but "to study the spiritual issues that were most important to me at the time . . . to find some answers." From 1974 to 1976, Gore studied law at Vanderbilt, planning to use the degree in tandem with his already budding career in journalism. "He vowed at the time," said a 1992 feature article in *Vogue*, that "he was not interested in politics, having been disillusioned by Vietnam, Watergate, and his father's embittering loss." Yet all the while, without a conscious plan to do so, he was heading toward politics.

CAREER HIGHLIGHTS

THE HOUSE OF REPRESENTATIVES

The young journalist's unexpected career move came in 1976, when the congressman from his home district decided to retire. The years of covering local government for the *Tennessean*, said Gore, "had rekindled my interest in public service. I felt intensely frustrated about policies and decisions I was writing about because I felt they were often dead wrong. But as a journalist I could do nothing to change them." Gore entered the Democratic primaries, winning by a narrow margin. He was victorious that fall in the general election, and went to Washington at the age of twenty-eight for what would be the first of four terms in the House of Representatives.

Gore gained a reputation there as a tough investigator, tenacious and thorough—skills he had gained in his work as a reporter. He involved himself in a variety of issues, ranging from organ transplants, to housing for the poor and disadvantaged, to legislation concerning the TVA (the Tennessee Valley Authority, a government corporation devoted to the economic development of the Tennessee River and surrounding areas). He was not, however, without his detractors, most of whom claimed that he loved the limelight and chose his issues specifically for the best media coverage.

THE SENATE AND BEYOND

Gore began a two-year-long campaign for a Senate seat early in 1983 when Howard Baker, Jr., the Tennessee Republican and majority leader, decided not to seek reelection. "Given his record and name, [Gore] was able to build considerable momentum while [the divided] Republicans squabbled among themselves," says *Current Biography*. Gore ran hard and won easily, but a cloud fell over the victory. His sister Nancy, a tireless worker through the years on her brother's behalf, died of lung cancer before the 1984 election, without ever knowing that he had come full circle to claim what many called his "political birthright."

In the Senate, as in the House, Gore was a workhorse. While he served on a number of committees with diverse interests, he was mainly concerned with environmental topics and arms control. He labeled himself a "raging moderate," looking for a balance, he said, between "national power and security on the one hand, and long-term human survival on the other." Gore diligently studied complex issues, talked with experts, and impressed his peers with his uncanny ability to absorb and process the most scientific details of new technologies. He was recognized as an authority in his specialties.

Gore's driving ambition pushed him to seek another level of government in 1988 when he entered the presidential primaries, but he was unable to define either his policies or himself. Appearing distant and awkward, often even smug, he campaigned, says Bill Turque in *Newsweek*, with a "confusing hash of messages: hawkish Southerner, champion of Israel, environmental protector." Gore withdrew from the race, wounded and humbled. The dismal failure of his campaign, coupled with a ghastly accident that almost took his small son's life, led him to "confront some difficult and painful questions about what I am really seeking in my own life, and why."

Albert III, then six years old, had darted in front of a car, and was thrown thirty feet into the air and dragged across the pavement before his horror-stricken father's eyes. He lay in the gutter, said Gore, with his eyes open in the "empty stare of death." Young Albert recovered after extensive surgery and a lengthy hospital stay; during the first several weeks after the accident, his parents kept a constant vigil at his bedside. The Gores say now that the trauma, and the subsequent counseling they underwent, has helped them to deal with the emotional aftermath and to reassess their priorities.

It was during the little boy's hospital stay that Gore began to write *Earth in the Balance: Ecology and the Human Spirit*, his best-selling book in which he notes the parallel between "the global environmental crisis and [his own] inner crisis that is, for lack of a better word, spiritual." Also, in 1992, Gore was an official U.S. representative to the Earth Summit in Rio de Janiero, Brazil.

THE CLINTON-GORE TEAM

Some called the choice unwise—Bill Clinton of Arkansas asking Al Gore, another Southern, moderate-liberal Baby-Boomer, to join him on the Democratic ticket in the 1992 presidential election. The decision turned out to be an inspired one. Balancing one another's strengths and weaknesses, the two men pooled their considerable resources for a buoyant campaign that led to ultimate victory.

Clinton was an expert on domestic and economic issues, and Gore was knowledgeable about foreign affairs. The president-elect had avoided the draft, but his running mate was a Vietnam veteran. Clinton's experience was limited to state administration—Gore knew his way around the nation's capital. Clinton had been forced to confront allegations of infidelity, while the Gore marriage stood up to scrutiny. The governor of Arkansas was an exuberant man of the people, but the senator from Tennessee was just beginning to test his new-found public ease.

At every national party convention, there are balloons, flags, and singing, but the Democratic celebration took on a new and different tone last July in New York. Youth was in charge for the first time in decades, noted the media, and as Hillary Clinton and Tipper Gore danced to Fleetwood Mac's "Don't Stop (Thinking About Tomorrow)," the change had already begun. In the final count, it was the shared energy, the idealistic but focused approach to thorny issues, and the fever for politics that brought together a winning team.

MARRIAGE AND FAMILY

Al Gore has been married since May 19, 1970, to Mary Elizabeth Aitcheson, known as Tipper, the nickname she acquired in babyhood from a favorite nursery rhyme. The couple met at a dance late in Gore's senior year at St. Albans and, after only a few dates, knew that they would one day marry. Like her husband, Tipper comes from a privileged background and also attended a private prep school in Washington. She holds both undergraduate and graduate degrees in psychology and has worked as a professional photographer. Tipper Gore is well known for her controversial campaign against profanity and violence in rock music, and for her success in forcing record companies to attach warning labels to albums with explicit lyrics. She is the author of a 1987 parents' manual, *Raising PG Kids in an X-Rated Society*.

The Gores have four children—Karenna, nineteen; Kristin, fifteen; Sarah, thirteen; and ten-year-old Albert III, whose chilling brush with death was emotionally described by his father at last year's Democratic National Convention.

Before the Gore family moved into the vice-presidential residence in Washington, they lived in suburban Arlington, Virginia. They also have a farm in Tennessee, across the Caney Fork River from the elder Gores.

MAJOR INFLUENCES

Political life has been perhaps the biggest influence on Al Gore. Even in the post-Vietnam years, when his enthusiasm waned and he veered off into a career in journalism, he wrote about politics and government. He was strongly influenced by his powerful father, one of the great Southern liberals, and by his bright and resourceful mother, who has been called her husband's "political braintrust." Even Gore's late sister set an example of activism—she was one of the first two people to enlist in the Peace Corps and, before that, had worked for the United Nations at the 1958 World's Fair in Brussels.

HOBBIES AND OTHER INTERESTS

Al Gore is a tall, vigorous, man who jogs every day and stays in shape by playing pick-up basketball in the Senate gym when he is in Washington. At home in Tennessee, he and his athletic family run, play lacrosse, and swim (sometimes in the river, more often in a neighbor's pool). The cool reserve so evident in Gore's public persona disappears when he returns to his roots at the farm. He is loose and comfortable with old friends from his youth—"a regular guy," they say, with a hilarious sense of humor.

The Gores still worship at New Salem Baptist, the simple, clapboard country church that the vice president attended with his grandparents during his childhood.

HONORS AND AWARDS

One of Ten Outstanding Young Americans (Jaycees): 1980

WRITINGS

Earth in the Balance: Ecology and the Human Spirit, 1992

FURTHER READING

BOOKS

Who's Who in America, 1992-93
Who's Who in American Politics, 1990-91

PERIODICALS

Current Biography Yearbook 1987
New Republic, Mar. 7, 1988, p.5
New York Times, July 19, 1992, Sec. IV, p.30
New York Times Magazine, Oct. 25, 1992, p.40
Newsweek, May 2, 1988, p.25; July 20, 1992, p.30
Time, July 20, 1992, pp.28,30; Oct. 12, 1992, p.60; Oct. 19, 1992, p.34
U.S. News & World Report, July 20, 1992, p.37
Vogue, May 1988, p.50; Oct. 1992, p.316

ADDRESS

Office of the Vice President
The White House
1600 Pennsylvania Ave.
Washington, DC 20500

Cathy Guisewite 1950-
American Cartoonist
Creator of Daily Comic Strip "Cathy"

BIRTH

Cathy Lee Guisewite (GICE-wite), originator of the popular comic strip that bears her name, was born September 5, 1950, in Dayton, Ohio, to William Lee and Anne (Duly) Guisewite. The middle child in the family, she has two sisters, Mary Anne and Mickey. Guisewite's father, now retired, was an advertising executive who worked his way through college as a stand-up comedian. Her mother was an ad writer before giving up her profession to raise a family, and also once taught grade school.

YOUTH

Lots of stories about family outings, childhood friendships, and Girl Scout activities indicate Cathy's warm and happy upbringing. She was reared in the central-Michigan city of Midland. Life was simple and happy for the Guisewite sisters, and they learned by parental example that, even when problems arose, nothing was ever so bad that it could not be tempered by laughter.

"All my life," Cathy relates, "my parents have been wildly enthusiastic about anything creative my sisters or I did. Every time we made a greeting card—and we almost always made our own—Mom would say, 'Oh, this is good enough to be published.' Most mothers tape their children's work to the refrigerator door. Mom would send them off to the Museum of Modern Art."

Apparently, the cartoonist exaggerates only slightly about her mother's endless approval. This was a woman, says a 1987 *Chicago Tribune* feature story, "who was so impressed by one of Cathy's second-grade compositions that she submitted it to a magazine for publication (the rejection slip is one of Cathy's keepsakes)."

EARLY MEMORIES

Guisewite, who portrays the mother in her "Cathy" strip as an anxious, hovering, homebody figure, remembers a different kind of female parent from her own childhood. "When I was growing up," she confessed several years ago, "I resented my mom for not being the kind of mother who sat home baking all day. She didn't bake and she didn't knit and I felt mothers should do these things. Mom tended to be more cosmopolitan than the other mothers I knew. She took us to art museums and foreign films, and I hated everything she dragged us to. I wanted a fat little mother baking cookies."

Cathy's attractive mom, who bears little resemblance to the cartoon mother, told a *Woman's Day* writer several years ago that she knows that the older woman in the strip is Cathy's fictionalized ideal mom. "I've never had any problems over things that happen in the strip," she says. Anne Guisewite may not have been the typical cookie-baking mother of the 1950s, but her children concede that she always put their needs first— and was always ready with advice. "She [still] gives great advice," says Cathy. "Our relationship hasn't changed since I was eight: I beg for her advice, then I scream at her for giving it."

EDUCATION

Guisewite attended elementary and secondary schools in Midland, and graduated in 1972 from the University of Michigan with a B.A. in English.

It was while she was at college in Ann Arbor, "where the student body was larger than the population of her hometown," says *Weight Watchers Magazine*, "that she felt overwhelmed and turned to food for comfort." A small young woman, barely 5'2", she ate when she was depressed and when she was happy, finally tipping the scales at close to 150 pounds. The weight problem has long since been conquered, however, by the real-life Cathy, who transferred the obsession with junk food to her alter-ego.

Guisewite's degree in English has been followed by two honorary doctorates in humane letters (LHD), the first in 1979 from Rhode Island College, the second two years later from Eastern Michigan University.

FIRST JOBS

Detroit was Guisewite's first stop after college. She was a writer for Campbell-Ewald, an advertising agency, for a year, moving on to two other area agencies, Norman Prady, Ltd., and B. Doner & Company. Her unique view of human foibles was a talent well-suited to the world of advertising—and was, no doubt, a legacy from her upbeat parents.

CHOOSING A CAREER

Cathy Guisewite did not actually select cartooning as her life's work, at least not at the outset. She had been sending her parents illustrated stories of her life, with wry commentary on her problems and anxieties in the big city. Her mother, as always, considered the work good enough for publication. She seized on the idea for a comic strip, went off to the library for a list of cartoon syndicates, and pestered her reluctant daughter to submit samples. In 1976, Cathy sent some of her work to the first name on the list—Universal Press—mainly, she admits, to get her mother off her back. The response was prompt and positive. With a little book on how to draw cartoons (bought, of course, by Anne Guisewite, who believes that "a lack of training is just a detail to be overcome"), the fictional Cathy came into being. Anne feels that she nudged her daughter into a career—Cathy says she was "shoved."

CAREER HIGHLIGHTS

After seven months of doodling and experimenting, Guisewite was ready to go public. "Cathy" debuted on November 22, 1976. Guisewite kept her job in advertising for about a year, drawing the strip in the evenings and on weekends until she felt that it was well-enough established. The theme of the cartoon quickly touched a responsive chord with young, single, working women, and with her new endeavor looking like a sure bet, Guisewite moved operations to Santa Barbara, California, in 1976. There, in a spacious home/studio, she settled into the routine of creating and preserving a "Cathy" empire. Four years later she moved again, this time to Los Angeles, where she felt she could find more aggravating situations to inspire her.

The heroine of Guisewite's strip is a junior executive in an advertising agency who struggles with the conflicting demands of life as a single career woman. She is caught between the conventions of an older generation (an interfering mother!) and the liberal attitudes of her New Age friend Andrea. Added to that combination is Irving, her on-again, off-again boyfriend, and her boss, Mr. Pinkley, a composite of people Guisewite knew in her Detroit offices. The themes of the strip revolve amusingly around what the artist calls "the four basic guilt groups: food, love, mother, and career." Guisewite has established in "Cathy" a fictional character whose life experiences are loosely based on her own. This is the cartoon's secret appeal—its ring of believability in exposing everyday stresses, insecurities, and rejections.

MORE THAN A DAILY STRIP

The popularity of the "Cathy" strip has produced a thriving industry in its 17 years of existence. First, there were books of cartoon collections, then television productions (including a 1987 award-winning special on CBS), a launch into monthly magazine appearances (*Glamour*), the licensing of "Cathy" products, and books by Guisewite's real-life mother and sister.

The strip now appears in almost 1,200 newspapers. It balances decidedly feminist themes with stereotypical female situations, and Guisewite explains this as her attempt to "amuse and make a point at the same time." There is no hard or hostile line to the cartoon, although a number of conservative readers protested when "Cathy" took on a political edge in 1988 during the Bush-Dukakis presidential campaign. In response, several newspapers pulled installments of "Cathy" or moved them to editorial pages, positioning them near the "Doonesbury" cartoon. Jim Creighton, feature editor of the *St. Louis Post Dispatch*, one of the papers that pulled the strip, denied censorship at the time saying that Guisewite was "not playing fair" with her readers, and that political satire is "not what [the strip] is supposed to be."

The "Cathy" phenomenon goes on. The strip remains near the top of popularity polls, and its pudgy, harassed cartoon character adorns hundreds of products. For as long as its creator can laugh at her own insecurities, Cathy" will appeal to a readership that sees itself in her alter-ego.

MAJOR INFLUENCES

The comic strip "Peanuts," which she followed faithfully while growing up, has had a definite influence on Guisewite. While "Cathy" is not actually modeled after Charles Schultz' appealing little characters, there are certain recognizable similarities in the simplicity of art style, according to Guisewite, and "the way of bringing the insecurities of real life into a comic strip" forum.

Guisewite's parents, however, have been her real inspiration—and her loyal cheering section. They often appear in her strip in caricature, says *Savvy* magazine, "with her mother dishing out unsolicited advice while her father stands quietly by." The themes that are built around her mother poke fun at the classic, strained mother-daughter relationship, but are always written with humor and compassion.

MARRIAGE AND FAMILY

Guisewite lives in the Hollywood Hills above Los Angeles, where, until two years ago, she worked in a bedroom-turned-studio. When her growing business threatened to crowd her out of living space, she moved her work from home to an office in the city.

Unmarried, Guisewite took a brief sabbatical in 1992 to adopt a baby girl, whom she has named Ivy. "Now I have this fantasy," she says, "that I can work at home while the baby plays quietly." She has discovered, however, that the idea is unrealistic, and finds that she "gets hypnotized" by the new baby in her life.

Guisewite remains close to her parents and sisters through frequent visits and constant phone calls. She and her mother collaborated on a book in 1987—*Motherly Advise From Cathy's Mom*—with Anne handling the text and Cathy providing the illustrations. Another family effort, this time with sister Mickey doing the text, was published in 1993 and, in typical Guisewite fashion, is waggishly titled, *Dancing Through Life in a Pair of Broken Heels.* Cathy cracks wise: "We're all genetically programmed to obsess over the same things."

HOBBIES AND OTHER INTERESTS

When asked what kind of routine she follows, or whether there are outside interests in her life, the real Cathy slips easily into her counterpart role: "I would say that shopping is my favorite form of entertainment. I can also almost totally rationalize doing almost anything as getting material for the strip." The business of cartooning is more than a livelihood for Guisewite; it is, except now for Ivy, her preoccupation and her entertainment.

Cathy Guisewite concedes that her tastes remain modest—she enjoys simple things like movies, either at the theater or on television. Making lots of money with the strip, and with the books and an ever-expanding line of products that bear her name, hasn't changed her, say those who know her best. She keeps a low personal profile in spite of her success and revels in the fact that she can shop around in public places without being recognized.

SELECTED WORKS

"Cathy," 1976-

BOOKS

The Cathy Chronicles, 1978
What Do You Mean, I Still Don't Have Equal Rights??!! 1980
What's a Nice Single Girl Doing With a Double Bed??!! 1981
I Think I'm Having a Relationship With a Blueberry Pie! 1981
It Must Be Love, My Face Is Breaking Out, 1982
Another Saturday Night of Wild and Reckless Abandon, 1982
Cathy's Valentine's Day Survival Book: How to Live Through Another February 14, 1982
How to Get Rich, Lose Weight, and Solve All Your Problems By Saying ''No'', 1983
Eat Your Way to a Better Relationship, 1983
A Mouthful of Breath Mints and No One to Kiss, 1983
Climb Every Mountain, Bounce Every Check, 1983
Men Should Come With Instruction Booklets, 1984
Wake Me Up When I'm a Size 5, 1985
Thin Thighs in Thirty Years, 1986
A Hand to Hold, An Opinion to Reject, 1987
Why Do the Right Words Always Come Out of the Wrong Mouth? 1988
My Granddaughter Has Fleas, 1989
Reflections: A Cathy Collection, 1991

TV PROGRAM

"Cathy," 1987

HONORS AND AWARDS

Emmy Award: 1987, Best Prime-Time Animated Program, for "Cathy"

FURTHER READING

BOOKS

Guisewite, Anne. *Motherly Advice From Cathy's Mom* (illustrated by Cathy
    Guisewite), 1987
Guisewite, Cathy. *Reflections: A Cathy Collection*, 1991
Guisewite, Mickey. *Dancing Through Life in a Pair of Broken Heels* (illustrated
    by Cathy Guisewite), 1993

PERIODICALS

Chicago Tribune, May 10, 1987, Section 5, p.3; Nov. 16, 1988, Style section,
    p.8; May 3, 1992, WomanNews, p.5; Sep. 6, 1992, WomanNews, p.1
Detroit Free Press, Nov. 18, 1991, p.E1; June 21, 1993, p.E1
Editor and Publisher, Oct. 20, 1990, p.42
Ladies' Home Journal, Oct. 1991, p.44
Los Angeles Times, May 7, 1987, p.G10
New York Daily News, May 15, 1992, p.D9
Savvy, Jan. 1988, p.50

ADDRESS

Universal Press Syndicate
4900 Main Street
Kansas City, MO 64112

Jasmine Guy 1964-
American Actress, Dancer, and Singer
Starred as Whitley Gilbert in
"A Different World"

BIRTH

Jasmine Guy was born in Boston, Massachusetts, on March 10, 1964. Her father, Dr. William Guy, is a black minister at Friendship Baptist Church, the oldest black Baptist Church in Atlanta, Georgia, where the family later moved; he is also a religion and philosophy teacher at Morehouse College. Her mother, Jaye Rudolph Guy, is a white high school English teacher. Guy has one younger sister, Monica, who works as a television news producer in Atlanta. In addition, their parents cared for dozens of foster children in their Atlanta home while they were growing up.

YOUTH

When Guy talks about her childhood, she quickly reinforces the importance of her family's strong values: respect for intellectual achievement and disdain for superficial qualities. "Every year, I'd be nominated to be in the beauty pageant at school, and I wasn't allowed to take part. My mother didn't think pageants would validate my beauty or that they judged you on anything important like your mind or your talent. She felt they were male chauvinistic. It was very clear in my parents' minds what was important. There weren't a whole lot of shallow or superficial values floating around in my household." To this day, her own beauty is one subject she's not comfortable discussing. "I wasn't raised that way," she says. "In fact, growing up in Atlanta, I had a strong spiritual and cultural upbringing. . . . My parents aren't prudes—far from it. But they instilled in me a strong set of intellectual values. Our family is close. My younger sister, Monica, like myself, is highly motivated. . . . We both loved bringing home report cards filled with A's. We've always had a mission."

Despite this strong foundation, Guy sometimes had trouble coming to grips with her racial identity. While her parents taught her to respect both races, the kids at school weren't so openminded: "I remember getting into several fights in grade school because black kids would think I thought I was pretty because I had light skin and long hair. They said I always tried to talk properly. But I wasn't trying to seem better. I just wanted to be me." These troubles continued into her high school years, when her father says she went through a personality shift, trying to act black. "She was holding herself back, not developing her full potential. She was doing it to fit in. It drove me crazy when she spoke bad English—it wasn't even an imaginative dialect, it was just *bad*. But I could tell she was hurting. I told her to just go on her own way and be herself."

Guy now demonstrates a clear sense of self-respect when talking about racial issues: "People always talk about my 'exotic' looks as if they're complimenting me, but I view these kinds of compliments as ignorant. Yes, my mother is white, but she's also a fascinating woman who has many talents. The same can be said about my father. When you start labeling people by color, that diminishes them to nothing else. That's the worst kind of racism I can think of."

EDUCATION AND DANCE TRAINING

Guy began dancing at age five, taking hours and hours of lessons throughout her childhood. She continued her training at Northside High School of the Performing Arts in Atlanta, dancing and acting in musicals at Morehouse College. By that time, she knew she wanted to continue on the stage. After graduating from high school in 1980, she turned down a scholarship from Spelman College in Atlanta to move to New York City to join the Alvin Ailey dance company.

FIRST JOBS

Guy spent two years with Alvin Ailey, doing the impossible—living in New York City on $75 a week. It was tough. "New York was a rude awakening. It was lonely and scary, but I couldn't afford those big city fears . . . . I was pursuing my dream of becoming a dancer. So I put my paranoia in my pocket, fought the smelly ol' subway and just kept training."

She soon got a break, winning a part as a dancer on the TV show "Fame" and working in Los Angeles. She stayed for 10 episodes before returning to New York because, in her words, "they treat us like scenery, and I knew in my heart I could do better." She returned, for a while, to the Alvin Ailey company, and then became a gypsy, a dancer who moves from one show to the next, often appearing in the chorus line. She danced in the touring companies of *The Wiz* and *Bubbling Brown Sugar*, danced off-Broadway in *Leader of the Pack*, and moved up to a principal role in the off-Broadway show *Beehive*, a 1960s musical revue. She also made cameo appearances on the television shows "The Equalizer," "Loving," and "Ryan's Hope."

Guy's first film was *School Daze* (released in 1988, but filmed before she was cast in "A Different World"). This controversial movie about the importance of skin color on a fictional college campus—how black is black enough?—was directed by Spike Lee, a friend from her days on stage at Morehouse. Guy played a light-skinned Wannabee, for wanna-be-white. "The role was difficult for me because it brought back ugly memories," Guy has said. "Again I had to face the reality of how the world sometimes views people only on outward appearances. I don't like being prejudged."

CAREER HIGHLIGHTS

Guy's big break came in 1987, when she was selected for the NBC television series "A Different World." A spin-off from "The Cosby Show," the series was initially intended to showcase the college exploits of one of the daughters, Denise Huxtable, played by Lisa Bonet, the original star of the show. At first Guy auditioned for the role of Denise's roommate at fictional Hillman College. She lost that part, and left to tour Europe in a musical. After her return to the States, she was called back to NBC for a second audition in August 1987, this time for the character of Whitley Gilbert. As she tells it, "In the meantime I'd been to Paris, where I did a sixties-style show that nearly did me in. I was so burned out I couldn't stop crying. When I got to California to read for the show the second time, there was a roomful of people, including the head of the network. I swallowed hard, and gave it all I had, and 15 minutes later was told to start working."

"A Different World" premiered in 1987. It had the good fortune to follow the ratings powerhouse "The Cosby Show" and was a success with viewers from the beginning. Set at Hillman College, a black university modeled on Spelman College, "A Different World" chronicled the lives and relationships of a group of students. Guy's Whitley was a comic character, a spoiled, superficial rich girl obsessed with her appearance. Critics were lukewarm, describing the show as formulaic and insipid. And when Lisa Bonet became pregnant and left after the first season, many expected the show to fail. Guy's consistently humorous performance as Whitley earned a lot of the credit for the show's continued success, as did the hiring of Debbie Allen as the show's director. In recent years, "A Different World" has moved beyond the typical sit-com format to cover such serious issues as blacks in the military, date rape, apartheid in South Africa, AIDS, and the riots in Los Angeles. In addition, individual characters have been allowed to develop more depth and their relations with one another have been strengthened, particularly that between Whitley and Dwayne Wayne (played by Kadeem Hardison).

Because her first big success was as Whitley, many viewers confused the actress with the character she plays. Yet her colleagues on the set were quick to disagree. "Jasmine isn't Whitley," according to Dawnn Lewis (who played Jaleesa Vinson). "She's not catty, she's not hurtful, she's not spoiled." In fact, critics have since discovered that she is a multi-dimensional performer. Her role in Eddie Murphy's *Harlem Nights* (1989) offers proof, as she played the cool and calculating Dominique La Rue. And her debut album, *Jasmine Guy* (1990), astonished those who had confused Jasmine with the spoiled and pretentious Whitley. Described as a mix of musical styles, including R & B, hip-hop, funk, ballads, and jazz, *Jasmine Guy* surprised and pleased many critics. Guy has also appeared in several other TV productions, most recently the mini-series "Queen" (1993), which relates the life story of the grandmother of Alex Haley, author of *Roots*.

Her portrayal of the slave Easter, Haley's great-grandmother, confirms the range of her talent.

In May 1993, NBC announced its plans to cancel "A Different World." Guy has been working on a new project, a pilot for a TV show called "Boy Meets Girl." In this show, which focuses on two families, one black and one white, she plays a waitress. The future of the program is still uncertain. Yet with her wide-ranging talents as an actress, dancer, and singer, Guy is sure to land on her feet.

MAJOR INFLUENCES

Guy has said that she was inspired by several dancers, including Donna Wood and Mari Kajiwara from the Alvin Ailey company, and Maniya Barredo from the Atlanta Ballet.

MARRIAGE AND FAMILY

Guy is single. While she stresses the importance of family, questions about her own family plans seem to lead to discussions of her career: "I'll want a baby, I know that. I love my little cousins, I love kids, I practically live through my friends' children. I'm extremely maternal. I'm monogamous by nature, and I'd love a strong, long-term relationship with a man. But right now my career is terrifically stimulating—you might even say overwhelming. I've worked hard and, having achieved a little, I find it hard not to want to work harder to achieve even more."

PERFORMANCES/CREDITS

TELEVISION

"A Different World," 1987-93
"Stompin' at the Savoy," 1992
"Queen," 1993

FILMS

School Daze, 1988
Harlem Nights, 1989

RECORDINGS

Jasmine Guy, 1990

HONORS AND AWARDS

NAACP Image Award: 1990, Best Actress in a Comedy Series, for "A Different World"

FURTHER READING

BOOKS

Who's Who among Black Americans, 1992-1993

PERIODICALS

Ebony, June 1988, p.68
Essence, Aug. 1988, p.46
Jet, Dec. 12, 1988, p.56; May 10, 1993, p.60
People, Nov. 9, 1989, p.123
Philadelphia Inquirer, Dec. 3, 1989, p.F1
TV Guide, Jan. 21, 1989. p.28

ADDRESS

PMK
955 S. Carillo Dr., #200
Los Angeles, CA 90048

Anita Hill 1956-
American Law Professor
Key Figure in the Confirmation Hearings
of Supreme Court Justice Clarence Thomas

BIRTH

Anita Faye Hill, the Oklahoma law professor whose 1991 testimony
of sexual harassment in the workplace ignited a fierce public
debate, was born July 30, 1956, near the small town of Morris in
rural, east-central Oklahoma. She is the youngest of Albert and
Erma Hill's 13 children, who range in age from 36 to 64. Her
brother Winston, once a blues singer in Los Angeles, is now
minister of the Baptist church in Lone Tree, the community where
the family has lived and farmed for decades.

YOUTH

The little girl who helped her 12 siblings with chores on the family farm could have never imagined the national controversy she would help shape. The acreage they worked, raising cattle and cash crops, is often described as a hardscrabble farm—one that yields a meager living through strenuous labor. The farmhouse was small for such a large family, but considering the broad span in sibling ages, it is doubtful that all the children slept under the same roof at one time. The Hill family was especially close-knit; if there ever was serious tension or undue squabbling, no one seems to recall it now.

Albert and Erma Hill were modest and devout parents who expected much of their children. A rigid moral tone prevailed in their household, and education was firmly stressed. Sunday was church day. The entire family worshiped toget.er at Lone Tree Baptist Church down the dirt road from the farm. In this community, Anita was—and still is—known by her middle name, Faye.

Friends and former classmates invariably remember the youngest Hill child as being sweet, earnest, religious, and scrupulously honest. "It's been instilled in her mind from day one to be truthful," her brother Bill told the *New York Times* during the furor of the 1991 Senate hearings, when Anita Hill accused Supreme Court appointee Clarence Thomas of sexual harassment (unwanted advances of a sexual nature). "It would be pointless," he added, "for anyone who came out of this house to fabricate anything about anyone . . . . There was none of that."

EARLY MEMORIES

Anita Hill is an intensely private person who rarely speaks of her personal life, even of the early years, to any but her closest friends. She makes only brief public reference to her youth in saying, "My childhood was one of a lot of hard work and not much money. I was reared in a religious atmosphere in the Baptist faith."

EDUCATION

Hill attended a small segregated village school for black children only, until she was 14. Then, when segregated schools in the outlying districts were absorbed into the central system, she entered the mostly white junior high classes in the neighboring town of Morris.

Always an excellent student, Hill continued to flourish in her new surroundings. She is remembered as having a quiet and somewhat reserved nature, yet she was active in school affairs and genuinely popular among her peers. She was student council secretary at Morris High School, a member of the National Honor Society, the Pep Club, and the Future Homemakers of America. When Hill was named valedictorian of her 1973 graduating class, she was only the latest in her family to earn such an honor. Four of her siblings had been valedictorian before her, and still another had once been salutatorian.

Hill moved on to Oklahoma State University in Stillwater, where she majored in psychology and graduated with honors in 1977. She was accepted at several of the country's best law schools and decided on Yale, where she studied under a scholarship from the NAACP (National Association for the Advancement of Colored People). She lived in an off-campus apartment during her years at Yale, and her social life then, as now, was kept private. Hill earned her law degree in 1980, again with honors. Former classmates recall her diligence and her decency. In *Capitol Games*, their book about the Supreme Court nomination, authors Timothy Phelps and Helen Winternitz quote a fellow student from those days, Jerry Miranowski, who made what the authors consider the most telling comment of all about her. "She was great," says Miranowski. "You're probably tired of hearing that, but if there was one person I would absolutely believe of the one hundred and seventy-five of my law-school classmates, that person would be Anita Hill."

FIRST JOBS

Hill interned with a local judge while she was an undergraduate student at Oklahoma State, and it is probably this experience that directed her toward the study of law. She later held a summer job, between her second and third years at Yale, at the Washington law firm of Wald, Harkrader & Ross, where she would return after graduation.

CAREER HIGHLIGHTS

After graduation, Hill worked for a year at the Washington firm, and her associates there found her to be serious and reliable. She eagerly left private practice, however, when offered the job of special counsel to Clarence Thomas, the young black lawyer who had recently been appointed assistant secretary in the Department of Education's office of civil rights. The year was 1981, and Hill's politically liberal friends were surprised to see an avowed feminist working in the conservative administration of President Ronald Reagan. But what they failed to consider then was that, in many ways, Hill and Thomas were not so different in their basic beliefs and values. "Much of [his] up-by-the-bootstraps life story has its equivalence in hers," said *Time* during the dramatic public debate over Thomas's fitness to sit on the Supreme Court. "And just as his reputation for integrity makes the charges against him hard to believe, her reputation makes them hard to dismiss."

During that first year of working with Thomas, Hill continued to live a quiet social life in sophisticated Washington. Thomas asked her out a few times and, later, his behavior toward her in those days would be vividly detailed at his Supreme Court confirmation hearings.

In 1982, following what she considered her "best judgment" in furthering her career, Hill moved on with Thomas to the Equal Employment Opportunity Commission (EEOC) when he was appointed chairman. Then, the following year, after accompanying him to a civil rights seminar in Tulsa, she decided to make a change in her life by accepting a position as a law professor at Oral Roberts University. Hill changed jobs again in 1986, this time to teach law at the University of Oklahoma, also in Tulsa. She was granted a full professorship with tenure after only four years (instead of the usual six) on faculty. Hill specializes in commercial law.

THE SENATE JUDICIARY HEARINGS

Professor Hill would have remained relatively unknown beyond the classroom had her former EEOC boss not been nominated by then-President George Bush for a seat on the Supreme Court. In the early autumn of 1991, Clarence Thomas, by now a federal appeals court judge, was facing almost certain confirmation to the higher bench. But news was leaked of sexual harassment charges against Thomas that Hill had privately made to Senate investigators, and what would have been a routine vote turned into new hearings—and a public spectacle unprecedented in Senate halls.

Surrounded by her elderly parents, seven other members of her immediate family, and the network news cameras, Anita Hill stood poised before the 14 white male judiciary committee senators to relate her story of Thomas's alleged harassment during the early 1980s. Her accusations were graphic and shocking. "He told me of his own sexual prowess," she said in calmly stated testimony, "and spoke about acts he had seen in pornographic films . . . . I am not given to fantasy. This is not something I would have done if I was not absolutely sure of what I was saying . . . . I felt that I had to tell the truth."

Judge Thomas's denials were as angry and emotional as Hill's accusations were cool and measured. He called the hearing "a travesty, a circus, a national disgrace," reported *Newsweek*. Witnesses appeared for both sides, further muddying the issue of who was lying and who was telling the truth. In the end, Hill's testimony failed to derail support for Thomas. He was confirmed in a close vote and sits today on the Supreme Court.

Anita Hill is back in the classroom, undaunted by the merciless grilling she endured at the hands of the all-male Senate Judiciary Committee. Her "courage and grace under pressure" were noted by *Glamour* in citing her as a 1991 Woman of the Year. Hill herself says only, "I am hopeful that others who may have suffered sexual harassment will not become discouraged by my experience, but instead will find the strength to speak up."

And indeed, those Senate confirmation hearings proved to be both a revelation and an inspiration for many. Hill's experience before the panel became a catalyst for many women, who were determined to demand scrutiny of the issue of sexual harassment and to redress the inequality of women's representation in Congress. Saying that men "simply didn't get it," women were inspired to become part of the political process and to run for office in record numbers at the local, state, and national level during the 1992 election. This, in the opinion of many commentators, is Anita Hill's legacy.

MARRIAGE AND FAMILY

Professor Hill is single and lives alone in a modest brick house not far from the university campus. She leads a low-key social life, but is friendly with her colleagues and joins them regularly in dining out. Hill remains close to her parents and siblings and is faithful to her religious upbringing. She is a member of Tulsa's Antioch Baptist Church.

MAJOR INFLUENCES

Friends and associates agree that the most influential element in Anita Hill's life has been the proud and rigidly moral atmosphere of the family in which she was reared. Among the many who were interviewed at the time of the riveting Senate hearings was Professor Leisha Self, an Oklahoma law-school colleague, who told the *New York Times* that "the steel inside of Anita that makes her as strong as she is comes from her family." All of the Hill children shared in the work during their years on the farm, and were ingrained with a firm respect for parents, church, and school.

HOBBIES AND OTHER INTERESTS

In spite of her recent public exposure, Professor Hill is not openly political. "Those who know her," says *Time* magazine, "describe her as both a conservative and a feminist, but not an ideologue [an advocate of particular theories] in either area." Her interests lie mostly in the contract law she teaches and in the work she does on the faculty senate and dean's committee. In addition, Hill is a member of the President's Advisory Committee on Minority Affairs at the university. Until recently, she was on the board of the Women's Resource Center in Tulsa, providing legal advice on matters of domestic violence and sexual abuse.

Hill enjoys both classical music and jazz, and also is a sports fan. Friends say that the Chicago Bulls basketball team is her favorite.

WRITINGS

"The Nature of the Beast," *Ms.* magazine, 1992 (based on remarks delivered in late 1991 as part of a panel on sexual harassment and policymaking at the National Forum for Women State Legislators)

HONORS AND AWARDS

Human Rights Award (City of Norman, Oklahoma): 1991
Glamour Woman of the Year: 1991 (one of ten)
Bill of Rights Award (ACLU Foundation of Southern California): 1992 (shared with actress Barbra Streisand)

FURTHER READING

BOOKS

Chrisman, Robert, and Robert L. Allen, eds. *Court of Appeal,* 1992
Morrison, Toni, ed. *Race-ing Justice, En-gendering Power,* 1992
Phelps, Timothy M., and Helen Winternitz. *Capitol Games,* 1992
Simon, Paul. *Advice and Consent,* 1992

PERIODICALS

Glamour, Dec. 1991, p.78; Mar. 2, 1992, p.30
Ms., Jan./Feb. 1992, p.32
Nation, Nov. 4, 1991, p.540
National Review, Nov. 4, 1991, p.14
New York, Oct. 28, 1991, p.30
New York Times Biographical Service, Oct. 1991, p.1064
New York Times Book Review, Oct. 25, 1992, p.1
Newsweek, Oct. 28, 1991, p.26; Oct. 21, 1991, p.26; Dec. 2, 1991, p.8
People, Oct. 28, 1991, p.41
Publishers Weekly, May 4, 1992, p. 20
Time, Oct. 21, 1991, p.35; Oct. 28, 1991, p.30; Apr. 6, 1992, p.25; May 11, 1992, p. 11

ADDRESS

University of Oklahoma
The Law Center
300 Timberdell Rd.
Norman, OK 73019

Ice-T   1957?-
American Rap and Rock Performer
Star of the Film *New Jack City*, and
Controversial Writer/Singer of "Cop Killer"

BIRTH

Ice-T, called "the godfather of hardcore rap," was born Tracy Marrow in Newark, New Jersey, in the late 1950s. Believed to be a good ten years older that most rappers, he seems reluctant to reveal his exact age. Tracy's mother died of a heart attack when he was seven, and his father was killed five years later. He then went to live with an aunt in Los Angeles when he was around twelve. He took his pseudonym from the author Iceberg Slim. Not even close friends call him Tracy.

YOUTH AND EDUCATION

Marrow first moved to Windsor Hills, a middle-class section of Los Angeles. He began to hang out with a tough crowd on the streets of South Central (the area where the 1992 riots occurred). A teacher at Crenshaw High School remembers him as a mild-mannered young man whose mischief was little more than trying to sneak into basketball games, but the rapper's own recollections have a harder edge. "Yeah," he says, "I was involved with the gangs then . . . . I became a street hustler . . . . I'd run the streets doing petty thievery . . . we would get away with a lot of things." Ice-T was shot twice, once during a jewelry heist that went awry and once in a drive-by shooting in South Central.

ON GANGS

These episodes helped him decide to get away from gang life. "When I got shot I got kinda worried," he remembers. "I thought I was a dead man, but couldn't even go to the hospital [because] the police would get involved. That's when I thought about getting out. Y'see, the key in the ghetto is simply not to care . . . . Now I look back at things that were real scary, but I wasn't scared then."

Ice-T claims that the nation became fixated on gangs when they spread their mayhem into white neighborhoods, and that law enforcement officials weren't concerned when the violence was contained in the poorest black and Hispanic locales. "My attitude is you have to make crime equally wrong anywhere," says the former gang member. "You can't make like it's O.K. to steal in one particular neighborhood because it starts to breed. . . . [If] you let one room in a house get dirty soon the dirt spreads into the other rooms. And that's what happened in L.A."

With his occasional stints in jail threatening to turn him into someone with no way out, Ice-T finally reformed when his girlfriend became pregnant and he realized that he had no life to offer a child. He signed up for a four-year stint in the army as a way to turn his life around. He still believes that others can leave their destructive lifestyles behind, and he works to help them turn around. "I'm out to fight that line-em-up and kill-em attitude that people got toward the gangs . . . . I think if I can become these kids' friend maybe I can push them out."

CHOOSING A CAREER

In 1982, Ice-T returned to Los Angeles after his stint in the army and rejoined his compatriots in South Central. Finding the early rap sounds inspiring, he recorded a single, "The Coldest Rap," for a local independent label. He received only $20 for this effort. He was, however, gaining a reputation as a rap pioneer. Instead of rapping about parties and women to a tight beat, Ice-T was convinced by friends to extend his old "rhymes about crimes" slogans. "I started doing that," he recalls, "and that's when I invented another style of rap."

Having drifted back into a criminal lifestyle, and performing at clubs "just for fun and to get girls," Ice-T was once again in danger of being caught up in the death-trap of gang violence. He wasn't sure he could handle it. "I never really was a violent person," he claims. "No matter what part of the hustle you get into, though, eventually violence comes into it . . . . The fact that I didn't want to kill nobody made it unsafe for me, because that little hesitation might take you out." Nevertheless, the feeling that he had been taken in with the recording "The Coldest Rap" made him reluctant when approached for a movie deal. "But the guys in my crew were like 'Go for it man,'" he remembers. "'You got a chance. White people like you, Ice.' We were supposed to be going to Palm Springs the next day to rob jewelry stores. We were on our way, and they said: 'You ain't going . . . . You going to that audition.'"

CAREER HIGHLIGHTS

Still unable to get a record deal with a major label, Ice-T took matters into his own hands. He formed the Rhyme Syndicate to promote himself and fellow rappers on the theory that they could at least record independently and control their own destinies. When his work impressed Sire Records (part of Warner Communications) in New York, he released his *Rhyme Pays* in 1987, got several friends signed, and watched rap explode into a much wider audience. While being the first album to be voluntarily stickered to warn parents of explicit lyrics, *Rhyme Pays* was no dirty party record. It was an explosion of anger, violence, and insight that began the "gangster rap" trend. Never had music been so charged or frightening. "Ice-T tells it the way he sees it," said Britain's *Melody Maker*. "Every song he's ever written annihilates any possible middle ground, forces us to take sides. If you end up hating him, it'll be for exactly the same reasons that others love him. Rap's never been this naked."

On both *Rhyme Pays* and its successor, *Power* (1988), Ice-T made it clear that he would not surrender to others' conceptions of what music should be. "I'll die before I do mainstream," he has said. "If you doing mainstream, that means you ain't saying s---." He has been accused of advocating a brutally sexist attitude and condoning racial violence. In fact, his public persona is one that is belligerently anti-estabilishment and often seems designed to be deliberately off-putting to what he perceives as the white, conservative power structure. Along with other "gangstas" such as N.W.A. (Niggas With Attitude), he insists that his message is that racial and gender problems are, in fact, class problems. He frequently expresses disdain for the phrase "it's a black thing," and asserts that conservative power brokers are worried more by unity than violence. "Soon as you start focusing and going right after people, people get scared," he said in 1991. "If all you're saying, is, "I'll kill you, I'll kill him, no one's scared . . . . Unity and racial harmony, that scares people more than Black Power."

As the audience for his music grew, Ice-T went from being scarcely noticed outside of the music world, to running afoul of parents, politicians, rock critics, and even members of his own profession for his explicit lyrics. One group in particular, the Parents' Music Resource Council, founded by Tipper Gore (now wife of the U.S. vice president), took exception to his songs. He has fought back with more venom than has any other performer. He believes that the censorship issue is a smokescreen to keep children from hearing challenging material and to cover up matters that truly are damaging youth. "Why don't they have a Parents' Homework Resource Center, where parents stay home and help kids with their homework?" he asked. "Or a Parents' Non-Drinking Center?" His *The Iceberg/Freedom of Speech . . . Just Watch What You Say* (1989) was a sustained attack on the censors he describes as "a bunch of bitches playing records backwards." But such industry insiders as David Geffen of Geffen Pictures, director Ivan Reitman, and Disney Studios, which was once considering him for a starring role in a project, have denounced or distanced themselves from him.

In 1990, Ice-T starred as a policeman in the critically acclaimed film, *New Jack City*. His song from the movie—"New Jack Hustler"—was an anti-drug anthem nominated for a Grammy award. He joked that his acting ability came from "repeated late shows in front of police flashlights," claiming his innocence. He also produced an anti-gang record and video, "We're All in the Same Gang." The crowning achievement of his rap career so far, though, is *O.G. Original Gangster* (1991). With tighter rhythms and less antagonistic lyrics, he brought his rap to a new level with this recording, his fourth straight gold record. *O.G.* is more explicitly anti-violent than anything he has ever done. Critical acclaim in the rap press, and even in the parts of the white rock press that had been hostile to him, was nearly universal. But Ice-T hadn't lost his anti-establishment edge: he was proud of the fact that the record was Number 1 for weeks on the charts at Harvard. "It scared the hell out of white folk," he said. "I mean, these are the kids who will be the senators and the Supreme Court justices of tomorrow. They'll be sittin' up there on the bench with Public Enemy T-shirts." In 1991 he also co-starred with Denzel Washington in the little-noticed film, *Ricochet*.

189

CONTROVERSY ARISES

In 1992, having long expressed a desire to play rock-and-roll, Ice-T formed a punk-metal band, Body Count, with several friends. They had performed without incident on the previous year's Lollapalooza Tour (a grouping of alternative rock bands). But when their album *Body Count* was released, a huge storm of controversy broke with criticism of the song "Cop Killer." The song's character describes his anger at the police and fantasizes about killing one. Then-Vice President Dan Quayle, the actor Charlton Heston, police groups, and investors recommended a boycott against Warner Communications, which had released the album. Notably, some black police groups defended the song and Warner's right to release it. Warner's president, Gerald Levin, wrote an impassioned defense of free speech in the *Wall Street Journal*, and Ice-T and his supporters pointed out that many white performers (including Arnold Schwarzenegger and Eric Clapton) had glorified police killing in their work.

The controversy was further inflamed when rioting broke out in Ice-T's old neighborhood of South Central after four white Los Angeles police officers accused of beating Rodney King, a black man, were acquitted, and the worst riots in American history took place amid a call for scrutiny of the issue of police brutality.

After increased pressure including, ironically, death threats, Ice- T voluntarily withdrew the song from the record. With the version that included "Cop Killer" coming off the shelves, a run on stores almost instantly tripled the sales of *Body Count*. The band itself continued to tour without incident, but Warner has since drawn back from its public support of this controversial artist. In January 1993, it refused to release Ice-T's rap album *Home Invasion*, severing its contract with him.

The long-term effects of this controversy remain unclear. Critics point out that, while such pressure on corporations could make them more wary of signing certain types of new acts, established artists will likely find a new outlet for their music. Ice-T is among those who have done just that. He was signed soon after his release from Warner's Sire label by Los Angeles-based Priority Records, which has, says *Time*, "built a financial fortune and a reputation as the music industry's House of Raunchy Rap." In the mean time, Ice-T continues to inspire controversy for the fury of his message.

MAJOR INFLUENCES

Ice-T credits such early rappers as the Sugar Hill Gang with inspiring his work, but still has created his own style. He speaks particularly well of Public Enemy. In rock, he listened to such heavy-metal bands as Black Sabbath and has worked with Jane's Addiction and Megadeth.

MARRIAGE AND FAMILY

Ice-T lives with his longtime girlfriend, Darlene, and their son, Little Ice, in a newly purchased home on Los Angeles' Sunset Strip. He and Darlene also have a 15-year old daughter.

HOBBIES AND OTHER INTERESTS

The controversial rap star directs his energy into several businesses, including a limousine company, a Porsche shop, and a recording and video studio. Although he strives to maintain his nonconformist image, he works extensively in anti-gang and anti-drug efforts in the inner cities and schools. When not keeping in touch with his "out-crowd," Ice-T enjoys his home, cars, and dogs.

RECORDINGS

Rhyme Pays, 1987
Power, 1988
The Iceberg/Freedom of Speech . . . Just Watch What You Say, 1989
O.G. Original Gangster, 1991
Body Count, 1992
Home Invasion, 1993

FILMS

Breakin', 1984
Breakin' 2: Electric Bugaloo, 1984
New Jack City, 1990
Ricochet, 1991

HONORS AND AWARDS

Key to the City of Atlanta: 1990, for anti-violence tour of high schools
Grammy nomination: 1992, for "New Jack Hustler"

FURTHER READING

PERIODICALS

Chicago Sun-Times, Feb. 2, 1993, p.27
Detroit Free Press, Feb. 14, 1993, p.1C
Los Angeles Times, July 19, 1992
Melody Maker, Feb. 18, 1989, p.18; Apr. 1, 1989, p.17; Sep. 28, 1991, p.45
National Review, July 20, 1992, p.36
New York Times, June 19, 1992, p.C24

Newsweek, Aug. 10, 1992, p.50
Rolling Stone, May 16, 1991, p.83; July 9, 1992, p.15; Aug. 20, 1992, p.30; Sep. 17, 1992, p.32
San Francisco Chronicle, July 21, 1991, p.29 ("Sunday Datebook")
Time, June 22, 1992, p.66; July 20, 1992, p.88; Mar. 15, 1993, p.63

ADDRESS

United Talent Agency
9560 Wilshire Boulevard
Beverly Hills, CA 90212

Darci Kistler   1964-
American Ballerina
Principal Dancer with the
New York City Ballet

BIRTH

Darci Anna Kistler was born June 4, 1964, in Riverside, California, to Jack B. and Alicia (Kinner) Kistler. Her father is a physician, and her mother, once a French teacher, now sells real estate. Darci was the youngest of five children, and the only girl. Her older brothers, who later became wrestling champs, were a rugged, competitive group, and Darci, every bit as athletic, aggressive, and daring, joined them in their love of sports, waterskiing, playing football, even dirtbiking.

193

YOUTH

Darci began dance classes at the age of six, inspired by a performance of the famous ballet duo Dame Margot Fonteyn and Rudolph Nureyev, whom she'd seen in Los Angeles, and by a tutu given to her by a friend to wear on Halloween. "It was a ratty little thing, from the dime store, but I loved it," she recalls. "I loved frilly things. And once I got that tutu, I knew I had to take ballet lessons."

EARLY MEMORIES

The world of ballet offered a distinct contrast to her home life: "It was so feminine, so *pink*. In my family, everything was masculine. I had four older brothers, and everything was sport: wrestling and dirtbiking and dirty sneakers everywhere." She also remembers the first time she learned of the New York City Ballet. In 1972, when she was eight, she saw an article on the company in a copy of *Vogue* magazine: "It showed Mr. Balanchine standing at the barre and, around him, all these beautiful girls . . . . To see these girls—so beautiful, so feminine. And the article said that Mr. Balanchine could walk into an elevator and know who had been in it, because he knew who wore what perfume. Well, for me, at that age— *perfume!* I fell in love."

EDUCATION

Darci attended the local grade schools in Riverside. Always drawn to music, she began to study clarinet in the second grade and also sang in the chorus—she once thought of becoming an opera singer, but knew her talents were elsewhere.

THE EDUCATION OF A DANCER

Darci enrolled in dance classes at six, starting with tap and scarf dancing, but ballet soon became her passion. At the age of 12, she began studying with Irina Kosmovska in Los Angeles, which required a 150-mile commute from her Riverside home. Kosmovska was also a teacher at the School of American Ballet in New York City, the training ground for dancers for the New York City Ballet, one of the finest dance companies in the world. The NYCB was founded in the 1930s by George Balanchine, an immigrant from Russia and one of the most distinguished choreographers of the twentieth century. "Everything [Kosmovska] taught us was 'Balanchine says . . ., Balanchine says . . . .' Just like at the school. All I had in my head was Balanchine."

Darci began a series of three summer workshops in New York City with the School of American Ballet, and in 1978 she was given a full scholarship to train at the school. So, at the age of 14, she moved to

New York, taking dance classes and continuing her academic studies at the Professional Children's School, although she never finished her high school degree.

The first time she saw Balanchine, she thought it might be her last. She and two other students had been called to a rehearsal for *Le Bourgeois Gentilhomme* so that one could be picked as an understudy, to learn the dance in case the ballerina in the role could not perform. "Everyone was there," she recalls, "Balanchine, Nureyev, Jerry Robbins, Peter Martins, Patricia McBride—just everybody. And I couldn't sit still. I was very nervous. So way back in the back, in a corner, I started to practice to the music, thinking no one could see me. But I kicked my leg up so high that my bottom leg went out from under me and I fell down. It made the loudest noise, and every one of those people looked at me and laughed."

But her precocious talent overshadowed this youthful glitch, and in 1980 she danced the lead in *Swan Lake* in the School workshop, giving a performance that delighted the audience and deeply impressed Balanchine. So much so that in 1980, when Kistler was 15, he selected her to leave the school and join the NYCB as an apprentice. She became his last "baby ballerina," one in a distinguished line of the greatest dancers in the company, who had been chosen by Balanchine to work closely with him, to learn directly from him the dances he had created.

CAREER HIGHLIGHTS

Her rise within the company was extraordinary. She became a soloist in 1981 and was made a principal in 1982, at age 17 the youngest dancer to reach the level of principal in the company's history. Unlike other major dance companies who rely on "star power" and big names to draw crowds, the NYCB divides its dancers into three categories: member of the corps de ballet, soloist, and principal dancer. The dancers' names are listed alphabetically in the performance programs to highlight the concept of the company as an ensemble, not a collection of stars.

Balanchine was old and ill when he began working with Darci; he was 76, she was 16. He knew he didn't have much time left, and he knew he wanted to work closely with her. Her teacher at the School, Alexandra Danilova, protested that she was too young: "I told Mr. Balanchine that I thought Darci should stay at school another year, but he told me that he wanted her to work with *him*. I think he had the presentiment that he would die soon . . . . If she wasn't so talented and he wasn't so sick, he probably would have left her in school another year."

Darci was strong, young, and diligent. She was also an exuberant dancer, who took sheer delight in the thrill of dance. Her superb technique combined with a deep musicality, something that is essential in a Balanchine

195

ballerina, and inspired critic Clive Barnes to exclaim: "She rides with the music as if it were a roller coaster." Of her approach to dancing at that time, Darci said this: "I enjoy dancing the way somebody else enjoys diving off a cliff into the ocean . . . I do it for that one moment of ecstasy. I may go three months at a time and never feel that outburst—and then something will happen and I'll go straight to heaven."

Balanchine taught Darci many of the major roles he had created for such famous NYCB stars as Suzanne Farrell, Merrill Ashley, and Gelsey Kirkland. But he also taught her more than steps: "Balanchine told me three things, and they're really very simple," she says. "Be in the moment. Be yourself. Don't act." Soon she was distinguishing herself in such roles as the Adagio in *Symphony in C*, the solo part in the *Walpurgisnacht Ballet*, roles in *Divertimento No. 15* and *Who Cares?*, as well as the Sugar Plum Fairy in *The Nutcracker*. Such critics as Jennifer Dunning of the *New York Times* praised her "clarity, ideal proportions, and the fluency of her long line." Rudolph Nureyev described her this way: "Have you seen that new one—seventeen years old—Darci Kistler with the New York City Ballet? Such aggression in her legs, by her feet. There are four other top ballerinas on stage and she's the one you're looking at, and she's not terribly pretty. But there's the devil inside. She already knows how to move to make everybody watch."

In a book of recollections on Balanchine published recently, Kistler said this: "I knew Balanchine as a master, as a teacher. His teachings and his ballets, all of the things he said to me, echo. I didn't have a deep personal relationship with him, but I got enough to live a whole life on."

THE INJURY

In early 1983, Darci slipped on a piece of duct tape during a rehearsal, injuring herself far more severely than was at first known. Doctors diagnosed a bad sprain, and when they discovered, months later, that it was in fact a broken ankle, Kistler was confronted with an injury that almost ended her career. Also, in April 1983, Balanchine died. Direction of the company now fell to two men: Jerome Robbins, a major choreographer whose works include some of the finest in the repertoire of the NYCB as well as such Broadway hits as *West Side Story*, and Peter Martins, a veteran dancer with the NYCB who had been Balanchine's hand-picked successor.

Over the next two years, Kistler underwent two operations on her ankle. Her condition was complicated by the discovery of a bone spur, a piece of chipped bone that had lodged in the joint. She faced a long recovery during which she tried to regain her strength, knowing that if, and when, she returned to the company, she would no longer be able to dance the way she did before, that her characteristic abandon would have to be tempered with a more careful approach.

KISTLER'S RETURN TO DANCE

Her return to the stage in 1985 was tentative: she continued to struggle with the injury, and she had to cancel many performances. But she was determined to return to dancing. "It makes you fearless, overcoming an injury. If you've faced not being able to do what you really want to do, there's nothing more to be afraid of." She continued to dance, but was often in pain and found it difficult to regain her former strength. She also endured other injuries to her shoulder, elbow, and back while trying to make a comeback. Yet despite these physical setbacks, critics and audiences alike began to notice a maturity to her dancing, remarking on its graciousness, elegance, and delicacy. "Other ballerinas are a feast for the eyes," wrote Arlene Croce of *The New Yorker* in 1990, "Kistler is a drink for the eyes, a tonic for the senses, instantly inspiriting and ever so mildly psychedelic."

"I love to take class and work, work, work," Kistler said in 1990, but after years of work, and a dazzling 1990 and 1991 season, she was forced to take another leave from dance, from June of 1990 to the following spring. She went home to California to recuperate, and after physical therapy and rest, returned to the NYCB and to the role of Princess Aurora in *Sleeping Beauty* in a new staging by Peter Martins. The role was terribly demanding. "I worked steadily for two months to get back in shape enough to dance that role, and they were probably the two hardest months of my life. That's when you talk about bitterness and frustration—working and working to gain strength, but always having to be careful not to rehurt your foot." Despite all the obstacles, she was a great success in the role, and has gone on to new roles and continued acclaim.

"Dancing is like this endless train ride, and you never want to get off the train," says Kistler. "Dancing breathes life into you. The more you do it, the more you have to do it . . . . Things in you get chipped away— mannerisms, attitude, things where, before, you couldn't admit you were wrong. And by giving up those things in yourself, you end up doing more. You become part of the ballet. You're not it—you're part of it. And so you just do it, and pretty soon it's all you want to do."

MARRIAGE AND FAMILY

Darci is still close to her mother, who is separated from her father. She was never close to her father, whom she feels ignored her and never encouraged her dancing.

In December 1991, Kistler married Peter Martins, now the sole head of the NYCB. They had been linked romantically when Kistler had first started with the company, but the relationship had not worked out. In the summer of 1992, their marriage made headlines when Kistler accused Martins of beating her. He was arrested, but Kistler later dropped the charges against her husband, and they issued a statement saying that they would seek professional help.

HOBBIES AND OTHER INTERESTS

When she's not rehearsing or performing, Kistler enjoys playing the piano and playing with her pet cockatoo, Eagle. She also likes to read, especially poetry, science fiction, and biography.

HONORS AND AWARDS

Capezio Dance Award: 1991
Dance Magazine Award: 1992

FURTHER READING

BOOKS

Tracy, Robert. *Balanchine's Ballerinas,* 1983
Who's Who in America, 1992-93

PERIODICALS

Connoisseur, June 1989, p.105
Current Biography Yearbook 1991
Dance Magazine, Feb. 1991, p.49; May 1991, p.16; Apr. 1992, p.16
Interview, May 1992, p.123
New York, Mar. 12, 1990. p.74; Apr. 29, 1991, p.24
New York Times, Feb. 2, 1990
New York Times Biographical Service, Nov. 1980, p.1555
New Yorker, Jul. 3, 1989, p.76; Feb. 26, 1990, p.118
Newsweek, Aug. 3, 1992, p.57

People, Nov. 23, 1981, p.44
Vogue, Feb. 1991, p.222; June 1986, p.63

ADDRESS

New York City Ballet
New York State Theater
Lincoln Center Plaza
New York, NY 10023

k.d. lang 1961-
Canadian Singer
Recording Artist Whose Work Includes
Absolute Torch and Twang and *Ingenue*

BIRTH

Katherine Dawn Lang (later legally changed to k.d. lang), was born on November 2, 1961, in Edmonton, the capital city in the western province of Alberta, Canada. When she was about six months old, the family moved to Consort, a small prairie town (pop. about 670) about 200 miles southeast of Edmonton. Her father, Fred, owned the local pharmacy, and her mother, Audrey, taught second grade for 20 years in the town school. k.d. is the youngest child in the family, with one brother, John, and two sisters, Jo Ann and Keltie.

YOUTH

In Consort, a small town where everyone knows each other, lang is remembered as an unconventional kid. "My parents brought me up with no limitations," lang recalls. "They supported my self-confidence and never said, 'Only boys can do that.' I rode motorcycles. I played sports. I did whatever I wanted to." Her earliest ambition was to be a roller derby queen, and she would often practice skating at her father's pharmacy, careening wildly through the aisles. It was there, too, that she first learned to shoot. As her dad recalls, "She had her own .12 gauge shotgun, and we'd practice target-shooting in the drugstore. We'd lay at the front door and shoot through the doorway through to the dispensary at the back. I never took her to a shooting match without her coming home with a prize." Despite their early closeness, lang has not seen her father since her parents' divorce when she was 12.

Music was always a part of family life—her father listened to Percy Faith, her mother enjoyed Broadway show tunes, her brother and sisters played contemporary hits, and everybody studied classical music. With her mother's encouragement, lang began taking piano lessons at age seven. Each week they drove to the Theresetta Convent in Castor, 60 miles away. According to her teacher, Sister Xavier, "The tears came to my eyes when I heard her sing." "I loved it," lang now says. "I knew what I wanted to be the day I had my first piano lesson. I fell in love with music, and I'll stay in love forever." She didn't much like to practice, though, and she quit piano lessons by age 10, which she later regretted. At age 13, she got her first guitar. She soon started playing at weddings, dances, and talent contests. For her first paying gig, at a local service club's Las Vegas Night, she earned $25.

EDUCATION

During high school, lang was editor of the yearbook and a top athlete, winning medals in track, javelin, and basketball. Team road trips would always find her at the back of the bus, playing guitar and singing. Once, while driving back from a meet, she even persuaded the bus driver to stop along the route at a talent show, where she wowed them with her singing.

After graduating from high school, lang left Consort to attend Red Deer College. During the day she studied music, but at night she dabbled in performance art and avant-garde music, once staging a 12-hour reenactment of a heart transplant using chopped vegetables for the heart. As she recalls, "It was sort of like being a beatnik. There was poetry reading and music 24 hours a day. I was living what I thought I had missed by missing the '60s." lang left Red Deer without graduating, charging that the rigid program stifled her creativity.

CHOOSING A CAREER

For lang, the decision about a career was made early and easily: "Most of my life I've studied music and practiced it. I started writing songs as a kid and played piano and guitar. Not to sound self-righteous, but I knew I'd be successful. There's been absolutely no point of beginning for me. It's been constant. Look," she adds, "if you say you're going to go to school to become a nurse, you do it. I said I was going to be a singer, and I just went and did it too."

FIRST JOBS

Despite this certainty, lang lacked direction after she left school. Then in 1982, she appeared in the musical *Country Chorale* in Edmonton in a part modeled after the legendary country singer Patsy Cline, who died in a plane crash in 1963. "Nobody was blown away by her acting," according to the director. "But she had such a strong presence that people couldn't take their eyes off her." Listening to Cline's records to prepare for the role, lang began to identify with the late, great singer.

lang soon formed a band, the reclines (in honor of her idol), hired a manager, developed a stage act, and began playing in clubs around Edmonton and later across Canada. She also made her first record, *A Truly Western Experience* (1984), on an independent label. Critics and audiences were captivated by her energetic performances and outlandish cowpunk appearance, wearing cropped hair, old-fashioned glasses, square dance skirts, and cowboy boots with the tops hacked off. Most of all, though, they loved her voice, warm, vibrant, and soaring. She sang heartbreaking ballads and country and western swing standards—or torch and twang, as she called it—but with a sense of humor. Her flamboyant stage shows offered, in her words, "a hootenanny wing-ding Daddy-O of a good time." With her golden voice, her on-stage antics, and her claim to be the reincarnation of Patsy Cline, she quickly captured the attention of the press, first in Canada and then throughout the United States. Signed to a major record label, lang was on her way to stardom.

CAREER HIGHLIGHTS

It wasn't an easy climb. lang has released four recordings since that first independent recording, charting a gradual evolution in her musical style. Initially she continued with traditional country music on the boisterous *Angel with a Lariat* (1986) and on the romantic *Shadowland* (1988). This critically acclaimed record was produced by the legendary Owen Bradley, who had produced Patsy Cline's recordings as well as those of Brenda Lee, Loretta Lynn, and Kitty Wells. After hearing lang sing on "The Tonight Show," Bradley was so impressed that he came out of retirement to work with her. A collection of country "weepers" with Bradley's characteristic lush string arrangements, *Shadowland* showcases lang's amazing voice and earned for this newcomer widespread respect. Her follow-up recording, *Absolute Torch and Twang* (1989), features acoustic steel guitars and fiddles for a more traditional country sound. This award-winning record combines the torch of passionate ballads with the twang of steel guitars. Together, *Shadowland* and *Absolute Torch and Twang* established her place in country music.

Yet lang's success has been consistently undermined by her controversial image. Much of the conservative country and western establishment in Nashville was suspicious of her nonconformity. Many were offended by her humorous renditions of old standards, feeling that she was poking fun at them. And as lang's stage persona evolved, as she gradually dropped her outlandish clothes and subdued her stage antics, some questioned what was real and what was just an act to gain attention. A longstanding vegetarian, lang also alienated country fans with her comments for the People for the Ethical Treatment of Animals (PETA), a U.S. animal rights group. In a TV ad for their 1990 campaign, lang said, "If you knew how meat was made, you'd probably lose your lunch. I know. I'm from cattle country. That's why I became a vegetarian. Meat stinks, and not just for animals but for human health and environment." These comments angered many throughout cattle country in the U.S. and Canada, including neighbors from her home town.

Perhaps the most controversial part of lang's image was her purposely androgynous looks. lang clearly didn't fit the typical image expected of a female country star. In her words, "the first rule of country and western stardom is 'The higher the hair, the closer to God.' I tried, but it just wasn't me." Instead, she says, "I like to look androgynous because I don't like to use clothes as a sexual tool, and my career has benefitted from the fact that I've bucked gender stereotyping." In fact, in a 1992 interview in *The Advocate*, lang confirmed longstanding rumors that she is a lesbian, though she refuses to discuss her personal life. She had been reluctant to disclose this fact, lang said, because of the repercussions for her mother, who was hounded during the "Meat Stinks" campaign.

All of these factors together contributed to an image that threatened to overshadow her talent and that alienated many potential fans. While critics touted her recordings and fans loved her live performances, most radio stations refused to play her music, thereby limiting her audience and her record sales. "I think I've been successful," lang once said. "I play to sold-out audiences and I play my music in uncompromising terms. I think that's as successful as one can ask for. In terms of formulated success, having hit singles and selling lots of records, that's not where I'm successful."

Ultimately, the world of country music became too confining, and lang decided to chart a new direction. After releasing *Absolute Torch and Twang,* she took two years off from the music business and acted in a film, *Salmonberries* (1991), about two women who come together in a small town in Alaska. While the film wasn't widely distributed, lang's performance earned generous praise. She returned to recording with *Ingenue* (1992), a collection of ten introspective songs about love and loss written by lang and her collaborator, Ben Mink. "*Ingenue* is based on my experiences of falling in love," lang confides, "and it's the most personally revealing record I've ever made. The writing is totally autobiographical, naked and real— if I was toothpaste and you squeezed me, you'd get *Ingenue.*" On a record that transcends standard genres, lang moves beyond country to encompass the influences of jazz, blues, and even Indian sitar music. Critics have marveled at her voice, "a golden voice that could fill the Grand Canyon," according to one, and compare her singing here not to Cline, but instead to Judy Garland, Edith Piaf, and Dinah Washington. With this spectacular transformation from cowpunk queen to jazzy torch singer, her fans can only wait and wonder what will come next.

MAJOR INFLUENCES

The list of singers that lang claims as influences is long and eclectic, evolving along with her stage persona. First and foremost, of course, was Patsy Cline, yet she has also cited such diverse figures as Anne Murray, Peggy Lee, Joni Mitchell, Karen Carpenter, Ella Fitzgerald, Billie Holliday, and Sarah Vaughn.

HOME AND FAMILY

lang spends most of her time on the road and little time at home. "I get itchy if I'm in one place too long," she claims. "I don't really feel like I'm ever at home anywhere." When she isn't touring, lang divides her time between two homes. She has a rented house in a modest neighborhood in Hollywood Hills, California, and a 12-acre farm outside Vancouver, British Columbia, where she keeps her animals: one pig, two goats, three horses, and four dogs.

RECORDINGS

A Truly Western Experience, 1984
Angel with a Lariat, 1987
Shadowland, 1988
Absolute Torch and Twang, 1989
Ingenue, 1992

FILMS

Salmonberries, 1991

HONORS AND AWARDS

Juno Awards: 1985, Most Promising Female Vocalist of the Year; 1987, 1988, 1989, Best Country Singer; 1989, Female Vocalist of the Year
Canadian Country Music Awards: 1989, 1990, Entertainer of the Year; 1988, 1989, Best Female Vocalist; 1989, Album of the Year, for *Shadowland*; 1990, Album of the Year, for *Absolute Torch and Twang*
Rolling Stone Magazine Music Awards: 1987, Best New Singer; 1988, Best Singer; 1989, Best Artist, Country
Gemini Awards: Best Performance in a Variety or Performing Arts Program or Series—1988, for "1987 Canadian Country Music Awards"; 1990, for "k.d. lang's Buffalo Cafe"
Grammy Awards: 1988, Best Country Vocal Collaboration (with Roy Orbison), for "Crying"; 1989, Best Female Country Vocal Performance, for *Absolute Torch and Twang*; 1992, Best Female Pop Vocal Performance, for "Constant Craving"
American Music Award: 1992, New Artist/Adult Contemporary
Canadian Recording Industry Association: 1990, Female Artist of the Decade

FURTHER READING

PERIODICALS

Alberta Report, Dec. 3, 1984, p.38
Chatelaine, Jan. 1988, p.54; Sep. 1992, p.60
Chicago Tribune, July 5, 1989, Sec. 7, p.5
Current Biography Yearbook 1992
Edmonton, Nov. 1985, p.22
People, July 4, 1988, p.94
Saturday Night, June 1990, p.27
Us, May 1992, p.46
Vanity Fair, Aug. 1993, p.94
Western Living, Sep. 1992, p.27

ADDRESS

Warner Brothers
P.O. Box 6868
Burbank, CA 91510

33800 Station "D"
Vancouver, B.C. V6J 5C7

Dan Marino 1961-
American Professional Football Player
with the Miami Dolphins
NFL Leader in Yardage and Touchdown
Passes Among Active Players

BIRTH

Daniel Constantine Marino, Jr., was born in Pittsburgh, Pennsylvania, on September 15, 1961, the first of three children of Dan Sr., a truck driver for the Pittsburgh *Post-Gazette*, and Veronica (Kolczynski) Marino, a homemaker. He has two sisters, Cindy, who is two years younger, and Debbie, five years his junior.

YOUTH

Marino grew up in Pittsburgh's working-class Oakland district, just five miles from downtown. "I was a city kid all the way," he says. "When I was a kid I could stand on my porch and literally touch the house next to ours. The entire neighborhood was like that. People lived close, they stayed close." Marino's neighborhood was racially and ethnically mixed, allowing Dan to learn tolerance for many different perspectives and lifestyles.

He also learned football early. Since his dad worked nights, he had plenty of time to play with his son and teach him the game, which the younger Marino describes as "the biggest thing in my early development." The focus of these lessons was getting Dan to throw without any wasted motion. Despite his youth and lack of arm strength, "my dad said if I worked on it the right way, I'd be able to throw it a lot better once I got bigger and stronger. He made me practice the right way. It was good advice." Dan's mother saw potential, at least in attitude, as well. She recalled to sportswriter Bob Rubin that little Danny called everything a ball—"he even called light bulbs balls."

Marino began playing organized football in the fourth grade at St. Regis elementary school, just across the street from his home. As a developing quarterback, he was fortunate to be on a passing team even then. While most teams at that level used the run on almost every play, St. Regis even experimented with the shotgun, a formation in which the quarterback stands several yards behind the center to facilitate the quick release of passes. In addition to their supervised activity on the school field, Dan and his friends played on the street, three or four to a team, whenever they got the chance. Baseball figured in Dan's life, too. He played in Little League as a kid, and became so adept at the game that he later starred on his high school team.

Marino's early sports background does not end there. In sports-crazy Pittsburgh, which was known in the 1970s as the "city of champions," there were opportunities to watch the winning Steelers and Pirates, and even to rub shoulders with the players. Pirates stars Willie Stargell and Donn Clendenon shared an apartment next door to Dan's grandmother, and often went to her house for family picnics and barbecues. While Marino now asks other celebrities for autographs, as a youngster he was unimpressed. He says that Stargell was "a real nice guy, but mostly I just thought of him as the guy that lived next door to my grandmother."

As a boy, Dan enjoyed singing, despite an inability to carry a tune, and he also liked to watch television (his favorite show was "Lassie"). The family often went fishing together.

EARLY MEMORIES

While he generally avoided trouble growing up, Dan's love of throwing got him into a few scrapes—accidents like broken windows, for instance. An especially embarrassing incident occurred at elementary school when a game of tossing an orange with a friend got out of hand. "I picked up the orange and returned it to Dominic," he says. When his friend ducked, the orange split open and splattered across the blackboard just as the teacher walked in. Although this was hardly a major delinquency, the errant throw earned Dan and Dominic a suspension.

EDUCATION

Dan Marino had some early problems with academics. He spent more time playing and thinking about sports than doing his schoolwork, and his grades suffered as a result. His teacher at St. Regis warned his parents that if he didn't shape up he probably would not graduate. Dan buckled down on his studies just enough to get into the high school of his choice, nearby Central Catholic. There he maintained a "B" average, and was able to further his dreams of an athletic career.

Marino started for Central Catholic freshman football team, was a backup quarterback for the varsity as a sophomore, and was the starting quarterback in his final two years. He was named to *Parade* magazine's All-America team in 1978. Dan also starred in baseball, leading his high school team to the state championship game. His combined pitching record was 25-1, and he hit over .500 for his junior and senior years.

After graduating from Central Catholic in 1979, Marino went on to the University of Pittsburgh. He received his B.A. there in 1983.

CHOOSING A CAREER

By his senior year in high school, it was clear that Marino was headed toward a professional career—the major question was which sport he would choose. That year the Kansas City Royals drafted him in the fourth round, projecting him as a power-hitting third baseman. In addition, many colleges coveted his powerful arm for their football teams. Yet he chose Pitt because it was close to his home and because Coach Jackie Sherrill used a pro-set, pass-happy offense that would showcase Dan's skills. "I not only wanted to play football," he says, "I wanted a college education. I couldn't see throwing away college, or football, for baseball." It was certainly a wise choice.

In his 1986 autobiography, *Marino!*, which he wrote with Steve Delsohn, Dan says that even though he gave up baseball, he couldn't get it out of his blood. "I'd been playing since I was small, and I loved it," he admits, adding, "I still miss baseball to this day. . . and there are times when I feel like picking up a bat and getting in some cuts."

CAREER HIGHLIGHTS

THE PITT PANTHERS

Marino started playing quarterback for his college team, the Pitt Panthers, in his freshman year. As a mid-year replacement for injured starter Rick Trocano, Marino led the Panthers to an 11-1 record and a Fiesta Bowl win over Arizona. His 15 touchdown passes in his sophomore year helped Pitt to another 11-win season. His junior year was his best and most satisfying. Ranked number one for most of the season, the Panthers won their first 10 games behind Marino's outstanding play. Dan completed the year with nearly 3,000 yards passing and a Pitt record of 37 touchdown throws. The devastation of a 38-14 loss to archrival Penn State in the final regular-season game was soothed by a thrilling 24-20 victory over Georgia in the Sugar Bowl. Marino's winning TD pass was his third in the sensational game.

The next season, Marino's senior year, was a major disappointment. His stats slipped, the Panthers lost three games, and an ugly (and untrue) rumor circulated that Dan had a drug problem. He kept his head up, however, as his draft prospects drifted away. "If you ask me if I think the season was a total loss," he says, "I'd answer 'no way.' I learned more that year, about football and about dealing with life, than during any other time in my life." Despite the controversy and the lack of perspective on the part of Pitt fans at the team's slide, Marino came out of college with an impressive list of statistics. His college career totals set school records for passing yards (8,597) and touchdown passes (79), while his team went 42-6. He is considered Pitt's greatest quarterback ever and one of its two or three best players.

THE MIAMI DOLPHINS

When the Miami Dolphins selected him in the 1983 NFL draft as the twenty-seventh pick, and sixth quarterback chosen, Coach Don Shula was one of the most surprised. "We just never thought Dan would be around when it was our turn to draft," he told *Sports Illustrated*. Shula's confidence paid dividends that no one could have imagined when Marino had one of the best rookie seasons in league history. Playing spectacularly in backing up David Woodley, Marino earned his first start in the Dolphins' sixth game. He has been the quarterback ever since. He won the conference passing championship and became the first rookie quarterback ever to start in the Pro Bowl, leading Miami to a divisional title.

Never has the term "sophomore jinx" seemed so foolish as in 1984. Marino served notice in the Dolphins' first game. He threw five touchdowns and completed 75 percent of his passes with no interceptions in leading Miami to a 35-17 win over the Washington Redskins. He tore up the league through 15 more regular-season games, ending with 48 touchdowns and only 17 interceptions. He threw for over 5,000 yards (a record) that year and led the Dolphins to the Super Bowl against Joe Montana and the San Francisco 49ers. That 38-16 loss could be Marino's last trip to the Bowl, but there was no question: Dan Marino had arrived.

The records kept piling up. Protected by a stellar offensive line and a quick release, throwing to star receivers Mark Clayton and Mark Duper, Marino rocketed to superstardom. After only 10 seasons in the pros, he is at or near the top of nearly every all-time passing category. Among active players, he is first in attempts, yardage, and touchdowns. He is already fourth on the all-time yardage list and on a pace to vault to the top in just four years. He has more 3,000-yard seasons than anyone in the history of the game, and also more seasons with 20 or more touchdown passes. And, since his first start, he has never missed a game. Whatever qualifiers might be offered (that he plays for a passing team with a very good line and fine receivers, for instance), it is widely agreed that Dan Marino is a great quarterback. There is little doubt that, by the end of his career, many will call him the best of all time. In fact, some are already doing just that.

Marino has not, however, done what every player dreams of—win a Super

Bowl. In fact, he has been to the playoffs only three times since his second pro year, and has suffered through several poor-to-mediocre seasons. Though a neglect of the defense and running game caused the Dolphins' problems, Marino knows he can suffer in comparison with Pittsburgh's other three famous quarterbacks: Terry Bradshaw (who played there) and Joe Namath and Joe Montana (who grew up there) have taken their respective teams to the top. Marino is optimistic that he can do the same. "I think we're heading in the right direction," he says of the Dolphins. "We're a good team. I don't think we're a great team yet, but we could be heading that way." Despite being knocked out of the 1992 play-offs, Miami's 11-5 finish and divisional title went a long way toward proving him right.

Needless to say, the Dolphins have a dangerous man at the most important position. As explained by Foge Fazio, one of the coaches at Pitt: "If you could build a quarterback from scratch, he would look and act just like Dan Marino."

MAJOR INFLUENCES

Aside from his parents, whom he reveres, Marino's greatest influence has been Dolphins coach Don Shula. When the Pitt star first arrived in Miami, Shula forced him to call his own plays, a highly unusual charge for a rookie. "It made me learn a lot quicker," says Marino. "The fact that he put the pressure on me to learn fast was a major factor." Shula's confidence that Dan could overcome his mistakes helped the young quarterback to become one of the best almost from the moment he stepped on the field.

MEMORABLE EXPERIENCES

Having failed to win the big one as a pro, Marino can look back to the 1982 Sugar Bowl for inspiration. Trailing Georgia 20-17 with only thirty-five seconds left, and facing fourth-and-five from his own thirty-five, Marino had to gamble that tight end "Downtown" John Brown could get open. Dan threw the ball "as hard as I could"—an astonishing 70 yards in the air—and Brown snared it in the Georgia end zone. Final score: Pitt 24, Georgia 20. Another shock came on the sideline. The normally reticent Sherrill planted a big kiss on Marino's cheek, saying "Dan, I love you." Marino tells of the moment: "For a second I was speechless. 'Well, Coach,' I finally replied, 'I love you, too.'"

MARRIAGE AND FAMILY

Faithful to his roots, Dan Marino married his Pittsburgh sweetheart, Claire Veazey, in 1985. Claire was a student at Carnegie Mellon University when he was at Pitt. The Marinos have four children: Daniel Charles, six; Michael Joseph, four; Joseph Donald, three; and Alexandra Claire, one. The family makes its home in Fort Lauderdale, Florida.

HOBBIES AND OTHER INTERESTS

A fine golfer, Marino reports a passion for the game. His teammates describe him as a "regular guy," despite his celebrity and huge salary. He and Claire still enjoy socializing with old friends from Pittsburgh who visit frequently. Dan has worked with charities involving muscular dystrophy, leukemia, retarded children, and the needy. He is active in the National Italian-American Hall of Fame, and his love of Italian food has never left him.

HONORS AND AWARDS

Parade All-American (high school, first team): 1978
All-American: 1981
Most Valuable Player (Sugar Bowl): 1982
NFL Rookie of the Year: 1983
Pro Bowl: 1983-87, 1991
Jim Thorpe Trophy (Newspaper Enterprise Association): 1984
Sporting News NFL Player of the Year: 1984

WRITINGS

Marino! (with Steve Delsohn), 1986

FURTHER READING

BOOKS

Rubin, Bob. *Dan Marino, Wonder Boy Quarterback,* 1985
Marino, Dan with Steve Delsohn. *Marino!,* 1986

PERIODICALS

Current Biography Yearbook 1989
Inside Sports, Aug. 1987, p.21; Oct. 1987, p.26
Newsweek, Jan. 21, 1985, p.62
Sport, Dec. 1991, p.20
Sports Illustrated, Sep. 1, 1982, p.28; Sep. 10, 1984, p.15; Jan. 14, 1991, p.20
Time, Jan. 21, 1985, p.64

ADDRESS

Miami Dolphins
4770 Biscayne Boulevard
Miami, FL 33137

Rigoberta Menchu   1959-
Guatemalan and Quiche Indian Activist
Winner of the 1992 Nobel Peace Prize

BIRTH

Rigoberta Menchu (Menchú in Spanish; pronounced men-CHOO) was born on January 9, 1959, in Chimel, a small village in El Quiche, a province in the northwestern part of Guatemala, on the border of Mexico. Her parents, Vicente and Juana Tum Menchu, were Indian peasants. Rigoberta was the sixth of ten children; only she and two sisters have survived the poverty and cruelty of their society.

GUATEMALA - BACKGROUND AND HISTORY

Menchu has lived during a period of great instability in her native land. Guatemala has long been shaken by political unrest and social repression, throughout this century and long before. The history of this country has been shaped by several contributing factors: the history of the native Indians, their conquest by Spanish settlers, the eventual dominance of foreign economic interests, and the resulting economic and political conditions.

Guatemala was the center of Mayan culture, an Indian civilization that flourished from about the fourth to the ninth centuries A.D. It is believed that there were about one million Mayans, speaking perhaps some 35 different dialects. Theirs was an advanced civilization, with particular progress in the areas of writing, astronomy, and mathematics. No one knows why the Mayan civilization collapsed around 900 A.D. The Quiche Indians, including Menchu, are descendants of the Mayans.

In the 1500s, following Christopher Columbus's arrival in the New World, Spanish explorers conquered the Guatemalan Indians. The Spaniards set up a feudalistic system that forced Indians to pay taxes and to work on the Spanish-owned *haciendas* (plantations). This system has influenced Guatemalan society throughout the centuries.

The Indians have been denied participation in the political, economic, and social organization of Guatemala. Since it was granted independence by Spain in 1821, the country has been ruled by a series of repressive, military-controlled governments that have worked to safeguard the interests of the elite. Guatemalan society has long been divided along lines of race and class: *ladinos* (whites and those of mixed race) control the government, run the economy, and own almost all the land, while the Indians lack political and economic power. And in a country where agriculture remains the foundation of the economy, land ownership is key. The plantation system has continued, eventually controlled not by *ladinos* but instead by American business interests, notably the United Fruit Company, who hired the *ladinos* to run the plantations for them. While there have been a few efforts at reform, particularly during the late 1940s and early 1950s, these efforts have been stymied, usually by the military. In 1954, when the Guatemalan government, under the leadership of President Jacobo Arbenz Guzman, attempted land and labor reforms, including the expropriation of large plantations owned by foreign companies, the U.S. Central Intelligence Agency (CIA) intervened and sponsored a military overthrow of the government.

Since the mid-1950s, Guatemala has seen a succession of governments, most controlled either directly or indirectly by the military. For the most part, these governments have worked to maintain the status quo: to keep economic and political power in the hands of the *ladinos*, to keep the Indian population powerless, and to suppress dissent. An active opposition movement has sprung up, including armed guerrillas, or rebel fighters, in both the countryside and the cities. The government has responded with paramilitary groups and "death squads," determined to eradicate all resistance. Guatemala is widely considered the most brutal regime in Central America. During the past almost 30 years, according to international human rights' groups, 100,000 to 150,000 people have been killed, mostly by government security forces, 50,000 have "disappeared" and presumably been killed, 250,000 have been orphaned, and one million have been forced out of their homes. Guatemala has been pulled into civil war. It has been a time of increasing violence and unrest: labor and political leaders have been killed, foreign diplomats kidnapped, and in 1968, the U.S. ambassador was assassinated. This is the society into which Rigoberta Menchu was born.

MENCHU'S YOUTH

The best source for information about Menchu's early life is her autobiography, *I, Rigoberta Menchú*, first published in Spanish in 1983. The book is an oral history; Menchu told the story of her life, as well as the history of her people and her culture, to a Venezuelan writer, who transcribed and edited it. In the book, Menchu says, "My personal experience is the reality of a whole people." If that is true, the reality of her people is one of systematic oppression.

Menchu spent much of her early life in Chimel, a small village that her parents founded in the mountains of northwestern Guatemala. There were no roads, no cars, and for many years, no neighbors there; the nearest town, Uspantan, was about 15 miles away, and all goods were transported on horseback. Her parents had moved up into the mountains and founded the town when they were forced out of their home in town by the *ladinos*, who gradually took over. Eventually other Indians joined them. Vicente and Juana Menchu were elected the leaders of their community, positions with a long historical tradition in their Indian culture. In her autobiography, Menchu describes many of the beliefs and traditions that are sacred to the Guatemalan Indians, including the ceremonies for birth, marriage, and death, and the roles of the village leaders in all these events. Above all, their culture stresses the importance of the community.

The Menchu family had moved to the mountains to get their own piece of land to cultivate, but the rugged terrain made that very difficult. It took several years before the land started to produce a decent crop, and even then the vegetables would grow only about four or five months a year. So like many Indians, they became migrant laborers and went looking for work. They spent about eight months each year working on the *fincas*, huge plantations or estates in the lowlands along the southern coast of Guatemala, near the Pacific Ocean. This rich, fertile region contained primarily coffee and cotton estates. Large, enclosed trucks would come to the mountain region and transport about 40 Indians at a time, whole families along with their animals. The trip lasted several days, the drivers would make few stops, the trucks became dirty and foul, and Rigoberta hated it.

The Menchu family traveled back and forth between their home in Chimel and the *fincas*, planting, weeding, and harvesting the crops of others before returning home to try to grow corn on their own poor land. The Indians were very poorly paid on the *fincas*, and they would end up spending all their wages there on essential items bought at inflated prices at the company store. Like most Indians, the Menchu family was unspeakably poor; Rigoberta vividly recalls watching one of her brothers die of pesticide poisoning, and another die of malnutrition, while the family had no money for food, medicine, or doctors.

EDUCATION

Like most Guatemalan Indians, Menchu never attended school, which makes her current world stature all the more impressive. She grew up speaking one of Guatemala's 22 native Indian languages, but unable to read or write. She learned Spanish years later to be able to communicate more easily with a broader group of people, and to safeguard the Indians' interests.

FIRST JOBS

"In Guatemala," Menchu says, "we Indians have no childhood," and her experience certainly bears that out. She began working as a very young child. On the *fincas*, only those who worked were fed, while the little ones had to share their mothers' meager rations, so children started working while still very young. The first job she remembers, at about age five, was watching her two-year-old brother so her mother could work without interruption. By the age of eight, she was old enough to work on the *finca* herself. When she started out, she had to pick 35 pounds of coffee a day, picking each coffee bean by hand, one at a time; within a few years, her quota was up to 70 pounds a day.

When she was about 13 or 14, she left her community to go and work as a maid in the home of some *ladino* landowners in the city. The family constantly insulted and humiliated her. They gave her very little to eat, worked her very hard, and cheated her out of some of her pay. They also instilled in her the will to learn Spanish, so she couldn't be cheated or tricked again. After about a year, Menchu learned that her father had been sent to jail. She left her job and returned to the *fincas* to try and earn extra money to help him.

THE BEGINNINGS OF POLITICAL ACTIVISM

For years the Menchu family had been able to split their time between their own land and the plantations. After a while, though, according to Menchu, the family wasn't safe on even their own small plot of land. In the late 1960s, the landowners began coming into the mountains to harass the Indians, claiming that the land belonged to them or to the government, and that the Indians would have to pay them. As the leader of the community, Vicente Menchu, Rigoberta's father, tried to stop the *ladinos* from taking their land. He traveled to the capital to try to obtain title to the land from the government, but found no one would help him. Instead, he was sent from one place to the next to get papers, obtain signatures, hire a lawyer, but he was continually frustrated in his efforts. He had no money, no resources, and didn't speak Spanish well enough to negotiate. And he had no way of knowing that the government agents had been bribed by the landowners to obstruct his claims.

The Indians intensified their efforts, and their difficulties escalated. While Rigoberta was working as a maid in the capital when she was about 14 or 15, her father was arrested for the first time, charged with creating disturbances. He was sentenced to 18 years in prison but released after just over a year with the threat that he would be jailed for life if he continued to cause problems. While Vicente was in jail, the landowners came with gunmen to the Indians' mountain community and threatened them, ransacking and destroying their homes. Upon his release, Vicente Menchu continued to fight for title to the land. While traveling back from the capital, he was attacked by gunmen, kidnapped, tortured, and left to die in the mountains. He was found and was hospitalized for almost two years. After that he was in constant pain and was never able to work in the fields again. Still, he continued to fight. In 1977, Menchu was jailed a second time, given a life sentence as a political prisoner. By then he was well known and had won the support of the Catholic priests and nuns, the unions, and Indian groups. He was in jail for just 15 days. After his release he went underground, continuing his work in hiding. He was never able to return to live with the family.

The work of Vicente Menchu and other Indian leaders owes much to the Catholic Church. In the 1960s and 1970s, certain groups within the Church, both clergy and lay people, started working with the Indians and other peasants. The religious people taught the Indians how to read and write and how to organize unions and village cooperatives. Local leaders who are involved in the Church, called "catechists," have become the principal religious and political leaders of many Indian communities. Rigoberta Menchu was one such cathechist.

In the mid-1970s, Rigoberta began working with her father, to ensure that his work would continue even if he was killed. She often traveled with him, meeting those in the city, especially in the unions and Catholic organizations, who had tried to help him. After a time, she began working on her own. She visited other villages, showing them some of the defensive measures that she and her people had devised to fight off the armed intruders. She also began organizing workers on the *fincas* and helped with several strikes. The different Indian languages became a barrier, one that divided her from other peasants. Menchu continued practicing Spanish, and began learning the other major Indian languages as well.

During this time, Rigoberta was going through a period of upheaval, trying to understand why her people have suffered so much. She began to see that it was not just a problem for her family, her community, but instead part of a much larger problem. As she explains, "We began to understand that the root of all our problems was exploitation. That there were rich and poor and that the rich exploited the poor—our sweat, our labour. That's how they got richer and richer." With time, she came to understand how the exploitation occurred. "We began thinking, with the help of other friends, other *companeros*, that our enemies were not only landowners who lived near us, and above all not just the landowners who forced us to work and paid us little. It was not only now we were being killed; they had been killing us since we were children, through malnutrition, hunger, poverty. We started thinking about the roots of the problem and came to the conclusion that everything stemmed from the ownership of land. The best land was not in our hands. It belonged to the big landowners. Every time they see that we have new land, they try to throw us off it or steal it from us in other ways." Rigoberta became more involved in organizing, working with the Indians in her own community and with those toiling on the *fincas*.

THE FATE OF THE MENCHU FAMILY

Rigoberta's family was made to suffer greatly for their attempts to help their people. By the late 1970s, the Indians' efforts to resist the government had escalated into armed conflict. Many villages were occupied by armed troops, who attacked the Indians, demolished their homes, killed their farm animals, and destroyed their crops. Claiming that many Indians were guerrillas, the army kidnapped and killed them, often in public to frighten others. In 1979, they kidnapped Petrocinio Menchu, one of Rigoberta's brothers. They claimed that he was a guerrilla and tortured him for 16 days. The army then ordered all of the local Indians to come see the guerrillas. They trucked in a group of dreadfully abused peasants, showed each of their wounds to the Indians who had been ordered to watch, and then set them on fire. The army burned those people alive, as Rigoberta and her family watched.

Driven by their anger and despair, all of the Menchu family members became activists. Both parents, Vicente and Juana, left the family to warn Indians in other communities about what was happening. Vicente Menchu began working with a group that was trying to draw national and international attention to the abuses that the armed forces were inflicting on the Indians. Their group went to Guatemala City and tried to create publicity—they visited the national Congress, sent out news releases to the media, held press conferences, visited colleges, and even occupied a radio station and several offices. But no one in the government would meet with them. On January 31, 1980, 29 people, including Vicente Menchu, decided to occupy the Spanish embassy, still hoping to generate interest in their cause. Instead, 400 armed troops surrounded the embassy. When the protesters refused to come out, the troops, acting on government orders, locked the building and set it on fire. Thirty-nine people, protesters as well as embassy workers, were burned alive.

Three months later, Rigoberta Menchu's mother was killed. The army captured her, hoping to learn about the location of the guerrilla hideouts. Juana Menchu was raped, beaten, and tortured. Finally she was put on public view, left outside in the sun and rain and cold to die. The soldiers who stood guard until after she died wouldn't even let her family recover her body for burial.

EXILE IN MEXICO

By that time, Rigoberta Menchu's life was in danger, too. She couldn't stay in her own village, where the army could easily find her; but she didn't want to endanger others by staying with them. She traveled from place to place, staying with sympathizers. Because she was well known and easily recognized, she mostly stayed inside. But one day, she simply got tired of hiding and went outdoors. As she and a companion were walking down a village street, an army truck passed by, and as she recalls, "its occupants said my whole name. I knew what that meant for me. It meant that I'd be kidnapped or killed." The soldiers came by again and said they wanted to talk to her. Menchu and her friend ran and hid in a church, and managed to get away. She went into hiding, working as a maid in a nuns' home until her supporters could smuggle her out of the country.

Since 1981, Menchu has lived in exile in Mexico, making a few brief trips back to Guatemala. In 1986, civilian rule was reinstated in Guatemala after decades of military rule, although the army continues to hold much power. Since April 1991, the government and the rebel armies have been holding peace talks, which have been held up by the issue of human rights' abuses. Throughout her years in exile, Menchu has continued speaking out, at the United Nations and other international forums, to draw the world's attention to the plight of her people.

THE NOBEL PRIZE

Menchu's work also drew the attention of the Nobel committee, and in 1992 she was awarded the Nobel Peace Prize. According to the Nobel selection committee, "Rigoberta Menchu stands out as a vivid symbol of peace and reconciliation across ethnic, cultural and social dividing lines, in her own country, on the American continent and in the world." They also stressed the significance of their choice of Menchu, an activist for native rights, to win the award during the 500th anniversary of Christopher Columbus's arrival in the New World. The announcement of her selection for this prestigious award was coolly received by the Guatemalan government, which had accused her of supporting the leftist guerrillas. The president offered a brief statement of congratulations, but the foreign minister denounced the award, claiming that Menchu "is tied to certain groups that have endangered Guatemala."

MARRIAGE AND FAMILY

Menchu is unmarried. As she explains, "As a woman I have decided not to marry or have children. According to our traditions this is unacceptable; a woman should have children and we like to have them. But I could not endure it if what happened to my brother would happen to one of my children. From time to time, when I'm depressed, I wish my mother had had an abortion and never given birth to me. Before having children we have to change the situation . . . . I don't want a boyfriend because it would be one more reason to grieve. They would kill him for sure, and I don't want to cry anymore . . . . I am no longer the owner of my small existence; the world I live in is so cruel, so blood-thirsty, that it is going to annihilate me at any moment."

WRITINGS

I, Rigoberta Menchú: An Indian Woman in Guatemala, 1984 (first published in Spanish in 1983)

FILMS

When the Mountains Tremble, 1983 (narrator)

HONORS AND AWARDS

Nobel Peace Prize: 1992, "in recognition of her work for social justice and ethno-cultural reconciliation based on respect for the rights of indigenous peoples"

FURTHER READING

BOOKS

Fried, Jonathan L., and others (editors). *Guatemala in Rebellion: Unfinished History*, 1983

Menchu, Rigoberta. *I, Rigoberta Menchú: An Indian Woman in Guatemala,* 1984

PERIODICALS

Miami Herald, Nov. 2, 1992, p.C1
New York Times, Oct. 17, 1992, p.A1
Sacramento Bee, Oct. 17, 1992, p.A1; Oct. 18, 1992, p.A1
San Jose Mercury News, Oct. 17, 1992, p.A1
Washington Post, Oct. 17, 1992, p.A1

OTHER

"All Things Considered" Transcript, Oct. 16, 1992, National Public Radio

ADDRESS

Verso
29 W. 35th St.
New York, NY 10001

Walter Dean Myers   1937-
American Writer for Young Adults
Author of *Somewhere in the Darkness*

BIRTH

Walter Milton Myers (later changed to Walter Dean Myers) was born on August 12, 1937, in Martinsburg, West Virginia. His birth parents were George Ambrose Myers and Mary (Green) Myers. Mary was George's second wife, and the family included seven children. When Walter was two years old, his mother died while giving birth to his sister Imogene. His father was left to care for the newborn baby, Walter, and the older children, two brothers and four sisters. It was a very difficult time for the family: few jobs were available during the Great Depression, and even fewer were open to blacks.

In 1940, Florence Dean, who had been George Myers's first wife, came to visit with her new husband, Herbert Dean. They had moved to Harlem, in New York City, and they came back to West Virginia to take Florence's two daughters, who George had been raising, back home with them. To help out the struggling Myers family, they also took three-year-old Walter with them. The adoption was informal but permanent, and the Deans became, in every way, his "real" parents.

YOUTH

Walter Myers's foster parents, as he calls them, had little formal education. Herbert Dean left school in the third grade. He worked as a shipping clerk for U.S. Radium and always held down extra jobs to make ends meet, working for a moving company or in the shipyards loading and unloading cargo. He also loved to tell stories, stories that were sometimes so scary that Walter was afraid to be left alone with him.

Florence Dean worked in a factory, but she also found time while doing the housework to teach young Walter to read. As he recalls, "Those were good days. Sitting in that living room, the sun coming through the windows and her starched and ironed curtains. (My mother believed that if you could wash it, you could starch it and you could iron it.) . . . She would do housework . . . . And she would teach me to read. I was about four years old and what we read was *True Romance* magazine. She had an endless supply of *True Romance* magazines. I loved them. I didn't always understand them . . . . She also found some Classic Comics and we went through some of those. This was one of the greatest periods of my life with this woman."

Myers grew up in Harlem, on the island of Manhattan in New York City. Much of his early childhood there was quite pleasant. At that time in Harlem, crime, violence, and drugs were not the widespread problem they are today. Instead, Harlem was a real community where people knew one another and neighbors looked out for each others' children, where "anybody could yell at you," as Myers recalls. He spent much of his time playing games, like baseball and stoopball, with neighborhood kids. At the corner church, Church of the Master, he learned to play basketball in the basement, as he later described in *Hoops*; he also studied modern dance at the church, which later became the home of the Dance Theater of Harlem.

EARLY MEMORIES

Although his experiences outside of school were often pleasant, time spent at school, for many years, was very difficult. As a child, Myers had a severe speech impediment. His classmates teased him mercilessly, and he often responded by fighting. Finally in fifth grade, his teacher, Mrs. Conway, helped him out. "I had been suspended for fighting in class and had to sit in the back of the class while I waited for my mother to appear. The teacher, known for her meanness, caught me reading a comic under the desk during a math lesson. The teacher decided that if I was going to read then I might as well have something decent to read. Later, she brought to school a selection of books for younger people, and I was introduced to reading good books." Soon after, he discovered the local branch of the New York Public Library.

EDUCATION

With time, Myers's speech impediment improved, and for a while, his school experiences did, too. In junior high he was classified as a bright student and was placed in an accelerated program in which the students completed two years in one. He then attended Stuyvesant High School, an excellent school with a special emphasis on science. Unfortunately for Myers, he wasn't much of a scientist. He was turning into a good writer, though—he won prizes in an essay and a poetry contest.

But he was once again having problems at school. As he explains, "I assumed I would go to college and eventually take my rightful place in the world of bright, influential people. But as I neared the end of my junior year in high school, I saw that going to college would be financially impossible. I also began to recognize that my 'rightful place' might be defined more by my race than my abilities. I became depressed, disillusioned. What was the use of being bright if that 'brightness' didn't lead me where I wanted to go. I stopped going to school, at least on a regular basis . . . .

"I felt my life was falling apart, that I had no control over my destiny. I had won a minor prize in an essay contest; I also won a set of encyclopedias for a long narrative poem. But my family didn't seem to think it was a big deal. I was from a family of laborers, and the idea of writing stories or essays was far removed from their experience. Writing had no practical value for a Black child. These minor victories did not bolster my ego. Instead, they convinced me that even though I was bright, even though I might have some talent, I was still defined by factors other than my ability . . . .

"We begin to compromise our ideals as we see that they exist in a more and more abstract plane. Sometimes, when the ideal seems completely unattainable, we abandon it altogether . . . . A youngster is not trained to want to be a gasoline station attendant or a clerk in some obscure office. We are taught to want to be lawyers and doctors and accountants— these professions that are given value. When the compromise comes, as it does early in Harlem to many children, it comes hard."

And that compromise came both early and hard for Myers. As he began to see school as a dead end, he started questioning the value of education, skipping classes, and hanging out on the street. In 1954, at the age of seventeen, he dropped out of school and joined the army. Although he went to radio repair school, where he "learned nothing about radio repair," Myers says that he spent most of his three-year army stint playing basketball.

Later, Myers attended City College in New York. He eventually earned a B.A. in communications from Empire State College in 1984.

FIRST JOBS

After leaving the army in 1957, Myers returned to New York and entered his "starving artist period," living on unemployment and reading constantly. He eventually got a job at the post office, where he met his first wife, Joyce. They were married in 1960, and soon had two children. While working at the post office he started writing on a daily basis, submitting poems and stories to black publications. From the post office, he went on to a string of jobs, as a messenger, a factory clerk, and an employment supervisor for the New York State Department of Labor (1966-69). During this time, he was also trying to live like a bohemian, as he says, playing bongos all night in clubs while his wife stayed home with their two small children. Their marriage dissolved. Throughout, though, he was writing, and he gradually became determined to make a living at it.

CHOOSING A CAREER

Myers got his professional start in 1968, when he entered a picture-book contest for black writers sponsored by the Council on Interracial Books for Children. He entered that contest, he has said, "more because I wanted to write *anything* than because I wanted to write a picture book." Still, his book *Where Does the Day Go?* won the contest, launching his award-winning career as an author for young readers. But it wasn't until ten years later that he worked as a writer full-time. From 1970 to 1977, Myers worked at the publishing firm Bobbs-Merrill Co. as a senior trade editor, learning, as he once said, "about the business aspects of my craft." He was laid off from that position following a restructuring in 1977, and he has supported himself as a writer ever since.

CAREER HIGHLIGHTS

Myers is considered one of the foremost modern American authors for young adults. During the past 25 years, he has written over 30 titles that focus primarily on life for American blacks. *Where Does the Day Go?* (1969) was his first published book; with his second, *The Dancers* (1972), he changed his name to Walter Dean Myers, to honor his foster parents. For the first few years, he concentrated on picture books. From there, Myers has branched into young-adult novels in a range of genres, including humor, mystery, suspense, adventure, and realistic contemporary, considered his forte.

He made the transition to young-adult novels quite by chance. At a party in the mid-1970s, he spoke with an editor who had read and liked a draft of one of his short stories. Believing that it was actually the first chapter of a novel, she asked Myers to tell her about the rest of the story. Undaunted, Myers "made it up on the spot," and thus began his first young adult novel, *Fast Sam, Cool Clyde, and Stuff.*

Since that time, Myers has primarily focused on young-adult novels. Typically, these works portray contemporary African-American life in urban communities, usually Harlem. Some of his best, according to reviewers, include *Fast Sam, Cool Clyde, and Stuff, It Ain't All for Nothin', The Young Landlords, Hoops, Won't Know Till I Get There, Motown and Didi, Crystal, Scorpions, Fallen Angels, The Mouse Rap,* and *Somewhere in the Darkness.* His depiction of black life in urban America is widely praised as authentic. Life is often hard in Myers's fictional world, but he showcases its joys as well as its challenges. The stories focus on the themes of friendship, the importance of peer groups, strong father-son relationships, and life amidst adversity. He is considered a gifted writer and a skilled storyteller, equally adept at humor, suspense, and realism. He is particularly noted for his use of the rhythms of black speech. He especially uses this gift for dialogue to define the characters, which reviewers describe as believable, sympathetic, complex, memorable, and well-defined individuals.

Myers has been involved in several different projects lately. In 1991 he published *Now Is Your Time!: The African-American Struggle for Freedom,* a history of the black experience in North America written for the young-adult audience. He has three new novels out in 1992: *Mop, Moondance, and the Nagasaki Knights,* a sequel to the story about a baseball team begun in his earlier novel *Me, Mop, and the Moondance Kid; The Righteous Revenge of Artemis Bonner,* a humorous tale about a young man in the 1880s in the Wild West, and *Somewhere in the Darkness,* a dark and moving story of a young man's journey down South with the father, recently escaped from prison and critically ill, that he has never known. Myers has also created a new series entitled "18 Pine St.," named after the address of a pizza parlor and teen hangout. The novels in this series focus on a group of teenagers, with realistic stories about family, friends, and romance in urban America. As Myers explained, "African-American kids need a chance to read about situations that interest them—featuring characters that they can identify with." For each book in the series, he provides the outline and then supervises the writing by others. In addition, he has written a biography, *Malcolm X: By Any Means Necessary*, which is currently scheduled to appear in early 1993.

MARRIAGE AND FAMILY

Myers and his first wife, Joyce, were married in 1960, and within three years they had two children, Karen Elaine and Michael Dean. They later divorced. Myers married Constance Brendel on June 19, 1973; they have one son, Christopher. Myers and his wife live in New Jersey; all three of his children are now grown.

HOBBIES AND OTHER INTERESTS

Myers's favorite activity is writing. When asked what he likes to do to relax, he once responded, "Write. If I'm working on something and I feel like that day's over, I may write something else for fun." He also enjoys teaching writing to sixth, seventh, and eighth graders at a Jersey City school, as well as playing the flute and taking photographs.

Travel is another one of Myers's special interests. In 1974 and 1975 he toured Europe with his son Michael, who was then 12 years old. With wife Connie and son Christopher, Myers has visited Asia, Mexico, and South America. In some cases, material from his travels may find their way into his writings; his trip to Peru with Chris, for example, provided scenes for *The Nicholas Factor*.

WRITINGS

FICTION

Where Does the Day Go? 1969 (as Walter M. Myers)
The Dancers, 1972
The Dragon Takes a Wife, 1972
Fly, Jimmy, Fly!, 1974
Fast Sam, Cool Clyde, and Stuff, 1975
Brainstorm, 1977
Mojo and the Russians, 1977
Victory for Jamie, 1977
It Ain't All for Nothin', 1978
The Young Landlords, 1979
The Black Pearl and the Ghost; or, One Mystery after Another, 1980
The Golden Serpent, 1980
Hoops, 1981
The Legend of Tarik, 1981
Won't Know Till I Get There, 1982
The Nicholas Factor, 1983

Tales of a Dead King, 1983
Mr. Monkey and the Gotcha Bird, 1984
Motown and Didi: A Love Story, 1984
The Outside Shot, 1984
Sweet Illusions, 1986
Crystal, 1987
Fallen Angels, 1988
Me, Mop, and the Moondance Kid, 1988
Scorpions, 1988
The Mouse Rap, 1990
Mop, Moondance, and the Nagasaki Knights, 1992
The Righteous Revenge of Artemis Bonner, 1992
Somewhere in the Darkness, 1992

Myers is also the creator of the "18 Pine St." Series.

"THE ARROW ADVENTURE SERIES"

Adventure in Granada, 1985
The Hidden Shrine, 1985
Duel in the Desert, 1986
Ambush in the Amazon, 1986

NONFICTION

The World of Work: A Guide to Choosing a Career, 1975
Social Welfare, 1976
Now Is Your Time!: The African-American Struggle for Freedom, 1991

HONORS AND AWARDS

Council on Interracial Books for Children Award: 1968, for the manuscript of *Where Does the Day Go?*
Best Books for Young Adults (American Library Association): 1978, for *It Ain't All for Nothin';* 1979, for *The Young Landlords;* 1982, for *Hoops;* 1988 (2 awards), for *Fallen Angels* and *Scorpion;* 1990, for *The Mouse Rap;* and 1992, for *Now Is Your Time! The African-American Struggle for Freedom*
Coretta Scott King Book Award (American Library Association): 1980, for *The Young Landlords;* 1985, for *Motown and Didi;* 1989, for *Fallen Angels;* 1992, for *Now Is Your Time!: The African-American Struggle for Freedom;* Coretta Scott King Honor Book: 1993, for *Somewhere in the Darkness*
New Jersey State Council of the Arts Fellowship: 1981
National Endowment for the Arts Grant: 1982, 1989
Notable Children's Trade Book in Social Studies: 1982, for *The Legend of Tarik*
Parents' Choice Award for Literature: 1982, for *Won't Know Till I Get There;* 1984, for *The Outside Shot;* and 1988, for *Fallen Angels*

MacDowell Fellowship: 1988

Newbery Honor Book: 1989, for *Scorpions*; 1983, for *Somewhere in the Darkness*

FURTHER READING

BOOKS

Bishop, Rudine S. *Presenting Walter Dean Myers*, 1990

Contemporary Authors New Revision Series, Vol. 20

Something about the Author, Vol. 41

Something about the Author Autobiography Series, Vol. 2

Who's Who among Black Americans, 1992-93

PERIODICALS

Publishers Weekly, July 20, 1992, p.217

ADDRESS

Scholastic Books
730 Broadway
New York, NY 10003

Martina Navratilova 1956-
Czech-Born American Tennis Champion
Winner of Nine Wimbledon Singles Titles

BIRTH

Martina Navratilova was born October 18, 1956, in Prague, Czechoslovakia. Her father, Miroslav Subert, a Prague restaurant manager, and her mother, Jana, divorced when Martina was only three. Her maternal grandmother, Agnes Semanska, was the finest woman tennis player of her generation. Martina has a younger sister, also named Jana, who still lives in Czechoslovakia.

YOUTH

The family returned to the Krkonose Mountains shortly after

Martina's birth, and she learned to ski almost as soon as she could walk. After her parents divorced, Martina and her mother went to the village of Revnice (pronounced zhev-NEE-tzeh), outside Prague, to live in the Semanska ancestral home. She saw her father infrequently, his visits eventually stopping altogether. Only years later did she learn that her father, always regarded as a rather unstable man, had committed suicide when she was eight.

Martina's family signed her up at the local tennis club at Revnice, and there at the courts she met and grew to like a friendly man— Miroslav (Mirek) Navratil. She was surprised and delighted when she first noticed him talking to her mother. In 1961, Jana and Mirek married, enriching young Martina's life with the presence of a man whom she has always referred to as a "second father." Two years after the marriage, her half-sister, Jana, was born. At the age of ten, feeling awkward at having a father and sister with a different surname, Martina changed her name from Subertova to Navratilova ("ova" is the feminine gender ending). Although, in the Czech language, the accent should be on the third syllable of her name, she now accepts what she calls the "Italian" pronunciation, NAV-rah-ti-LOW-vah.

Navratilova frequently accompanied her parents to the tennis court, pounding the ball against the wall with a wooden racquet inherited from her grandmother. Frustrated with the fact that a wall could never be defeated, she was thrilled at the age of six when she first stepped onto the red clay court at Revnice. "The moment I . . . felt the joy of smacking a ball over the net," she recalls, "I knew I was in the right place."

While tennis was always Navratilova's best and favorite sport, she remembers being the "school jock." Tiny and all muscle, she displayed early the athleticism and fierce competitiveness that have made her a superstar. She loved to run so much that teachers would send her on errands to get them done quickly.

Navratilova's parents took different approaches to her fascination with tennis. Mirek Navratil always believed in his daughter's potential for becoming a great player. Her mother, while supportive, had resented being pushed into tennis by her own father and was too close to the game to be a good coach. "While [my father] was working me out," Martina recalls, "[my mother] would sit alongside the court, and if I missed a shot, she'd say, 'How could you miss that?' and I'd say, 'You're a player, *you* missed it before.' Meantime, my father would be saying, 'Here's what you did wrong.'"

TRAINING BEGINS IN EARNEST

When Navratilova was nine, she was admitted to George Parma's tennis school at Klamovka Park, on the edge of Prague. This was important not only because Parma was a superb teacher, but also because he had been one of Czechoslovakia's best players. Just as importantly, Klamovka was the only indoor tennis facility in that part of the country and, considering the long and harsh Czech winters, being able to practice year-round was a tremendous advantage. "If you didn't play for George Parma at Klamovka," asserts Navratilova, "you didn't become much of a tennis player." She remembers Parma as a patient coach, tutoring her once a week. She would rush from school to the commuter train to Prague, board a streetcar there, and walk up a hill to the courts. Sometimes, though, Parma would travel to Revnice to work with his young star—a "big occasion" for which Navratilova would replace her warm-up suit with a white tennis skirt. "I was so excited to work with him," she recalls, "that I'd chase balls until I ran out of breath."

That same year, Navratilova began playing in local and national tournaments, excelling against girls as much as three years older than she. A tournament in August 1968 was to affect her strongly, though, for reasons that had little to do with tennis. Czechoslovakia was at that time part of the Eastern Bloc controlled by the Soviet Union. Under the regime of Alexander Dubcek, Czechoslovakia had adopted a policy of "socialism with a human face"—in contrast to the totalitarian, bureaucratic version set forth by the Soviet Union. Mirek Navratil called Pilsen, where Navratilova was playing, at six in the morning, to tell her not to go outside. The Russian leaders had lost patience with Dubcek, and their Russian tanks were in Czechoslovakia's streets. The "Prague Spring," as the period of reform was called, was over, and Navratilova's tournament canceled. George Parma was in Austria that day, and he joined with 120,000 other Czechoslovakians in defecting. For Navratilova, it was time to concentrate on tennis and wait for the sport to provide travel opportunities.

The first such chance came in 1969 with a junior tournament in what was then West Germany. After a harrowing train ride through occupied Czechoslovakia, Navratilova dominated the German competition and received her first international publicity. Upon returning home, she captured her first national title (at the age of 14), winning Czechoslovakia's 14-and-under division. She became her country's top-rated player by winning the 1972 national title from Vlasta Vopickova in a stunning upset, 7-5, 6-4. By the time she was 16, the possibilities seemed endless. They were.

EARLY MEMORIES

When taking lessons in Prague, Navratilova would stay with her real father's mother, Grandma Subertova, who called her granddaughter "Zlata Holcicka"—golden little girl. Navratilova would sleep on a couch-bed in the small apartment, and the two would listen to the radio and do crossword puzzles. Proud as she was of Navratilova, Grandma Subertova didn't understand much about competitive tennis, but she provided support, inspiration, and comfort.

"She just loved me and encouraged me to enjoy life," Navratilova says. "Nobody has ever loved me so completely, so acceptingly, as Grandma." To this day, the memory is overpowering. She says in her autobiography that she still has recurring dreams about her grandmother, and notes: "I loved Grandma Subertova so much that she almost did not get into this book. Every time I started to talk about her, I would break into tears, and feel weak and tired inside."

EDUCATION

Martina Navratilova was a good student, for years juggling her tournament play with her studies at high school in Revnice. She was the third-best student there even though she had little time for her academic work. Her favorite subject was geography, where she could picture herself in some of the many cities she has since visited. Because of her defection to the United States in 1975, Navratilova never finished high school.

MAJOR INFLUENCES

As a young player, Martina idolized Billie Jean King and Margaret Court Smith, giants of the women's game during the 1960s and 1970s. And while her second father fired her ambition and confidence, it was George Parma who shaped her game. He noted that, even as a youngster, she preferred to rush the net and volley, so he taught her to use a one-hand backhand shot that improved her reach. He also instilled in her what little caution exists. "I'd try some fancy drop shot and George would raise his eyebrows or say, 'Just hit it back, Martina,'" she recalls. "I'd get in the groove and hit a few forehands. But if I saw an opening, I'd rush the net again, and he'd have to remind me that I was taking a lesson, not playing for the Czech championship."

Parma also gave Navratilova tips on playing in matches and reinforced her desire to compete internationally. Having suffered from politics and bureaucracy, he developed his young charge so as to quickly give her chances to compete against the top players, telling her to set her sights on being one of the best in the world. Mirek Navratil, however, set even higher targets, and he proved to be the better prophet. He had been telling his daughter ever since she was a little girl that she would one day win Wimbledon.

CAREER HIGHLIGHTS

After conquering the Czech women's field and playing several impressive tournaments in Europe, the young tennis star came to challenge America's best women on the Virginia Slims tour in early 1973. This first trip to the United States led to two discoveries: one, that she was competitive with all but the top players, giving Evonne Goolagong a sound match before losing 6-4, 6-4 in Hingham, Massachusetts; two, that she loved junk food. Navratilova usually stormed through the qualifying matches, and her power game ensured that she would win her share of them. And, "cutting my marathon eating swath through the New World," she gained 20 pounds, leading fans to call her "the great wide hope."

In Akron that year, Navratilova first encountered the woman with whose name hers will probably always be linked—Chris Evert. Two years Navratilova's senior, Evert was at that time a much more accomplished player and already one of the stars of the tour. Evert, known for her charming smile, pleasant demeanor, and vicious two-handed backhand, had been a semifinalist at both Wimbledon and Forest Hills (the former site of the U.S. Open) the previous year, and beat Martina 7-6, 5-4, 6-3. The match began a rivalry that lasted until Evert's recent retirement.

The Czech tennis federation thought enough of Navratilova's play to send her to the French Open, where she shocked Nancy Richey (then one of the world's best clay court players) with a 6-3, 6-3 defeat. She succumbed to Goolagong in the quarterfinals, 7-6, 6-4, but had garnered for herself an invitation to Wimbledon, the world's most prestigious tournament. She lost there in the third round to Patti Hogan. Returning to Czechoslovakia, Navratilova won a tournament at Pilsen, then closed out 1973 with another trip to North America. Her best showing here was a loss in the semifinals at Charlotte. Overall, it had been an exceptional year for such a young player, establishing her as a rising star.

The year 1974 was even better. Early on, Navratilova reached the finals of the Italian and German Opens, which are considered second-level tournaments. She joined the Virginia Slims tour and, in Orlando, notched her first tournament victory on this side of the Atlantic. Her match record on the tour was a respectable 13-9, putting her tenth in money earnings and gaining her *Tennis* magazine's "Rookie of the Year" honors. She closed the year with her best showing ever in a Grand Slam tournament, losing to Goolagong in the semifinals after beating Margaret Court for the first time.

Navratilova led the Czech women to their first victory in the Federation Cup (the women's equivalent of the Davis Cup) in 1975 with her first victory over Evonne Goolagong, 6-3, 6-4. With Chris Evert, she took four doubles championships. As a singles player, she reached the finals of seven major tournaments, including the French and Italian Opens, and became the second-leading money winner in women's tennis, bested only by Evert.

A NEW LIFE IN THE U.S.

Navratilova's biggest headlines in 1975, however, came with her defection to the United States on September 6. Having battled the Czech tennis federation for two years over her right to travel freely and keep the money she earned, and envying the freedom of American players, Navratilova made the difficult break with her family and her country. "I realized that I would never have the psychological freedom to play the best tennis as long as I was under their control," she commented after applying for political asylum.

Although 1976 began well with a Virginia Slims victory in Houston over Evert, her friend and nemesis, the year was to prove difficult. Persistent injuries and transition to Western life left Navratilova in a slump that denied her a tournament victory for nine months. She did capture the Wimbledon doubles crown with Evert, but was crushingly upset in the first round of the U.S. Open, the foremost tournament of her new country. After Janet Newberry defeated her 1-6, 6-4, 6-3, Navratilova collapsed in tears on the court. Six more Opens would pass before Navratilova could win one of her own.

Her rise to the top, despite this interruption, was to continue. Armed with a new dedication to training and the encouragement of friends, Navratilova stormed back over the next two years. She finished the 1977 women's professional tour in first place. The next year would feature the greatest triumph of a young career and the fulfillment of a childhood dream. After besting Goolagong in the Wimbledon semifinal, the stage was set for what later became almost a cliche: Navratilova versus Evert in the final. Coming back from a first-set loss, and defeat in the final two sets, Martina took the match 2-6, 6-4, 7-5. "I put my right hand to my forehead in disbelief," she relates, "and I could feel Chris patting me on the back and congratulating me." A few days later, Evert's four-year stranglehold on the world's number-one ranking had been broken—the 20-year-old adopted American was now the best woman player on the planet.

A DECADE OF VICTORIES

The win over Chris Evert was the first of what would be an unprecedented nine Wimbledon singles titles, added to eight doubles titles—with Evert and with her partner through the eighties, Pam Shriver. Navratilova captured the French Open twice and the Australian three times. But the win, after Wimbledon, that she wanted most proved to be the hardest to get. She had gained American citizenship July 20, 1981, but had never even made the finals in New York. She beat Evert to get there that year, but dropped the deciding match to Tracy Austin, 6-1, 6-7, 6-7, double-faulting at match point. Standing on the court after this heartbreaker, she admitted, "I wanted to crawl into a hole."

After being sick in 1982 and losing in the quarterfinals to doubles-partner Shriver, Navratilova's time finally came. She met Evert for the 39th time in a final, when they were even with 19 victories each. The setting—and the pressure—could not have been greater. The match wasn't even close. Navratilova won, 6-1, 6-3, in only 63 minutes. Winning 84 and losing 19 games, not dropping a single set and averaging just over 50 minutes per match, Navratilova had stormed her way to the championship of her chosen country, 11 years after conquering the title in the nation of her birth. On being told that she had accumulated $6 million for the year to date—a record—Navratilova joked, "I know New York is an expensive city to live in. Maybe this can go toward a down payment somewhere."

Only one goal remained: the Grand Slam. That came exactly one year later. First there was a win over Kathy Jordan in Australia, then consecutive wins over Evert in Paris, London, and New York. Navratilova had won the world's four most important tournaments in one calendar year. There were even suggestions that, with Evert's star fading, Navratilova might be so much better than the others as to make women's tennis unfair. That, with the rise of Steffi Graf and Monica Seles, proved untrue. But neither her inevitable decline in the late 1980s (interrupted by a stunning 1990 victory at Wimbledon), nor sensationalistic publicity about personal and legal problems, should eclipse the overpowering talent that led Martina to dominate women's tennis for nearly a decade. Ken Rappoport sums up her career succinctly in a *Saturday Evening Post* article: "She is said to be the best female tennis player ever. And the stats make that claim indisputable."

MARRIAGE AND FAMILY

Martina Navratilova's personal life has caused much controversy. The fact that she, a self-proclaimed bisexual, has publicly acknowledged her long-term love affairs with other women has led to what might have been private problems becoming front-page news. She was involved with novelist Rita

Mae Brown (the author of *Rubyfruit Jungle* and *Southern Discomfort*) in the early eighties, and then with former beauty queen Judy Nelson later in the decade. After her breakup with Nelson, the latter sued her, claiming that their "life contract" on videotape was the equivalent of a marriage. The two settled out of court, and Navratilova weathered the furious storm of publicity with considerable grace.

MEMORABLE EXPERIENCES

Navratilova realized what her struggle for citizenship meant to Americans after her loss to Tracy Austin at the 1981 U.S. Open. "I was still crying when the announcer called my name for the runner-up trophy. But then something marvelous happened: the crowd started applauding and cheering . . . . I knew that they were cheering me as Martina, but they were also cheering me as an American . . . . They weren't cheering Martina the Complainer, Martina the Czech, Martina the Loser, Martina the Bisexual Defector. They were cheering me. I had never felt anything like it in my life: respect, maybe even love."

HOBBIES AND OTHER INTERESTS

Navratilova is an avid reader, and enjoys movies, swimming, skiing (both on snow and water), and backgammon. She also is a confirmed animal lover, and her home shelters several pet dogs.

WRITINGS

Martina (with George Vecsey), 1985

HONORS AND AWARDS

Rookie of the Year (*Tennis*): 1974
Most Improved Player (*Tennis*): 1975
The Championships, Wimbledon: 1978-79, 1982-87, 1990, Ladies' Singles; 1976, 1979, 1981-84, 1986, Ladies' Doubles; 1985, Mixed Doubles
French Open: 1982, 1984, Women's Singles; 1975, 1982, 1984-88, Women's Doubles; 1974, 1985, Mixed Doubles
U.S. Open: 1983-84, 1986-87, Women's Singles; 1977, 1978, 1980, 1983, 1984, 1986, 1987, 1989, 1990, Women's Doubles; 1985, 1987, Mixed Doubles
Female Athlete of the Year (Associated Press): 1983
Honorable Citizen of Dallas: 1983
One of America's 100 Most Important Women: 1988
A Woman of the Year (*Ms.*): 1988

FURTHER READING

BOOKS

Navratilova, Martina (with George Vecsey). *Martina,* 1985

PERIODICALS

Current Biography Yearbook 1977
Ms., Feb. 1988, p. 58
New York Times, July 17, 1992, p.B7; Sep. 4, 1992, p.B9
Saturday Evening Post, Mar. 1988, p.50
Tennis, Apr. 1989, p.52; Mar. 1992, p.18
Time, July 2, 1990, p.62
World Tennis, July 1988, p.43

ADDRESS

International Marketing Group
One Erie View Plaza
Suite 1300
Cleveland, OH 44114

Phyllis Reynolds Naylor 1933-
American Writer for Children and Young Adults
Author of *Shiloh*, the 1992 Newbery Medal
Winner

BIRTH

Phyllis Reynolds Naylor, celebrated author of books written mainly for children and young adults, was born Phyllis Dean Reynolds on January 4, 1933, in Anderson, Indiana. Her parents, Eugene Spencer Reynolds and Lura Mae (Schield) Reynolds, reared their family during the difficult years of the Great Depression, moving around central Indiana as job opportunities arose for Phyllis's father. Eugene and Lura Reynolds had met at Anderson College (now a university), where they were preparing for a lifetime of church work—he in the ministry, she in religious education. When the nation's economy collapsed in 1929, Eugene was one of the millions of Americans forced to abandon career plans; he found work first as a grocer, and later went into sales.

Young Phyllis was the middle child in her family, coming between an older sister, Norma, and a younger brother, John. The books and stories that surrounded the children in their growing years and the interest in music and drama engendered by their parents contributed, not surprisingly, to the development of their own considerable talents. Norma's creativity showed itself in art and painting, and John became an architect.

YOUTH

Many of the stories that have brought success to Naylor in her adult years were inspired by memories from her own childhood. She grew up in what she describes as a "most ordinary family . . . descended from preachers, teachers, and farmers." From the people and experiences of her formative years have sprung novels enjoyed today by a generation far removed from the spartan lifestyles of the 1930s.

Naylor's father worked for various Midwestern companies, and she writes that, "by the time I entered high school, we had lived in eight different neighborhoods stretching across Indiana, Illinois, and Iowa." Vacations were spent either on an Iowa farm with her mother's parents, or in Maryland, where her paternal grandfather was both a farmer and the pastor of a small church, and her grandmother, an untrained nurse, cared for wards of the state in their home. These family elders, and others whose lives were connected with them, would later serve as models for characters in Phyllis's novels.

The Reynolds siblings were reared in a deeply religious home. Mealtime blessings, church music, and Bible stories were part of their everyday existence, yet entwined with the tedium of these routines was the warmth of simple pleasures. Naylor has tender memories of an understanding mother who would slip her a stick of gum or a mirrored compact to play with during a long and boring church sermon, and of a father who took her "walking to the woods . . . on a Sunday morning to see the gypsies and finding only their campfire. These are the memories of my childhood," Naylor now says, "that seem different from the experiences of young people today."

EARLY MEMORIES

Fear was a major element in young Phyllis's nature. Although her home life was secure, small worries and even irrational fears drained her emotions. The possibility of losing those she loved loomed as the most frightening thought of all. "So strong was my fear of being separated from Mother," she relates, "that I almost lost my life." She tells of having to cross railroad tracks on the way home from kindergarten, and how a train came by one day at the exact time she reached the tracks, cutting off her immediate access to home. "The thought of the train separating me from my mother was unbearable. And so I ran. I reached the other side only seconds before the train thundered by . . . . I can still see the horrified face of the engineer as he leaned out the side window."

Lura Reynolds accompanied her five-year-old child home from school for a while, then tempted her with candy in an effort to teach her to wait at the crossing should a train come into sight. The situation never repeated itself but, Naylor admits, "deep down I knew that if I [had been] once again put to the test, I would have run."

EDUCATION

Despite her fears, Naylor enjoyed school right from the start. Her kindergarten teacher would write down stories as the children told them, and young Phyllis's enthusiasm for spinning tales often left little time for others to have their chance as "authors." By fourth grade, Phyllis was caught up in storytelling: "Each day I would rush home from school to see if the wastebasket held any discarded paper that had one side blank. We were not allowed to use new sheets of paper for our writing and drawing, so books had to be done on used paper. I would staple these sheets together and sometimes paste a strip of colored paper over the staples to give it the appearance of a bound book. Then I would grandly begin my story, writing the words at the top of each page and drawing an accompanying picture on the bottom. Sometimes I typed the story before stapling the pages. And sometimes I even cut old envelopes in half and pasted them on the inside covers as pockets, slipping an index card in each one, like a library book, so I could check it out to friends and neighbors. I was the author, illustrator, printer, binder, and librarian, all in one."

Naylor attended elementary schools in both Muncie and Anderson, Indiana, before the family moved to Joliet, Illinois. There she went to junior high and high school, graduating in 1951. She tells of being asked to try out for the honor of class poet, since she already had begun to write for a church paper and for a few small magazines. Remembering now the "dreadful" poem she submitted, Naylor says she is convinced that she won only "because no one else wanted the job."

In college, Naylor put aside childhood dreams of such diverse careers as missionary or actress. Although she longed to be a writer, she doubted that she could really make a living at it. So she attended Joliet Junior College, preparing for a teaching career. She taught elementary school briefly, but in resuming her education some years later, she changed direction. In 1963, she earned a bachelor's degree in psychology from American University in Washington, D.C.

MARRIAGE AND FAMILY

Naylor has been married twice. The early marriage which she describes vividly in *Crazy Love: An Autobiographical Account of Marriage and Madness* was to a brilliant young scholar named Thomas A. Tedesco, Jr. (Names and places were changed in the 1977 book to protect family members living at that time.) The couple had married on September 9, 1951, when Phyllis was only eighteen, but their union was doomed within a few years as the young husband fell victim to paranoid schizophrenia. The tragic experience ended with Tedesco's commitment to a state hospital. Phyllis, who had lost any hope for his recovery, divorced him in 1959. She reprised the experience, though, in writing *The Keeper* (1986), a novel about a teenager forced to cope with his father's mental illness.

Naylor has enjoyed a happy home life since May 26, 1960, the day she married for the second time. Her husband, Rex V. Naylor, is a speech pathologist whose advice and helpful literary criticism have been major elements in her success. The Naylors have two grown sons—Jeffrey Alan, a knowledge engineer for a computer consulting firm, and Michael Scott, who does video production work.

FIRST JOBS

During her painful first marriage, Naylor held a series of jobs. Besides her short stint as a third-grade teacher, she found work as a YWCA locker-room attendant, a clinical secretary, an editorial assistant, and an executive secretary. All during this time, she wrote and sold short stories to pay the bills as her husband descended into mental illness.

CHOOSING A CAREER

Throughout the 1950s, the hopeful young writer submitted stories to small magazines and church publications. She was paid a pittance for some, and she learned, too, about rejection slips. However, the need to support herself and her mentally ill husband kept her working at other jobs. "I did not know that writing would be my life's work until I was in my late twenties," the acclaimed author of 75 books says now.

CAREER HIGHLIGHTS

Although Naylor has been writing most of her life, she began her professional career in earnest in 1960. The security and stability of her second marriage and the decision to finish her education gave her the self-confidence she lacked throughout the trying years of the previous decade. Earlier, her work had appeared as written either by P.R. Tedesco or Phyllis Dean Reynolds (her full given name), but now, as Phyllis Reynolds Naylor, she struck out creatively with assurance and dedication. She did well enough, even in the beginning, to pay part of her American University tuition with revenue from her writing.

The Galloping Goat and Other Stories and *Grasshoppers in the Soup*, short story collections published in 1965, were Naylor's first offerings to find their way into public view. Soon she was spinning out a dizzying array of novels, picture books, and nonfiction, borrowing themes from the experiences of her own life and polishing the tales with her thriving imagination. Versatility quickly became the hallmark of her work. A prolific author, Naylor writes for a wide range of audiences, from pre-schoolers to teenagers, and adults as well, with humor and compassion. She uses a wide range of forms and styles, including mystery and suspense, adventure, humor, realism, and fantasy. The settings vary from city to country and from the fourth century to the present. Despite such diversity, her works are consistently distinguished by their complex, believable, and individual characters. Her "Witch" and "York" trilogies, in particular, demonstrate a special sensitivity to the problems of childhood and adolescence. One of Naylor's most cherished projects is *Maudie in the Middle* (1988), a novel co-authored with her eighty-seven-year-old mother and based on the latter's recollections of her childhood in the early part of this century.

Honors started to accumulate as early as 1971, when *Wrestle the Mountain* became a Junior Literary Guild selection and was chosen also as Children's Book of the Year by the Child Study Association of America. More recognition followed through the next two decades, culminating in 1992 with the prestigious John Newbery Medal for *Shiloh*, the touching story of a boy who befriends a mistreated beagle. The story sprang from one of her own experiences. Visiting friends in West Virginia, she and her husband encountered a skinny, frightened, and mistreated dog while out taking a walk. They were unable to find its owner. Although her friends eventually adopted the dog, Phyllis was haunted by the experience and decided to write a story about it. According to Naylor, the story deals with justice— and the difficulty, for children and adults, of making ethical decisions in complex situations.

BOOKS FOR ADULTS, TOO

Although Naylor is known principally for her books for children and adolescents, she also has produced significant writings for adults. *Crazy Love*, the poignant story of a wrenching period in her life, was published in 1977, and it has brought more reader response than anything else she has written. In addition, she is the author of two adult novels, a book of essays, and an instructional volume titled *The Craft of Writing the Novel*.

Naylor often acknowledges how important writing has been in her own life: "On my deathbed," she asserts in *How I Came to Be a Writer*, "I am sure I will gasp, 'But I still have five more books to write!' . . . I will go on writing, because an idea in the head is like a rock in the shoe; I just can't wait to get it out." Her husband, Rex Naylor, concurs, as he says in a profile in *Horn Book Magazine*: "Writing is as necessary for her as eating or sleeping. She has taught this family the value of focus and perseverance. A rejected manuscript or an unfavorable but fair review simply spurs her to greater effort."

MAJOR INFLUENCES

Naylor credits her father with instilling in her the drive and persistence she exhibits to this day. He always believed that "you could accomplish anything you wanted if you really tried," she remembers, and it was the example of that positive approach to life that bolstered her in her most challenging times. Naylor's mother was a somewhat fearful person, much like her middle child, always cautioning, "What if, what if," but Eugene Reynolds's incurable optimism balanced what the author calls "drumbeats of alarm."

Several years of psychotherapy helped Naylor to set a new course in life and to stop agonizing over things she could not change. So, too, did her second marriage, which she claims was one of the best decisions of her life. "But mostly," she reflects, "it was that I had found myself—who I was and what I could do. I could write."

HOBBIES AND OTHER INTERESTS

Naylor says that there is always a book on her mind, even when she is not doing the actual creating or revising. "I have given up a lot for writing—oil painting, madrigal singing, dozens of books I'd planned someday to read," she admits, all the while insisting that the sacrifice is worth it.

In the moments that she can borrow from her busy career, she enjoys most being with her husband and family. A short trip or a weekend at the ocean are what she calls "joyful interludes."

ADVICE TO YOUNG WRITERS

Naylor offers these words of advice to aspiring writers: "Write the story only you can write—something you can really love or feel. Too many beginning writers try to write about something they don't know, like robberies, or travel to the moon. They can write about a young boy who really wants to write, or excel. This would ring true. Get them looking to their own life for tidbits and local color."

SELECTED WRITINGS

FOR YOUNG READERS

The Galloping Goat and Other Stories, 1965
Grasshoppers in the Soup, 1965
The New Schoolmaster, 1967
When Rivers Meet, 1968
Dark Side of the Moon, 1969
Ships in the Night, 1970
No Easy Circle, 1972
An Amish Family, 1974
Witch's Sister, 1975; *Witch Water*, 1977; *The Witch Herself*, 1978 (first "Witch" trilogy)
Walking Through the Dark, 1976
How I Came to Be a Writer, 1978
Shadows on the Wall, 1980; *Faces in the Water*, 1981; *Footprints at the Window*, 1981 ("York" trilogy)
The Boy With the Helium Head, 1982
A String of Chances, 1982
The Mad Gasser of Bessledorf Street, 1983; *The Bodies in the Bessledorf Hotel*, 1986; *Bernie and the Bessledorf Ghost*, 1990 (series)
The Agony of Alice, 1985; *Alice in Rapture, Sort of*, 1989; *Reluctantly Alice*, 1991; *All But Alice*, 1992; *Alice in April*, 1993 ("Alice" series)
The Keeper, 1986
Beetles, Lightly Toasted, 1987
Send No Blessings, 1990
Witch's Eye, 1990; *Witch Weed*, 1991; *The Witch Returns*, 1992 (second "Witch" trilogy)
King of the Playground, 1991
Shiloh, 1991

FOR ADULTS

Crazy Love: An Autobiographical Account of Marriage and Madness, 1977
Revelations, 1979
In Small Doses, 1979
Unexpected Pleasures, 1986
The Craft of Writing the Novel, 1989

HONORS AND AWARDS

Children's Book of the Year (Child Study Association of America): 1971, for *Wrestle the Mountain*

Golden Kite Award (Society of Children's Book Writers): 1978, for *How I Came to Be a Writer*

Notable Book Award (American Library Association), 1982, for *A String of Chances*; 1985, for *The Agony of Alice*; 1986, for *The Keeper*; 1991, for *Shiloh*

Child Study Award (Bank Street College of Education): 1983, for *The Solomon System*

Edgar Allan Poe Award (Mystery Writers of America): 1985, for *Night Cry*

Creative Writing Fellow (National Endowment of the Arts): 1987

International Book Award (Society of School Librarians): 1988, for *Maudie in the Middle*, co-written with the author's mother, Lura Schield Reynolds

Christopher Award (The Christophers, a religious organization that promotes Christian principles): 1989, for *Keeping a Christmas Secret*

Best Book Award (American Library Association): 1990, for *Send No Blessings*

John Newbery Medal (American Library Association): 1992, for *Shiloh*

FURTHER READING

BOOKS

Children's Literature Review, Vol. 17

Naylor, Phyllis Reynolds. *Crazy Love: An Autobiographical Account of Marriage and Madness*, 1977

Naylor, Phyllis Reynolds. *How I Came to Be a Writer*, 1987

Something about the Author, Vol. 66

Something about the Author Autobiography Series, Vol. 10

Twentieth-Century Children's Writers, 3rd ed., 1989

Who's Who in America, 1992-1993

PERIODICALS

Horn Book Magazine, July/Aug. 1992, pp. 404, 412

NEA Today, May 1992, p.9

The Reading Teacher, Sep. 1992, p.10

The Writer, Mar. 1986, p.12

ADDRESS

Macmillan Publishing Co.
Children's Book Group
866 Third Avenue
New York, NY 10022

OBITUARY

Rudolf Nureyev   1938-1993
Russian Ballet Dancer, Choreographer, and Director

BIRTH

Rudolf Hametovich Nureyev, considered by many to be the greatest male ballet dancer of the twentieth century, was born March 17, 1938, aboard a train bound for Vladivostok, in the former Soviet Union, where his father was a political instructor to Soviet soldiers. He was the fourth child of Hamet and Farida Nureyev, and the only boy. His sisters, Rosa, Rosida, and Lida, were traveling with their mother at the time of Rudolf's birth.

The Nureyevs were Tartar, rather than Russian, and that ethnic distinction was always important to Rudolf. "Our Tartar blood runs faster somehow, is always ready to boil. And yet it seems we are more languid that the Russians, more sensuous . . . . We are a curious mixture of tenderness and brutality."

YOUTH

Nureyev grew up in incredible poverty and deprivation. Soon after his birth, the Soviet Union entered into World War II (1939-1945), and his father joined the army. It was a time of tremendous famine throughout the Soviet Union. The family lived first in Moscow, where their home was bombed. They then moved to the small village of Tchichura, where the mother and her four children shared a room with two devout peasants. Farida was angry at their efforts to convert her children to Christianity, but Rudolf, driven by hunger, didn't mind praying with the old people, for they gave him food as a reward. "In those days stomachs were more often empty than not," he recalled in his autobiography. "Only potatoes mattered to me—they were worth their weight in gold, let alone their weight in prayers. The whole country was like a ravenous wolf." Indeed, his mother had once been attacked by wolves as she made her daily trek to find something for her children to eat, often trying to pawn shoes, belts, anything she could for food.

The family later moved to the city of Ufa in Bashkir, a remote Soviet republic east of the Ural mountains. There they lived with two other families—20 people—in one room. Nureyev remembered being a solitary child, playing alone and always loving trains and train stations. He also loved music and would sit and listen to the classical music broadcast on the radio for hours, even as a child of two or three.

EDUCATION

Nureyev attended kindergarten in Ufa, and the experience was a humiliating one. His mother had to carry him to school, for he had no proper shoes or other clothing. The children made fun of him and called him a beggar. He became acutely aware of the differences between those who had money and those who did not—of those who were fed and those who were hungry. He would sometimes faint from hunger during school. The experience made him even more distant from the other children, and he remembered no friends from his youth. He saw himself as solitary, different, and driven by a different destiny than those around him.

In his early years of grade school, Nureyev was an outstanding student. He began to dance at the age of seven, when he learned Bashkir folk dances. His talent was noted immediately by family friends and teachers alike. He knew, too, that he would be a dancer from the age of seven, when he attended his first ballet at the Ufa Opera House. "I shall never forget a single detail of the scene that met my eyes: the theater itself with its soft, beautiful lights and gleaming crystal chandeliers . . . . Something was happening to me which was taking me far from my sordid world and bearing me right up to the skies. From that unforgettable day when I knew such rapt excitement I could think of nothing else; I was utterly possessed. From that day I can truthfully date my unwavering decision to become a ballet dancer."

But there were many obstacles to overcome. His father, home from the war, wanted Rudolf's schooling to lead to a job that would help support the family; he wanted his son to have a masculine profession, to become a scientist or an engineer. He never understood the artistic temperament that drove his son, and he bitterly opposed Rudolf's ambition to dance. Rudolf's school work began to suffer as his obsession with dance grew. He had heard his teachers and his parents' friends say that he should go to Leningrad, to study with the Kirov Ballet, and he was determined to get there.

BALLET TRAINING

When he was 11, Nureyev began to study with his first real teacher, a woman named Udeltsova, who was then 70 years old. She had danced with one of the most famous ballet troupes of the twentieth century, the Ballet Russes, directed by Sergey Diaghilev in the early decades of the century. Its premier star was the great Vaslav Nijinski, to whom Nureyev would be compared throughout his career. "Child," Udeltsova said to Nureyev, "you have a duty to yourself to learn classical dancing. With such an innate gift, you must join the students at the Maryinsky Theater," calling the Kirov by its former, pre-Revolutionary name.

At 15, still without any training in classical ballet, he apprenticed to the Ufa Opera House dance troupe and performed in Moscow with them. In 1955, while on tour with the Ufa group, he auditioned for the Kirov. His audition judge had this to say to the young hopeful: "Young man, you'll either become a brilliant dancer—or a total failure. And most likely you'll be a failure." Nureyev knew what she meant: "I would have to work like mad." And he was willing to do anything to realize his dream.

At the age of 17, Nureyev began his formal training with the Kirov Ballet, the age at which most dancers, who begin at five or six, have completed their training and begun their careers. Nureyev, rebellious by nature, fought with the teachers constantly, and he refused to join the Komsomal, a communist student organization. He despised politics and had no time for anything that stood in the way of his dancing. His mercurial temperament and arrogance gained him many enemies throughout his career, for there were always some people who found his behavior intolerable from either a political or an artistic standpoint. His rebelliousness got him kicked out of his first class at the Kirov, and landed him in the class of Alexander Pushkin, who became a father figure to the young man. Pushkin's gentle but demanding methods worked well with eager but difficult Nureyev.

At 20, after only three years of professional training, he had offers from both the Kirov and the Bolshoi, the only other company in the Soviet Union to rival the Kirov. He chose the Kirov and became a soloist immediately, partnering the prima ballerina of the troupe, Natalia Dudinskaya, the wife of the head male dancer of the ballet, Sergeyev.

CAREER HIGHLIGHTS

The response of audiences and critics alike to the young dancer's debut was ecstatic. Nureyev was learning the classical repertoire at lightening speed and performing the roles with the power and abandon that always characterized his dancing. Yet his contempt for conformity—for either the established rules of the Kirov or the political pressures of Soviet society—stood in his way. For three years, as his ability and his popularity grew, so did the efforts of the Soviet government to control his actions. He remembered at this time that "a point had been reached where everything I did was interpreted with special significance." When he and a friend missed a train from Vienna back to Moscow after a performance, he was greeted with charges of insubordination, and he was subjected to what he termed "an organized campaign of calumny and almost daily denunciations over a period of three years."

When the Kirov was scheduled to perform in Paris in the spring of 1961, Nureyev never expected to be allowed to go with them. But Sergeyev, the Kirov's leading male dancer, had been asked to step aside in favor of a younger male dancer, to please the Parisian taste for young stars. That's how Nureyev arrived in Paris in 1961 and made the defining decision of his career.

DEFECTION TO THE WEST

The French press and public loved Nureyev, and the Kirov's performances in France were a tremendous success. In June, the troupe was scheduled to travel to London for the next leg of their tour. But as they were about to board the plane, Nureyev was told that he was to fly back to Moscow for a special performance at the Kremlin. "This, I knew, was the final coup of a three-year campaign against me," he recalled. "I had seen it coming all too clearly. I knew exactly where I stood and also what this immediate recall to Moscow would entail: no foreign travel ever again and the position of star dancer to which I was entitled in a couple of years would be forever denied me. I would be consigned to complete obscurity. I felt I would rather kill myself." So, with the help of a new friend in Paris, he ran from the Soviet agents who were following him into the arms of two

French policemen. "I want to stay," he said and was granted political asylum. He became the first of a distinguished line of defectors from the Kirov, including Mikhail Barishnikov and Natalia Makarova, who fled to the West in search of artistic freedom.

From his first appearances, Nureyev captured the attention of Western audiences, ballet lovers and novices alike. With his long hair and high cheekbones, he seemed almost as much a symbol of the defiant 1960s as a premier dancer. He attracted millions of new fans to ballet, who were drawn to his rugged, masculine presence, the athleticism, speed, and technical virtuosity of his dancing, and his innate theatricality. He became a superstar.

DANCING WITH FONTEYN

Nureyev's first dancing opportunities in the West came from the Marquis de Cuevas ballet company, and he was also asked to dance with a variety of European and American troupes. But it was a phone call from Dame Margot Fonteyn, the prima ballerina of the Royal Ballet in London, asking him to dance in a benefit for her company, that signaled his way to stardom in the West.

Nureyev and Fonteyn began dancing together in 1962, when he was 24 and she was 42 and considering retirement. Their legendary partnership, which lasted until the mid-1970s, revealed a magnetism and an artistic sympathy despite an age difference of nearly 20 years. "I don't care if Margot is a Dame of the British Empire or older than myself. For me she represents eternal youth; there is an absolute musical quality in her beautiful body and phrasing. Because we are sincere and gifted, an intense abstract love is born between us every time we dance together." They danced in such great classical roles as *Giselle, Swan Lake,* and *Sleeping Beauty.* They also distinguished themselves in two modern ballets that bore the signature of their special partnership: *Marguerite and Armand,* by Sir Frederick Ashton, and *Romeo and Juliet,* by Kenneth MacMillan. The MacMillan piece became known to a wide audience after it was made into a film in 1966. Fonteyn's memories of their alliance were equally heartfelt: "When I dance with him, I see not Nureyev but the character of the ballet."

He was a demanding perfectionist who saw the male role in ballet as something other than a platform for displaying a ballerina's technique. His range was stunning: in addition to the male leads in such nineteenth-century ballets as *Le Bayadere, Le Corsaire, Giselle,* and *Romeo and Juliet,* Nureyev performed the modern pieces of Frederick Ashton, Jerome Robbins, and George Balanchine. In a seemingly endless quest to test his talent, he worked with such modern choreographers as Rudi van Dantzig, Glen Tetley, Paul Taylor, Maurice Bejart, Jose Limon, and a giant of modern dance, Martha Graham. Balanchine saw Nureyev as limited by the classical roles he performed so well: "My ballets are too dry for you," he said. "Go and dance your princes. When you're tired of them come back." Graham saw no such limitations. "He doesn't permit himself to be limited," she said of Nureyev. "He wants to break the mold that the audiences have made for him to move into twentieth-century things . . . . He has an endless capacity for work." With the Graham company, he danced *Night Journey, Appalachian Spring,* and a work she created for him, *The Scarlet Letter.*

Nureyev traveled the world over to dance; he once said that instead of a nationality, his passport said "Dancer." He did become a citizen of Austria in the 1980s, but he truly was a dancer whose range and thirst for new challenges made him an artist of the world. His flamboyant superstar image also added to his international flair and appeal: he loved discos and hobnobbing with jet-setting socialites.

In his later career, Nureyev continued to tour widely and to dance when, in the opinion of most observers, his talent and technique were spent. Arlene Croce of the *New Yorker* noted in 1981 that "For some time, his appearances have belonged to the history of his career rather than to the history of his art." He seemed unable to cope with aging and with the end of his career. In 1989, he returned to the Soviet Union and to the

Kirov for a disappointing series of performances. Well past his prime, he "came at the twilight of his dancing career, in his fifties, already losing his form, and with ailing legs," said Soviet critic Inna Sklarevskaya. "The tragedy for the Leningrad audience was that its encounter with Nureyev came too late. We were removed from him in space, and now we are removed from him in time."

From 1983 to 1989, Nureyev directed the Paris Opera Ballet. He brought a higher standard to the company, but his frequent absences to continue to dance with other troupes and his insistence that he continue to dance roles that were clearly no longer within his range led to his departure.

Nureyev also tried his hand as a movie actor, with limited results. His performance as the lead in *Valentino*, the film biography of Rudolf Valentino, is noted more for its camp than its truthfulness. He later played a violinist in the movie *Exposed*, which was widely panned.

In 1989 and 1990, Nureyev played the role of the King of Siam in a U.S. road tour of the musical *The King and I*, cheered by some audiences and panned by most critics. His lifelong love of music led him to study orchestral directing in 1991, and he began conducting in that same year, making his New York debut directing Sergey Prokofiev's *Romeo and Juliet*.

In October 1992, Nureyev made his last public appearance, at the premiere of a performance of *La Bayadere* at the Paris Opera. He was obviously gravely ill and had to be helped to the stage. He received the Commander of Arts and Letters award from the Minister of Culture of France and a ten-minute ovation from the audience. He never appeared in public again. On January 6, 1993, Rudolf Nureyev died. His physician, saying he was speaking according to Nureyev's wishes, did not reveal the cause of his death. Later it came to light that he had died of AIDS.

MARRIAGE AND FAMILY

Although his name was linked with many stars from the world of dance, Nureyev never married, and he never had children. When he defected from the Soviet Union, the K.G.B. had tried to use his family to force him back, but he had not returned to the country of his birth until his mother became very ill in the 1980s. His sister Rosa, who was his closest relative, was with Nureyev during his final illness.

HOBBIES AND OTHER INTERESTS

Nureyev was a man consumed by dance, and he had little time for other things. He loved music, and at the end of his life was learning to conduct. He had homes in Paris, New York City, St. Bart's in the Caribbean, and also owned an island off the west coast of Italy that had once belonged to Leonid Massine, the famed choreograper of the Ballet Russes.

HONORS AND AWARDS

Dance Magazine Award: 1973
Capezio Dance Award: 1987
Commander of Arts and Letters (France): 1992

FILM CREDITS

An Evening with the Royal Ballet, 1963
Romeo and Juliet, 1966
Swan Lake, 1966

I Am a Dancer, 1972
Don Quixote, 1973
Valentino, 1977

WRITINGS

Nureyev, 1963

FURTHER READING

BOOKS

Barnes, Clive. *Nureyev,* 1982
Bland, Alexander. *The Nureyev Image,* 1976
Encyclopedia Brittanica, 1988
Gruen, John. *People Who Dance,* 1988
Nureyev, Rudolf. *Nureyev,* 1963
Philip, Richard, and Mary Whitney. *Danseur: The Male in Ballet,* 1977
Smakov, Gennady. *The Great Russian Dancers,* 1984
Terry, Walter. *Great Male Dancers of the Ballet,* 1978
Who's Who in America 1992-93

PERIODICALS

Current Biography 1963
Dance, Mar. 1962, p.42; May 1990, p.32; Aug. 1990, p.18
Esquire, Mar. 1991, p.124
New York Times, Oct. 10, 1992, p.A16; Jan. 7, 1993, p.C18
New York Times Biographical Service, Dec. 1981, p.1719; Aug., 1982, p.1053;
    July 1986, p.863
New Yorker, Aug. 4, 1986, p.77
People, Nov. 2, 1992, p.61

Shaquille O'Neal 1972-
American Professional Basketball Player
with the Orlando Magic
NBA Rookie of the Year in 1993

BIRTH

Shaquille Rashaun O'Neal was born March 16, 1972, in Newark,
New Jersey, the son of Army Sergeant Philip Harrison and Lucille
O'Neal. The third of six children, Shaquille has one brother and
four sisters. Harrison, a convert to Islam, chose his son's first two
names from an Arabic phrase meaning "little warrior," and insisted
that the child keep his mother's maiden name (the parents were
not married until after Shaquille's birth) so that the O'Neal side
of the family would not die out.

YOUTH

Shaquille had a strict upbringing as an "army brat," with his parents instilling in him a sense of responsibility and confidence. "I got spanked every day for a solid year," he remembers. "But I was a bad kid. I had it coming. At the time, I didn't see it. I didn't think they loved me. So one day, when all the other kids were out causing trouble, I picked up a basketball. I found a way out for myself."

While moving from army base to army base, Shaquille indeed did not always see things his father's way. He remembers getting into frequent fights and acting as the class clown. Philip Harrison, or "The Sergeant" (as O'Neal's college coach Dale Brown always refers to him), would have none of this. "I told Shaquille the world had too many followers," he often repeats in talking about his son. "What he needed was to be a leader. He'd see guys hanging out on the corner, and he'd know they were followers. I told him I'd whup him rather than have the guys on the corner whup him. I told him there's no half-stepping in this life." Shaquille didn't particularly mind the constant moving across the United States and Europe as a child, considering the difficulty of living at home in crime-ridden Newark. "The best part for me was just getting out of the city," he recalls. "In the city, where I come from, there are a lot of temptations—drugs, gangs."

When Shaquille was 13, the family was stationed at Wildflecken, (West) Germany, where Louisiana State University coach Brown was giving a basketball clinic. The 6'8" Shaquille approached Brown and asked him about a strength program for his legs that would aid him in jumping. Taking one look at O'Neal, the coach asked him his rank and how long he had been in the military. "I said, 'I'm not in the Army, I'm only thirteen.'" Shaquille remembers Brown exclaiming in astonishment, "Thirteen? Where's your dad? Where's your dad?" Dale Brown wrote to the boy throughout the next four years, and when it came time to choose among more than 100 college scholarships, "the Shaq" remained loyal and went to LSU.

Basketball and constant parental pressure finally had an effect on the somewhat undisciplined youth. "I had such a bad temper, I almost got thrown out of school," claims O'Neal, adding that "a few lickings from my dad got me out of that scene. He wore me out with a paddle." That no-nonsense attitude still prevails between father and son. "All you have to do is see Shaquille around his dad—he's 'yes, sir, no sir,' and that's it—to know how he got so tough and disciplined," says former LSU teammate Vernel Singleton.

EDUCATION

O'Neal's family finally settled in San Antonio, Texas, where Shaquille graduated from Cole High School in 1989. Having decided to do things his father's way, Shaq got good grades in his junior and senior years while leading Cole's basketball team to a combined 68-1 record. He enrolled on scholarship at Louisiana State University in Baton Rouge, but left a year early to turn professional. He has assured his father, however, that he will return to college to complete his degree in business.

CHOOSING A CAREER

Shaquille O'Neal has not always wanted his current career—as a youth, he aspired to be a dancer. Picking up a basketball because that's "what big kids did," he soon found his career choice made for him. The superlatives started rolling in, and the Shaq was projected as an NBA (National Basketball Association) star before he even left high school. Throughout his three years in college, the question was not *whether* he would be the league's number-one draft pick, but *when*. His combination of natural talent and a strong work ethic assured him of fame and fortune, and Shaquille stuck to his best game.

CAREER HIGHLIGHTS

THE COLLEGE SEASONS

In his freshman year at LSU, Shaq began to tote up big-time numbers, averaging 13.9 points and 12 rebounds per game. He also blocked 115 shots, setting a Southeastern Conference record. The year was nevertheless disappointing for the LSU Tigers, who had been predicted to win the SEC title. O'Neal, now 7'1", joined All-American guard Chris Jackson and another seven-footer, center Stanley Roberts, but "it was obvious," said *Sports Illustrated*'s Curry Kirkpatrick in a 1991 article, "that sharing the ball with [these two] . . . restricted O'Neal's development as a freshman." The Shaq commented after the season, "We were all messed up. I think we had too much talent." When Jackson and Roberts turned pro, opposing coaches began to dread facing a more mature Shaq who would have unquestioned leadership of the LSU team. After spending a summer hard at work, O'Neal made their nightmares come true.

"There's no comparison to him as a freshman," said Vanderbilt coach Eddie Folger after his team was trounced the next season by the Tigers. Georgia Coach Hugh Durham was even more impressed. *Sports Illustrated* quoted him at the time: "Last year you could play behind him and know he wasn't going to get the ball from those other guys. Now you have to front him or side him, and he muscles you out of the lane anyway. They just keep going to the mountain, going to the mountain. Shack [an alternate spelling of his nickname] may be unguardable." O'Neal was such a dominant player as a sophomore that NBA teams simply stopped scouting him, not wanting to waste time or money looking at a player that everyone knew would become one of the game's key centers.

O'Neal's sophomore year, during which he led the NCAA (National Collegiate Athletic Association) in blocked shots and rebounds while scoring nearly 30 points a game, led Bill Walton, former basketball great turned commentator, to write off comparisons. "He has the physical talent and personal discipline to be the best, the very best. . . . Believe me, he's not the next anyone. He's the first Shaquille." "I've seen the all-time great centers like Bill Walton, Kareem Abdul-Jabbar and all the rest, but they couldn't do the things as sophomores that Shaquille can do," commented Florida coach Len Kruger that season. "I don't know if there's ever been anyone like that kid." Still another coach, Jim Lynam of the Philadelphia 76ers, put it bluntly: "No question, he's a franchise."

Late that year, O'Neal, who had previously insisted that he would stay in college his full four years, began hinting that he might turn pro early. The money was not an issue—but college officiating was. Philip Harrison began worrying that the physical play his son was being subjected to might cause a serious injury. Coach Brown even compiled a tape of flagrant fouls against O'Neal that went uncalled. College rules made it far easier to triple- and even quadruple-team big men, and many felt that excessive roughness

was being used against Shaquille. "Unless we want to continue losing good big men early to the pros," Brown fumed, "we need to learn how to officiate big men in college basketball. It's ridiculous. I don't know if there's ever been a center in college so strong and agile. We shouldn't penalize him for that."

O'Neal decided to stay at LSU for one more year, largely because of his father's insistence. The Tigers got off to a slow start, having trouble finding a team strategy with as many as four players guarding O'Neal. Though they surged late in the season, a second-round loss to Indiana in the NCAA tournament ended Shaq's college career. O'Neal still led the nation in rebounds, blocking more than four shots per game and collecting nearly twenty-five points each night. He averaged 21.4 points and 13.6 rebounds for his LSU career.

Despite the fact that Shaquille wanted to finish college and have one more shot at a national championship, two factors pushed him to declare himself eligible for the 1992 NBA draft. First and foremost was the physical pounding that he still felt officials were letting other teams get away with as his expense. Also, O'Neal was anxious to move on to the next challenge. "I haven't had the chance to show all of my talents," he said at the time. "The NBA is more my game—banging and pushing, but man against man. I always said that when it wasn't fun anymore, it would be time to move on. And what I went through this year took a lot of fun out of the game."

THE ORLANDO MAGIC

As expected, O'Neal was chosen by the Orlando Magic as the first pick in the draft. Signing him to a contract was another matter, due to the NBA's complex salary cap—a system that attempts to create rough parity among payrolls and to control salary inflation. Shaquille and agent Leonard Armato showed every sign of driving a hard bargain, forcing the Magic to carve a niche for their franchise player by cutting money from elsewhere. In fifteen days, Orlando convinced five players to accept salary cuts, traded one who was unwilling to do so, and renounced the rights to another player. This maneuvering enabled them to sign O'Neal to a seven-year, $39.9 million contract. Along with income from endorsements, the Shaq is estimated to be a $70-million man.

His rookie season provided considerable evidence that he's worth it. Shaq was playing with the best centers in the game—New York's Patrick Ewing, San Antonio's David Robinson, and Houston's Hakeem Olajuwon—and at least holding his own. At 7'1" and 303 pounds, O'Neal is probably the most dominant physical presence in the game. "You know what he looks like?" quipped Olajuwon. "A bigger me." Teammate Greg Kite marveled at the 20-year-old superstar: "In all my years, I've never seen a package of talent like this. Patrick has a lot of strength and David Robinson is really quick, but nobody combines the strength and quickness that Shaquille has."

The season had its rough spots. O'Neal complained early and often that veteran centers were drawing more foul calls than he. Most coaches and observers scoffed at this claim, noting that Shaq actually was getting more calls than any rookie should expect. O'Neal let his frustration boil over against the rough-and-tumble Detroit Pistons in March. Annoyed at Detroit's strategy of fouling him every time he touched the ball during the final stretch of the game (O'Neal does not excel at the free throw line), he punched Pistons guard Alvin Robertson and was ejected, fined, and suspended for one game.

However, an occasional fit of temper and complaints about officials cannot mar a superb season. Collecting a game average of 24 points and 14 rebounds made Shaq's season the third-best ever for a rookie center, behind only Wilt Chamberlain and Kareem Abdul-Jabbar. Those two, observers note, had fewer talented big men with whom to compete. The fans recognized O'Neal's brilliance by voting him to start at center for the Eastern Conference All-Stars. He played well, garnering 14 points and seven rebounds in 25 minutes of play. The public has taken to Shaq off the court as well—he is seen in endorsements for countless products, and fans love him. His appeal, observers say, stems from the combination of his dominating on-court physical presence and his gentle, polite, off-court personality.

The end of the 1992-93 season was a roller coaster ride for the Magic. They improved their record to finish at 41-41, only to miss the playoffs in a tie breaker with the Indiana Pacers. At the time, no one in Orlando realized what good news this was. The NBA uses a weighted lottery system to determine the draft order, giving the poorest teams a better chance at getting the top pick. The Magic had only a one-in-66 shot at that honor. It came though, and Orlando selected first for the second year in a row. They took Chris Webber, an outstanding forward from the University of Michigan. Had they kept him, instead of using their pick for a prearranged trade with the Golden State Warriors, the Orlando front court would have been virtually unstoppable, and the Magic could have been bona fide contenders. They chose a different course of action, however, gambling that the three players received in the trade will be the support they—and the Shaq—need for another try at the championship.

MAJOR INFLUENCES

Shaquille O'Neal's character and work ethic come directly from his mother and father, with whom he stays in constant contact. He also remains close to LSU coach Brown.

MEMORABLE EXPERIENCES

Another Shaquille has already been born, although he is not related to the original. After seeing O'Neal play as a college freshman, Ernest and Rebecca Long, a Louisiana couple living in a small town near Baton Rouge, were so impressed that they named their first child Shaquille O'Neal Long. Deeply moved at the gesture, the Shaq arrived at their house unannounced to have his picture taken with the baby. He took his parents to visit, too, and keeps going back. The child's father told the *Orlando Sentinel* that "when Little Shaq hears the name on television, he just loves it."

HOBBIES AND OTHER INTERESTS

Shaquille is known as the team comedian and enjoys coming up with names for himself—"the Shaqnificent," "the Love Shack," and "Shaquille the Real Deal." He likes to play with his dog, Shazzam, listen to rap music, and spend time with his close friend and teammate Mike Hanson, with whom he shares an army-brat background. His favorite meal, for which he shuns the training table on game days, is a gargantuan combination of Blimpie sandwiches and Hawaiian Punch.

HONORS AND AWARDS

NCAA First-Team All-American: 1990
Southeastern Conference Player of the Year: 1990-91
Louisiana Amateur Athlete of the Year: 1992
NBA All-Star Team: 1993
NBA Rookie of the Year: 1993

FURTHER READING

PERIODICALS

Dallas Morning News, Mar. 17, 1993, p. B1
Florida Today, Feb. 21, 1993, p.A4
Forbes, July 20, 1992, p.18
New Orleans Time Picayune, Mar. 18, 1992, p. D1
Orlando Sentinel, June 7, 1992, p.A1; Mar. 31, 1993, p. B1
People, Dec. 16, 1991, p.142
Sport, Jan. 1993, p.52
Sports Illustrated, Jan. 21, 1991, p.38; Nov. 25, 1991, p.86; Feb. 10, 1992, p.28;
    May 18, 1992, p.42; Nov. 30, 1992, p.42
TV Guide, Apr. 24, 1993, p.16
USA Today, Feb. 22, 1993, p.B1
Washington Post, Feb. 26, 1993, p.F1

ADDRESS

Orlando Magic
1 Magic Place
Orlando Arena
Orlando, FL 32801

Janet Reno 1938-
American Lawyer and Veteran Prosecutor
First Female U.S. Attorney General

BIRTH

Janet Reno, the first woman to become attorney general of the United States, was born July 21, 1938, in Miami, Florida, to Henry and Jane (Wood) Reno. Her parents were both journalists, the Danish-immigrant father a police reporter for the *Miami Herald*, and the mother a writer for the now defunct *Miami News*. In a recent cover story on the nation's new top lawyer, *Time* reveals that Henry Reno, "tired of having his Danish surname, Rasmussen, mispronounced, picked his last name off a map of Nevada."

The Reno family, which included Janet's younger siblings—Robert, Maggy, and Mark—moved to the countryside beyond Miami when the children were young. There, with a pioneer spirit belying her own background, Jane Reno almost single-handedly built a house on the fringes of the Everglades.

YOUTH

Janet Reno's upbringing was unconventional, even by the most casual standards. She and Maggy and their brothers were reared in a world that "was closer in spirit to Dr. Seuss than it was to Dr. Spock," writes Meg Laughlin in *Lear's* magazine. They grew up in the midst of a strange menagerie of animals, reptiles, and exotic birds—a pride of peacocks among them—and visited the Miccosukee and Seminole Indians in their native environment. The Reno children were exposed to an adventurous lifestyle of canoeing, camping, and exploring that toughened them in body, while storytelling, music, and poetry fed them in spirit.

Young Janet, whose personality seemed more like that of her gentle (but often absent) father, learned to adjust to the eccentricities of her notoriously rough-and-tumble mother. She learned compassion and a sense of order from one, while absorbing the spark of nonconformity, the grit, and the certified genius of the other. It was a childhood with distinct advantages and disadvantages, and one that often made her feel different from her classmates. Yet, the richness of her upbringing gave Janet an awareness of her own worth and a respect for others that, friends say, have remained with her throughout adulthood.

Tall and athletic, Janet played sports at school, although she concentrated more on academics and leadership activities as she progressed through the grades. By all accounts, she was an excellent student. She laughingly acknowledges now that her fifth-grade teacher told her that she was bossy, and adds that her family still thinks she can be "opinionated and sometimes arrogant, and they would be happy to supply you with other words." There is no question, though, that young Janet was a born organizer, and her peers looked to her for a fair decision in any controversy.

EARLY MEMORIES

Reared in a frontier setting with basic comforts but few niceties, Janet especially enjoyed visits to her maternal grandmother's gracious Florida home. Writer Laughlin describes Daisy Wood as "a proper Southern lady who . . . lived among antiques and silver . . . wore pearls and gloves, and kept her lips buttoned. She never embarrassed anyone." Janet longed for the refinement she found there. Wistfully remembering her feelings as a young girl, Reno admits, "I loved it at her house. It was so different from home."

EDUCATION

After graduating from Coral Gables High School, Janet attended Cornell

University in Ithaca, New York, where she was active in student politics and earned spending money by waiting on tables in a student dining hall. She earned a B.A. in chemistry in 1960. By then, however, she had decided on a different career. She planned to be a lawyer like her maternal grandfather, George Washington Wood, Jr., in spite of her mother's initial objections. Mrs. Reno, says the *Miami Herald,* "had a taste for beer and a distaste for lawyers. She wanted Janet to be a foreign correspondent." But if her mother was scrappy and stubborn, so was Janet, who applied to and was accepted by Harvard Law School. In the end, her mother was supportive, as her father had been from the beginning. Janet received her LL.B. in 1963, one of only 16 women in a class of more than 500 men.

Reno was not interested in big-city practice, even with her prestigious Harvard degree, but wanted to return home to Miami. Representative Patricia Schroeder, the Democratic legislator from Colorado, remembers her fellow law student as "one of the few in the class who really had this idealism about public service," reports the *Los Angeles Times.* "I remember her talking about being from Miami and how she was going back . . .".

FIRST JOBS

Reno applied for a summer clerkship after law school but, in one instance, faced discrimination. "One law firm wouldn't give me a job because I was a woman," she relates, adding, "I [just] went out and got a job at another firm." That was at Brigham and Brigham, where she stayed until 1967. Ironically, fourteen years after her rejection because of gender, Reno was made a partner in the firm that had turned her away. "I know what it is like to finally have opportunity," she says.

MAJOR INFLUENCES

Jane Wood Reno was unquestionably the major force in her daughter's life. "We never really talked about role models or feminism," Janet says, but "she told me, 'You can do anything, be anything, regardless of whether you're a woman.'"

CAREER HIGHLIGHTS

From 1967 to 1971, Reno was in practice as a partner in Miami's Lewis & Reno, leaving there to become staff director for the judiciary committee of the Florida House of Representatives in Tallahassee. She ran unsuccessfully in 1972 for a seat in the state legislature. Undaunted by the loss, she involved herself in committee work for the revision of Florida's criminal code. The following year, veteran Dade County State Attorney Richard Gerstein offered her a job as his assistant. Reno insisted on telling him, reports the *St. Petersburg Times*, that her father was convinced that he (Gerstein) was a crook, and that she, also, had been a critic. "That's just why I want to hire you," he replied. It was an appropriate choice. During her three years as assistant state attorney, Reno reorganized the over-burdened juvenile system and, because of her proven management skills, became Gerstein's chief administrator. She returned to private law practice in 1976, joining Miami's distinguished Steel, Hector and Davis, the same firm that had failed to hire her out of law school.

STEWARDSHIP IN DADE COUNTY

With a well-documented reputation for professional competence and unquestioned integrity, Reno again entered the public arena. She was appointed state attorney for Dade County (which includes Miami) to serve out the term of the retiring Gerstein. A lifelong, liberal Democrat, she went on to win five elections in a politically conservative county. She served nearly fifteen years as prosecutor in a community rife with drugs, crime, and racial tensions—some say the toughest jurisdiction in the country—but the blunt-speaking, social-activist Reno faced up to the task. She endorsed innovative drug courts that emphasized treatment over jail time for low-level abusers; went after deadbeat spouses with such zeal that annual child-support collections more than doubled in Dade County; set in motion programs for better foster care and school dropout prevention; and formed a domestic violence unit that put spouse abuse on a par with other crimes. An especially creative accomplishment was in helping to establish a neighborhood resource team to work hand-in-hand with police patrols in poor neighborhoods, interviewing residents and aiding them in finding day care, jobs, and medical attention.

Reno's popularity grew, but she was not without her failures. One of her greatest setbacks happened two years into her tenure, when her office failed to win convictions against four white police officers charged in the beating death of a black man who had been stopped for a traffic violation. The acquittal stunned black Miami, and parts of the city went up in flames in the ensuing riots. The perception of racism had been fed. Reno became the target of fierce criticism and more than a few personal threats. She learned some important lessons from that experience, and eventually mended fences with the black community. Reno also taught herself Spanish through tapes and books so that she could relate more meaningfully to the city's mushrooming Latino population. She became so accessible to the public that she even kept her home number listed in the telephone book.

Other high-profile defeats marked Reno's years as state attorney—some of them relating to cases that the police felt had been handled poorly or not at all. On the whole, however, respect for the high-minded prosecutor as a person never wavered. The backbreaking caseload involving illegal immigration, drug trafficking, and corruption that passed across her desk would have buried a lesser attorney, say former associates, but praise for Reno's dedication to law and justice always outweighed reproach.

FIRST WOMAN ATTORNEY GENERAL

Janet Reno's selection as attorney general was the result of skill, hard work, and good fortune. When President Clinton's first two choices for attorney general were forced to withdraw because they had once employed illegal aliens as nannies and failed to pay Social Security taxes for them, it was only by benign timing that Janet Reno, his third choice, was available. Had she been approached in the early weeks after Clinton's election, she could not have heeded the call. Her mother was gravely ill, and friends say that Janet would never have left her side. "My mother was my best friend," Reno said again lately, as she has so often before, "and the most loving person I have ever known." As it was, after Jane Wood Reno died, and Zoë Baird and Kimba Wood were out of the running, Janet was then free to accept the president's nomination.

Bipartisan respect for her honesty and courage, "traits considered rare in Washington," says *USA Today*, made Reno's confirmation little more than a formality. She was sworn in March 12, 1993—the successor to 77 male attorneys general who had served before her. Her young niece and namesake stood beside her, holding the Bible. As attorney general, Reno is a member of the president's Cabinet and is the nation's top law-enforcement officer. The attorney general is the head of the U.S. Department of Justice, a part of the executive branch of government that is charged with enforcing federal law and providing legal advice to the president and other top government officials. The department includes such agencies as the FBI (Federal Bureau of Investigation), DEA (Drug Enforcement Administration), and INS (Immigration and Naturalization Service.)

Reno is winning acclaim for her bold approach to thorny issues, and she is only part way through her first year in office. Her agenda is what it has always been, except that now it is sketched on a broader canvas. "I serve as the people's lawyer, and adviser to the president," she explains, and, in those capacities, Reno vows that she will properly execute the law. In the few months she has been at the Department of Justice, she has already met several "moments of truth," says *Time*. Her most courageous stands have been in taking the heat for the disastrous assault on David Koresh and the Branch Davidians at their compound in Waco, Texas; in publicly protesting the handling of dismissals at the White House travel office (a subsequent investigation supported Reno's position); and in her slow and studied decision to take Islamic cleric Sheik Omar Abdel Rahman into custody for alleged terrorism. *Time* says that "Janet Reno does not rush to judgment," nor will she "be pushed by political considerations."

The new attorney general has law enforcement reformation on her mind, as well as the rebuilding of cooperation among government agencies. And always, she speaks of the needs of the young. "We've got to figure out how to . . . reweave the fabric of society around our children. . . . America has forgotten them," she states with a mixture of sadness and resolve, "and they are our future."

MARRIAGE AND FAMILY

One of Janet Reno's few large regrets is that she has never married and had children. With neither husband nor children of her own, Reno has become the focal point in a large, extended family of brothers, sister, seven nieces and nephews, and a raft of close friends. The siblings who shared her colorful childhood have carved out interesting careers of their own. Robert is a business columnist for *Newsday*, Maggy (now Maggy Hurchalla) is an elected commissioner in Martin County, Florida, and Mark is a merchant marine captain.

Janet Reno has an apartment in Washington, close enough to her office so that she often walks to work. However, her real home is the one where she grew up. Henry Reno died in 1966, and in the waning years of her mother's life, Reno assumed responsibility for the family home, which they shared until the older woman's death in December 1992. Much of the original property surrounding the house was sold by Janet's parents to finance their children's education, but the modest wood and stone house remains a refuge. Richard Gregory, one of Reno's former assistant state attorneys in Dade County, is quoted in the *Chicago Tribune*: "That house is symbolic of who Janet Reno is. . . . Unpretentious . . . Private . . . Simple. And she lives her life the way she feels comfortable."

HOBBIES AND OTHER INTERESTS

Janet Reno is a confirmed workaholic. When asked recently about her personal reading habits, she quipped, "Who has time to read?" She is known, however, to favor poetry, and is especially partial to the works of Rudyard Kipling. She keeps anthologies close at hand.

At home in Florida, Reno fills her free hours with canoeing, hiking, sailing, and other outdoor activities. She often surrounds herself with family and friends, enjoying conversation, music, and the simple food she prepares for frequent gatherings on the big porch.

HONORS AND AWARDS

Herbert Harley Award (American Judicature Society): 1981
Public Administrator of the Year (American Society for Public Administration, South Florida Chapter): 1983
Medal of Honor Award (Florida Bar Association): 1990

FURTHER READING

BOOKS

Who's Who in America, 1992-93

PERIODICALS

Chicago Tribune, May 17, 1993, Tempo Section, p.3
Lear's, July 1993, p. 48
Miami Herald, Dec. 22, 1992, p.B12; Apr. 20, 1993, p.A1
New York Times, Feb. 12, 1993, p. A1; Feb. 15, 1993, p.A12; Mar. 10, 1993,
   pp.A1, A10
Newsday, Feb. 12, 1993, p.3; Apr. 29, 1993, p.106
Newsweek, Feb. 22, 1993, p.26
Parade, May 2, 1992, p.4
People, Mar. 29, 1993, p.40
Time, May 10, 1993, p.46; July 12, 1993, p.20
U.S. News & World Report, Feb. 22, 1993, pp.14, 28; June 7, 1993, p.33
Wall Street Journal, Feb. 12, 1993, p.A3; Mar. 1, 1993, p.A16

ADDRESS

Office of the Attorney General
U.S. Department of Justice
Constitution Avenue & 10th Street, N.W.
Washington, DC 20530

Jerry Rice   1962-
American Professional Football Player with
the San Francisco 49ers
NFL All-Time Leader in Touchdown Receptions

BIRTH

Jerry Rice was born in the rural eastern Mississippi town of
Crawford on October 13, 1962. His father, Joe, a brickmason, and
his mother, Eddie, had seven other children, five boys and two
girls. Jerry was their sixth child.

YOUTH

Crawford, an all-black town of about 500 people near the small
city of Starkville, offered an idyllic place to grow up. Ralph Wiley
wrote in *Sports Illustrated* that Rice's childhood was "simon-pure.

No streetlights, or sidewalks, or traffic signs, or stadium concerts. No drugs, or crime, or sirens. No distractions." The family lived in a house that Joe Rice had built himself on the edge of a pasture, with few of the luxuries to which Jerry has now become accustomed.

The Rice children entertained themselves by playing games and sports, a favorite being chasing horses in the pasture until the animals tired enough to be caught and ridden bareback. Rice also helped his father by carrying bricks and mortar. While he describes his childhood as happy, he *does* remember that "when you live in Crawford, all you want to do is get out." He always believed that his now-famous hands would be his ticket to the "greener grass" on the other side. At first, though, he thought that more pedestrian manual skills would determine his career. He would "fix anything that was broken, toys, appliances. I wanted to open my own shop someday."

Rice credits his parents with the work habits that have lifted him a step above others in the National Football League (NFL). "I take a lot of pride in everything and try to be the best in what I'm doing," he says. "Every time I step on the football field, it's not like a job to me; I really enjoy it. Working with my father taught me the necessity of hard work. On my mother's side, I'm a caring person. I guess that's why I've been successful."

EARLY MEMORIES

Rice remembers practicing his phenomenal speed in chasing horses. "They didn't just come to you," he explains. Also, without a ride to football practice, he had to find a way to quickly travel the five miles to school in the early morning and back home again. He ran. "That's what made me," he claims, "running those back dirt roads and country fields."

EDUCATION

Rice graduated in 1980 from B.L. Moor High School in Crawford. He began playing football there after a rare instance of misbehavior. During his sophomore year, the assistant principal caught him cutting class. When Rice heard his name called, he took off running. Noting his speed, school authorities decided to give Jerry a choice: punishment or sports. Sports it was. While Eddie Rice didn't object to her son's participation as a forward on the basketball team or as a high-jumper on the track team, she had difficulty accepting the more violent sport of football. "I didn't love it," she remembers, "but the more I fought it, the more determined he was, so I gave it up. You just never know what God has in the storehouse for you."

Playing many positions, including quarterback and tackle, Rice showed great promise as a football player. Only one college coach showed up to recruit him, though—Archie Cooley, from all-black Mississippi Valley State

University in Itta Bena. Cooley was impressed, and decided to play Rice at wide receiver where his hands and speed could be put to their best use. Jerry attended MVSU for four years, but did not graduate.

FIRST JOBS

Rice's summer jobs with his father provided unintentional conditioning that would later prove invaluable. Pushing a brick-filled wheelbarrow in Mississippi's stifling heat was an upper-body strength builder that could hardly be matched in a gym, and it increased Jerry's stamina as well. Most important, though, was the work with his hands. "I would be standing on this tall scaffold," he recalls, "and they would toss the bricks up to me. I was catching bricks all day. One of my brothers would stack about four bricks on top of each other and toss them up. They might go this way and that, but I would catch all four. I did it so many times, it was just a reaction." This was good enough to impress his father. "Jerry handled bricks better than any workers I ever had," Joe Rice told the *Sporting News*.

CHOOSING A CAREER

"Until my junior year at Mississippi Valley, I thought I was going to be an auto mechanic or TV repairman," Rice relates. "A pro football career was just a fantasy." However, the records piled up to such an extent that the pro scouts had to notice, even at a tiny school in Division I-AA. Over

four years, Rice caught 214 passes for 3,295 yards and 50 touchdowns, 28 in his senior year alone. He achieved this despite being double-teamed throughout his college career. Such phenomenal success was possible because Coach Cooley, seeing Jerry's talent, installed a new offense—the "stack," a no-huddle forerunner of the run-and-shoot so popular today in pro football. "Some teams go for three yards and a cloud of dust," Cooley told *Sporting News* in 1985. "We think three plays and a touchdown."

Jerry Rice caught the attention of Bill Walsh, the innovative coach who had recently guided his San Francisco 49ers to two

Super Bowl championships. "As soon as I saw him run and catch," Walsh told *Sport*, "I knew that if we didn't get him, someday we'd be playing against him." After Rice was the MVP of the 1984 Blue-Gray all-star game, the Niners were forced to trade three draft picks to move up far enough to choose Rice. They snagged him in the first round with the sixteenth overall pick, just beating out the Dallas Cowboys, who were waiting to choose him with the seventeenth. That choice is certainly more popular now than it was in 1985, when many Bay Area fans felt that Rice would not be able to perform well against a top-quality NFL defense.

CAREER HIGHLIGHTS

Rice's rookie year did not at first look to be the opening chapter of a storybook career. Driving to training camp in a new BMW with a license plate reading WORLD (because in college he caught "everything in the world"), he began to struggle with the 49ers' triple-scripted offense. "At Mississippi Valley," he says, "I had the option of running any route I wanted, and I became accustomed to that freedom. I had to adjust." Rice dropped 15 passes that year, largely because of concentration problems. "He'd be the first to admit that every time he touched the ball that first year, he wanted to go all the way," quarterback Joe Montana remembers. Montana was not discouraged, though, and told *Sport*, "There's a difference between a guy who's catching the ball and then dropping it, and a guy who can't catch."

Rice showed the world which category he belonged to on December 9, 1985, in a game against the Los Angeles Rams. He grabbed a 66-yard touchdown pass and totaled 10 receptions for 241 yards. Freddie Solomon, the veteran player Rice was drafted to replace, had seen enough to retire after the season. Jerry had rebounded from a poor start to earn 927 receiving yards in 49 catches, a team record for a rookie. He was named Rookie of the Year by UPI (United Press International) and the NFL Players Association.

Even this stunning late-season success, however, did not prepare fans for the explosiveness that Rice would demonstrate in 1986. His 1,570 receiving yards and 15 touchdowns led the league and broke team records, and his 86 catchs led the NFL. His yardage total was the third highest in league history. Rice's efforts got him to the Pro Bowl and earned him recognition by *Sports Illustrated* as NFL Player of the Year.

SPECTACULAR SEASONS

The strike-shortened 1987 season represented an even greater leap for the third-year star. In only 12 games, Rice set an NFL record for touchdown receptions with an astonishing 22. His 138 points made him the first wideout to capture the scoring crown since 1951, and represented the highest point total ever achieved at the position. He gained 1,078 yards for the year, traveled again to the Pro Bowl, and was named the league's Most Valuable Player. An unusual poor game against the Minnesota Vikings in the playoffs eliminated the 49ers from the Super Bowl chase. Rice had become the league's most feared opponent, but had not yet led his team to the big prize. He vowed to change that.

Change it he did, in a most spectacular way. After gaining 1,306 yards during the 1988 regular season to again lead the team, Rice for the first time turned it up in the playoffs. Bringing down the ball for five total touchdowns against the Vikings and the Chicago Bears was only a taste of the heroics to come. In one of the most exciting Super Bowls ever, Rice caught 11 Joe Montana passes for 215 yards and a touchdown. His three receptions during the last-minute 49er drive set up the touchdown that beat the Cincinnati Bengals with only 34 seconds left in the game. Rice's Super Bowl-record yardage earned him the game's MVP award, and the Niners had their third championship of the decade.

Rather than basking in the glow of his MVP award and the Super Bowl victory, Rice became embroiled in controversy. Upset that Montana and the retiring Walsh were getting the most media coverage, Jerry complained to reporters. He implied that racism was involved, a charge that upset many fans and was hotly denied by local editors. "Being MVP doesn't necessarily mean you are the news lead of the paper," commented San Francisco *Examiner* executive editor Larry Kramer, who pointed out that Montana had engineered his third Super Bowl victory. Rice later turned down the heat, saying, "It was just the respect of being the MVP I wanted. Really." It is respect that none could begrudge him, and that he has continued to earn.

The 49ers clinched the Team of the Decade title in 1989, due in no small part to Rice's abilities. Leading the league with 1,483 yards and 17 touchdowns, Rice once again brought the Niners to the Super Bowl. There he set a record with three touchdown catches as his team routed the Denver Broncos 55-10 for new coach George Seifert. The Niners became only the second team, after the Pittsburgh Steelers, to win four Super Bowls. Jerry again went to the Pro Bowl, and was elected by his peers to the All-Star team of the 1980s.

Rice caught 100 passes in 1990, including a record-tying five touchdown catches in a single game against Atlanta. Leading the league again with 1,502 yards, he was named Player of the Year by *Sports Illustrated*. Talk was beginning to center around career totals, and many suggested that Rice was the best player to ever play his position, while still in only the sixth season of his career. Rice played down the hype. "There's still a lot that has to be proven," he said. "To be the ultimate receiver one day, I

have to hold all the records for receptions, for yardage, for touchdowns
. . . . Right now, Steve Largent [formerly of the Seattle Seahawks] is
the best."

HEADING FOR ALL-TIME RECORDS

Despite his modesty, Rice has spent the last two years taking important
steps toward the top. With 80 catches in 1991 and 84 in 1992, he totals
610 for his career, putting him on pace to break Largent's record of 819
sometime in 1995. His 24 touchdowns over the last two seasons already
have placed him in the all-time lead in that category, with 103 in just eight
seasons. In total yardage, he now has 10,273, just about 3,000 (less than
three average Rice-years) off Largent's all-time total. Nothing short of a
severe injury is likely to stop Jerry Rice from sitting atop all three major
receiving categories. "Best ever" no longer seems too great a compliment.

Having signed a three-year deal with the 49ers, Rice hopes to break the
records in San Francisco. Former teammate Dwight Clark remembers years
of awe in watching Rice. "The first time I saw him, he was the best I *ever*
saw, and I learned how to turn on the television set at an early age. Jerry's
like a Mike Tyson, a Michael Jordan, a Joe Montana. He's a step above
the field." Clark adds that with his tactical speed, leaping ability, and great
hands, he is a joy to watch. "If football is theater, Jerry Rice is a leading
actor. His world is one of grace and fear. Each performance may be his
last. The next performance may be his best."

MEMORABLE EXPERIENCES

In 1989, just prior to the Super Bowl, Rice suffered with a recurrence of
a sore ankle that had plagued him throughout the season. A year earlier
he had said, "I don't think about how many touchdowns I scored. I don't
think about the yardage . . . . I just want to go to the Super Bowl." Now,
in his first opportunity, he was listed as questionable. But he didn't play
as if he were hurt. He caught 11 passes, including a sensational 27-yarder
on the final, winning drive. "What Rice did this windy evening," wrote
Thomas Boswell in the *Washington Post*, "warps the imagination and
redefines what is possible." Rice himself was so moved by finally reaching
the top that he needed time alone before joining his teammates and the
press. Standing by a row of lockers, he had to bend over to hold back
his tears.

MARRIAGE AND FAMILY

Jerry Rice and his wife, Jackie, live in Redwood Shores, California,
with their three-year-old daughter, Jacqui, and two family pets—Max, a
Rottweiler, and Casio, a poodle. They also spend considerable time in
Crawford, where Rice has built a new home for his parents.

HOBBIES AND OTHER INTERESTS

Rice enjoys soul music, dancing, luxurious sports cars, and designer clothes. "He's got some clothes," jokes his father [that] "I don't even know what they are."

HONORS AND AWARDS

Blue-Gray Classic Most Valuable Player: 1984
NFL Rookie of the Year: 1985
Pro-Bowl: 1987-93
NFL Most Valuable Player: 1987
Sports Illustrated Player of the Year: 1987, 1990
Sporting News Player of the Year: 1987, 1990
Super Bowl XXIII, Most Valuable Player: 1989
Pete Rozelle MVP Trophy (*Sport*): 1989
Associated Press All-Pro First Team: 1992
Football News All-Pro Team: 1992

FURTHER READING

BOOKS

Encyclopedia Brittanica Book of the Year, 1988

PERIODICALS

Boston Globe, Jan. 20, 1989, p.A5
Boys' Life, Nov. 1989, p.34
Current Biography Yearbook 1990
New York Times, Dec. 3, 1990, p.C1
San Jose Mercury News, Oct. 28, 1990, p.A1
Sport, Nov. 1989, p.19; Jan. 1992, p.31
Sporting News, Sep. 25, 1989, p.8; Dec. 24, 1990, p.5
Sports Illustrated, Jan. 30, 1989, p.30

ADDRESS

San Francisco 49ers
4949 Centennial Boulevard
Santa Clara, CA 95054

Mary Robinson 1944-
Irish President
Lawyer, Activist, and Politician

BIRTH

Mary Terese Winifred Bourke, the first female head of state in Ireland's history, was born May 21, 1944, in Ballina (Bally-NAH), a small County Mayo market town in the western part of the Republic of Ireland. The third of five children and the only daughter of physicians Aubrey and Tessa (O'Donnell) Bourke, she grew up in prosperous circumstances with older brothers Aubrey (deceased) and Oliver—who, like their parents, became doctors— and younger brothers Henry and Adrian, who would follow their sister into the law. Mary's late mother gave up the practice of medicine to rear a family; her father has continued to be active in his profession for more than fifty years.

YOUTH

Being the only girl in a family of boys was a lesson in self-reliance for young Mary. "It was fight your own battles and fight them hard, or be swallowed," her brother, Henry, told *Vanity Fair* last year, adding that Mary learned to take hard knocks and stand up for herself. She was an independent, headstrong young girl, and stories of her willfullness during the early years have been confided by members of the family. In one instance, when told by her mother to take her little brothers away from the house and out for a walk, she defiantly led them several miles into town just to register her resentment.

The Bourke children led a privileged life. They grew up with what Mary now remembers as a "sense of harmony." The special benefits that prosperity provided were coupled with parental encouragement toward higher education and the professions, regardless of gender. Expectations for Mary were no less than those for her brothers—a rare circumstance in the male-dominated Ireland of the 1950s. Townspeople of Ballina who knew the intense little girl of those days say that her strengths and ambitions were nurtured within the family circle. The family encouragement only fortified a self-confidence that Robinson today admits was unusual. "I didn't have doubts about whether I could do things because I was a girl. I don't ever remember having those thoughts." Educated privately, the Bourke children were usually content with their own company and, even during their university years, shared a home in Dublin where they were looked after by their former nanny.

Many humorous tales have surfaced about the unrestrained partying at their Dublin living quarters, once the home of nineteenth-century poet and dramatist Oscar Wilde. Its very name, Wilde House, became a worrisome implication for the Bourke parents. Friends from student days say, though, that Mary was the one who could strike a balance between fun and responsibility. An intensity of purpose was even then the determining factor of her personality.

EARLY MEMORIES

From her youngest years, Robinson has bristled at overbearing authority. A lingering resentment about a particular injustice in childhood is apparent as she tells about being punished at school. "I wrote an essay at seven or eight years of age," she says, "and used the word 'consequently'. . .The teacher didn't believe I'd written it. I still recall the deep wound I felt at being accused. It was probably the point at which I realized those in authority didn't have a monopoly on wisdom."

CHOOSING A CAREER

Astronomy was one of Robinson's first enthusiasms, and there was a time when her scientific curiosity made medicine a likely ambition. However, as a girl always eager to argue her point of view—and to win concessions—she eventually gravitated toward the law. She and her younger brothers would often sit all day at local trials, absorbing the techniques of the courtroom. When the time came for her to decide on a career, law was a natural choice.

"I think I was always interested in the law," she says now. "My grandfather [Adrian Bourke, a Ballina solicitor] had a passionate commitment to justice. He . . . believed in the integrity of the law." It is often noted that Robinson's belief in the legal system as an instrument of social change and protection of individual rights is rooted as much in Grandfather Bourke's influence and example as in her own idealism.

EDUCATION

This early interest in the law, combined with the family tradition of educating women for the professions, led her parents to give her every possible advantage. She was sent to the exclusive Mount Anville in Dublin, a Catholic boarding school run by the religious order of Mesdames of the Sacred Heart. From there she went on to Mademoiselle Anita's, a finishing school in Paris, to perfect her French. Most children of the Irish upper class are encouraged to become conversant in French, and all Irish students must be educated in their ancestral language—Irish Gaelic, a Celtic tongue—as well as in the official English.

After Paris, Robinson enrolled at prestigious Trinity College (the formal name is University of Dublin) although, as a Roman Catholic, she had been strongly advised by her bishop not to study at what was then considered a predominantly Protestant institution. Such strict admonitions are now rare. Graduating in 1967 from Trinity with honors in French and law, she also earned the degree, first class, of barrister at law that same year from King's Inn, Dublin. In Ireland, as in Great Britain, a distinction is made between *barristers*, who argue cases at court, and *solicitors*, who represent clients in legal matters.

Through a fellowship at Harvard University in Cambridge, Massachusetts, Robinson earned an LL.M. (master's degree in law) in 1968.

CAREER HIGHLIGHTS

Impressed by what she refers to as an "exciting" and "refreshing" taste of activism at Harvard in the tumultuous political atmosphere of the late 1960s, Mary Robinson returned to Ireland with renewed vigor for her chosen profession. She joined the Trinity law faculty in 1969, becoming, at only 25, the college's youngest-ever professor. She was elected to the Irish Senate (Senead Éireann) that same year—again the youngest member and also the first Catholic to fill one of Trinity's three traditional senate seats.

Conservative Ireland would experience a new kind of legislator over the next two decades. Robinson became an outspoken advocate for women's rights, voting privileges for 18-year-olds, the legalization of divorce and birth control, and the right to obtain abortion information. The hotly debated divorce ban still stands, however, in spite of her impassioned efforts during 20 years in the senate, and abortions are still illegal in Ireland. Robinson served on committees dealing with a broad range of social issues, gaining a reputation "that marked her," wrote Kevin Cullen in a 1991 *Boston Globe* article, "as a maverick in polite circles, a bloody eedjit [idiot] in others."

Armed with a natural stubbornness, Robinson repeatedly refused to cave in to ultraconservative and outdated arguments against her proposals. She became the gadfly in Ireland's political scene, provoking and irritating with her bold and passionate speaking. When hate mail poured in during her attempt in the 1970s to legalize contraception, she was shaken but undaunted, and asserts now, "That taught me, if you believe in something, you must be prepared to pay the price." She admits to one regret, nevertheless, about the contraception issue, that her position caused embarrassment for her parents.

Robinson championed liberal issues at home and in the European courts, making a name for herself as a defender of human rights and feminist causes. Among her numerous appointments were to the Advisory Board of the Common Market Law Review, where she served from 1976 to 1990, and the International Commission of Jurists at Geneva, from 1987 to 1990.

Although Robinson was defeated twice in bids for election to the Dáil, the Irish Parliament's powerful lower house, she retained her longtime association with the Labour Party until 1985, when she resigned to protest its endorsement of the Anglo-Irish Agreement. She felt that the treaty unfairly excluded the concerns of the Protestant Unionists of Northern Ireland. Robinson resigned her senate seat in 1989 to focus on legal work and her commitment to the Irish Centre for European Law, which she and others (her husband among them) had founded the previous year.

In spite of her break with Labour five years earlier, Robinson was approached in 1990 to run for the presidency as that party's candidate. Her former political associates recognized in her traits of both quality and strength. She accepted the challenge and, with her husband, embarked on an energetic, cross-country tour, her campaign song, "Mrs Robinson," blaring from loudspeakers atop the campaign bus. The strangely symbolic Simon and Garfunkel song was more appropriate than it would seem, notes Cullen of the *Globe*, explaining that "few would remember the characters in [the movie] *The Graduate* who served as the song's inspiration: a woman who seduces an inexperienced young man. . . . But in a way, Robinson is the mature woman seducing a naive nation, encouraging it to indulge in pluralism, to shed itself of isolationism and clerically imposed mores, and to embrace more fully its European identity."

A NEW KIND OF PRESIDENT

The November day in 1990 that Mary Robinson won the presidency of Ireland was a political and cultural turning point for that historically conservative country. She defeated the ruling Fianna Fáil Party candidate, Brian Lenihan, by garnering a mere 52 percent of the vote. But in the ensuing years, Robinson has captured an approval rating that comes close to being unanimous. She is the seventh, and first woman, president of Ireland (which has been a republic only since 1949), and is the first popularly elected head of state in 17 years. The constitution allows the presidency to be filled by appointment if all political factions agree on a candidate, and the post often has been bestowed as a reward for party loyalty. "I was a directly elected candidate," says Robinson, "and I find it encouraging that the people chose someone with my track record."

The political system in Ireland is markedly different from that in the U.S. In the Irish parliamentary form of government, it is the Prime Minister, not the President, who is the nation's leader. The constitutional restraints on the Irish presidency make it a largely ceremonial position, yet Robinson is using her formidable skills to redefine the role. Once regarded as reserved and standoffish, she has unmasked a personal warmth known previously only to family and friends, and its effect on those with whom she connects is making a significant difference. Without official clout, she is, nevertheless, a highly visible symbol of hope. Robinson speaks out for building a stronger economy that would slow the emigration of Ireland's youth—and she keeps a lighted candle in the kitchen of her private quarters for their return to their homeland.

Mary Robinson openly courts the friendship of Northern Ireland, striving to find a middle ground in which Catholics and Protestants can co-exist in mutual tolerance. After centuries of conflict between the Catholic and Protestant peoples of Ireland, she has become the voice of a changing nation whose people are beginning to recognize, says Foreign Minister Richard Spring in a recent *Detroit News* story, "that the conflict is not so much about religion as about age-old politics and cultural differences, with religion as a distinguishing marker."

MARRIAGE AND FAMILY

Married since 1970 to Nicholas Robinson, a fellow lawyer whom she has known since their undergraduate days at Trinity, Ireland's head of state balances her professional duties with a warm and somewhat guarded family life. She and her husband have three children—Tessa, 21, William, 19, and 12-old Aubrey—and make their home at Áras an Uachtaráin, the presidential mansion in Dublin's Phoenix Park.

Nick Robinson is a strong ally of his energetic wife. An expert on historical preservation, an author, and once a political cartoonist for the *Irish Times*, he has taken a leave of absence from the Centre for European Law at Trinity to aid the president in both her professional and family obligations. He does, however, retain chairmanship of the Irish Architectural Archive. The presidential spouse is quoted in a 1992 *Vogue* feature story as being "quite happy to simply make the analogy to the countless able women who have put their support behind male political leaders. If they can do it, why shouldn't a woman expect the same from her husband?"

While the separation between faiths is no longer inflexible in modern-day Ireland, such was not the case when Mary Bourke married Nicholas Robinson 23 years ago. Her staunchly Catholic parents refused to attend her marriage to a member of the Church of Ireland, which is an Anglican denomination similar to the American Protestant Episcopal Church. Reconciliation between the Bourkes and the Robinsons came soon after the marriage, however, and the families remain on close and affectionate terms.

HOBBIES AND OTHER INTERESTS

Throughout her adult life, Mary Robinson had been characterized as an aloof overachiever—"a bit of a grind," said *The New Republic*—but, behind the scenes, she was known as witty and charming, devoted to family and close friends. Her personal appeal came to light only after she began her campaign for the presidency. With a new hairdo and a glamorous wardrobe visibly softening a rather austere image, Robinson surprised voters with her easy smile and attentive ear toward their concerns. In the brief three-year period since her election, she has become, says Richard Coniff in *Town & Country*, "the most widely admired public figure in Ireland's modern history."

Robinson is well versed in the literature and culture of her native land. Her reading interests are both avid and broad, extending far beyond the legal writings which have been so much a part of her career.

HONORS AND AWARDS

Mayo "Man of the Year" (first female recipient): 1991, County Mayo,

Ireland
Honorary Order of Australia: 1992

FURTHER READING

BOOKS

Finlay, Fergus. *Mary Robinson: A President With a Purpose*, 1991
International Who's Who, 1992-93

PERIODICALS

Boston Globe, Oct. 20, 1991, Sunday Magazine, p.14
Chicago Tribune, Dec. 16, 1990, p.1; Oct. 11, 1991, p.6
Current Biography Yearbook 1991
Maclean's, Nov. 19, 1990, p.30
Ms., May/June 1992, p.16
People, Nov. 26, 1990, p.57
New York Times, Dec. 27, 1990, p. A4; July 2, 1992, p. A4; Jan. 15, 1993, p.A29
Time, June 29, 1992, p.62
Town & Country, Feb. 1993, p.60
Vanity Fair, July 1992, p.120

ADDRESS

Office of the President
Áras an Uachtaráin
Phoenix Park
Dublin 8, Ireland

Winona Ryder 1971-
American Actress
Co-Starred in *The Age of Innocence, Bram Stoker's Dracula, Edward Scissorhands,* and *Heathers*

BIRTH

Winona Ryder (originally Winona Laura Horowitz) was born October 29, 1971, in Winona, Minnesota. Her unusual first name comes from her birthplace, where her mother was visiting relatives at the time. Her mother, Cindy Palmer Horowitz, runs a video production company, while her father, Michael Horowitz, currently runs Flashback Books, which specializes in counterculture books. Winona is one of four children: she has an older sister and brother, Sunyata and Jubal, from her mother's first marriage, as well as a younger brother, Uri.

YOUTH

Ryder had a rather singular, unconventional childhood. Her parents, who had settled in San Francisco, were part of the counterculture community of the late 1960s; they lived in the Haight and hung out with Allen Ginsberg and Timothy Leary. Leary, who is Winona's godfather, describes the couple as "hippie intellectuals and psychedelic scholars." During those years, her father, a rare book specialist, worked as an archivist for Leary, and her mother pursued her interests in Buddhism and macrobiotics. When Winona was about ten, the family moved to a 300-acre communal plot of land in northern California, which they shared with seven other families.

"It wasn't as hippie-do as it sounds," according to Ryder. "A lot of people, when they hear the word *commune*, connect it with, like, everyone's on acid and running around naked. This was more like this weird suburb, if suburbs were really cool. It was just a bunch of houses on this chunk of land; we had horses and gardens. You have so much freedom, you can go roaming anywhere. We didn't have electricity, which was weird, but it was great to grow up that way. We didn't have TV, so you'd have to *do* stuff. My friends' names were Tatonka, Gulliver, and Rio. We'd have hammock contests, sit around and make up stories, make up weird games. I don't know—it was a weird, weird childhood. I mean, it was great."

EDUCATION

Like the rest of her childhood, Ryder's education was a bit unconventional. After about a year on their communal land, the family decided to move to be closer to the father's job in the city and the children's schools. They settled in the suburban community of Petaluma, where the elder Horowitzes still live, and Winona started junior high there. With her short hair and offbeat clothes, she soon felt that she didn't fit in. On her third day at her new school, some kids mistook her for a boy, called her a faggot, and beat her up. She started studying at home, and eventually enrolled at the other junior high in Petaluma. But she also started taking an acting class at the prestigious American Conservatory Theatre (A.C.T.) in San Francisco. She was 13. "We weren't thinking of her being professional," says her mother. "We just wanted her to be happy, to be around more imaginative peers."

Ryder loved her classes at A.C.T. As she later recalled, "they'd give us these weirdo plays like *The Glass Menagerie*, and there were always these twelve-year-old girls playing these *women*. So I asked if I could find my own monologue to perform. I read from J.D. Salinger's *Franny & Zooey*. I made it like she was sitting, talking to her boyfriend. I had a connection with Salinger-speak; the way she talked made sense. It was the first time that I felt that feeling you get when you're acting—that sort of *yeah!* feeling."

That monolgue caught the attention of a talent scout, who recommended Ryder for a part in the movie *Desert Bloom*. She lost out on that part, but the casting agent was so impressed that she sent Ryder's audition tape along to an agency, which immediately signed her. She soon landed her first part, in the movie *Lucas*, which was filmed during her eighth-grade summer vacation. It was for this film that she chose her professional name, Winona Ryder.

Over the next several years, Ryder continued to combine acting with her education, mostly through independent study with a tutor. She graduated from high school with a 4.0 grade point average. When asked if she had thought about taking a break from acting to attend college, Ryder responded, "Yeah, I've thought about it. But my education hasn't stopped. I read all the time, and I'm still learning, I'm not worried that my IQ is going to drop because I'm not going to college. I really love acting and making movies right now . . . And I don't want to knock college, but I went to visit a friend at a college, and I got there and it was like frat hell or sorority hell or whatever it is called. It felt just like [high school] . . . . There were the same sort of obnoxious cliques. It was all the same, just a little bit older."

CAREER HIGHLIGHTS

Over the past six years, Ryder has appeared in over ten films. While these films have achieved varying levels of critical and popular success, Ryder's performances are consistently praised. She has typically chosen offbeat roles in dark comedies, usually playing a teenager in a "coming of age" story. Her first big hit was *Beetlejuice* (1988), directed by Tim Burton. She played Lydia, the strange, death-obsessed daughter who always wears mourning clothes. *Heathers* (1989) features Ryder as Veronica Sawyer, in a part that she considers "*the* role of my life." This black comedy, one of Ryder's favorite movies of all time, has become a cult hit as well. Veronica, "whose teen angst bull has a body count," according to the actress, keeps murdering her popular and arrogant friends, then making it look like suicide. Although Ryder was acclaimed for this performance, the movie became controversial because some viewers believed that it glamorized teen suicide.

Ryder's next important role came in *Edward Scissorhands* (1990) in which she was again directed by Tim Burton. She plays Kim, the high school cheerleader who falls in love with the strange mechanical man, played by her real-life fiance Johnny Depp. The creation of a scientist, Edward has scissors for hands. According to Ryder, "*Edward Scissorhands* is a beautiful Gothic romantic story with a lot of real-life feeling. Edward expresses the negative self-image possessed by so many—especially in adolescence. The desperate feeling that everything you do is wrong, everything you touch you destroy." In *Mermaids* (1990), directed by Richard Benjamin, Ryder plays Charlotte, the religious daughter of a careless, sexually promiscuous mother played by Cher. A teenager with wildly conflicting feelings, Charlotte is torn between her Jewish roots, her interest in Catholicism and desire to become a nun, and her new-found sexuality. For Ryder, "What I related to about Charlotte is that she's inconsistent. One day she'll be obsessed with Catholicism, but the next day she'll be obsessed with Joe the gardener. And the *next* day she'll want to be an American Indian. I had really been going through stuff like that. I would think, I'm going crazy! I don't know what I want! I don't know who I am!'"

Ryder's current work marks her debut playing an adult woman rather than a teenager. Her most recent film, *Bram Stoker's Dracula* (1992), was directed by Francis Ford Coppola and co-stars Gary Oldman, Anthony Hopkins, and Keanu Reeves. As the title suggests, the movie was based on the nineteenth-century novel by Bram Stoker, rather than on previous Hollywood treatments of the story. Ryder was the impetus for the project: she gave the script to Coppola, hoping that he would direct what she felt would be an "epic movie." She plays Mina, an English school teacher and the lover of the vampire Dracula. Ryder describes the movie as "a love story, a fantasy, very, very surreal." She has also completed work on *The Age of Innocence*, based on the Edith Wharton novel of the same name. This film, directed by Martin Scorsese and co-starring Michelle Pfeiffer and Daniel Day-Lewis, is expected to be released in late 1993. With these films, according to *Esquire* magazine, "Ryder is set to become the most prominent and powerful movie actress of her generation. She is about to become a star in the old-fashioned sense, a classic combination of glamour, talent, and ambition."

MAJOR INFLUENCES

Ryder speaks frequently of her great respect for her parents, Cindy and Michael Horowitz. "They're great people to hang around. They're both incredibly smart and intellectual and they could have become very wealthy but they struggled to pay the bills and stuck to what they want. That has to do with how I make my decisions. If they taught me anything, it's to trust myself and go with what my gut tells me."

MARRIAGE AND FAMILY

Ryder, who is unmarried, recently moved from her home in Southern California to New York City. She has been involved with actor Johnny Depp since 1989; the two became engaged about five months after they first met.

Their relationship has been avidly covered in the press, although both Ryder and Depp have tried to guard their privacy. Recently, there has been widespread conjecture about their on-again, off-again relationship, and their future plans are unknown.

FAVORITE BOOKS AND MOVIES

Ryder typically lists *Brazil, My Life as a Dog,* and *Heathers* as her favorite movies. When asked about her favorite book, there is no hesitation: "My all-time favorite novel is [J.D. Salinger's] *Catcher in the Rye.* It's my bible. I bet I've read it 50 times . . . . It's funny. I read it at age 12—and I didn't get it. Then I tried it again when I was about 14. And wow, it was gospel. I was crushed when I found out a whole generation had loved it before me. I thought it was just my book."

HOBBIES AND OTHER INTERESTS

Ryder's hobbies include reading, watching movies, traveling, and listening to alternative music (The Replacements is her favorite band). She particularly enjoys writing—she keeps a journal, and has also written a screenplay and short stories.

MOVIES

Lucas, 1986
Square Dance, 1987 (shown on TV as *Home Is Where the Heart Is*)
1969, 1988
Beetlejuice, 1988
Great Balls of Fire, 1989
Heathers, 1989
Edward Scissorhands, 1990
Mermaids, 1990
Welcome Home, Roxy Carmichael, 1990
Night on Earth, 1992
Bram Stoker's Dracula, 1992
The Age of Innocence, 1993

FURTHER READING

BOOKS

Who's Who in America, 1992-93

PERIODICALS

Esquire, Nov. 1992, p.114
Interview, Dec. 1990, p.86
New York Times, Dec. 9, 1990, p.H11
Rolling Stone, May 18, 1989, p.69; May 16, 1991, p.45

San Francisco Chronicle, Nov. 12, 1992, p.E1
Seattle Times, Dec. 9, 1990, p.J3
Seventeen, Oct. 1988, p.93
Vogue, Nov. 1992, p.294

ADDRESS

PMK Public Relations
1776 Broadway, 8th Floor
New York, NY 10019

Jerry Spinelli 1941-
American Writer of Books for Children and Young Adults
Author of *Maniac Magee*, the 1991 Newbery Medal Winner

BIRTH

Jerry Spinelli was born on February 1, 1941, in Norristown, Pennsylvania. His parents were Louis Anthony Spinelli, a printer, and Lorna Mae (Bigler) Spinelli. Jerry has one brother, Bill.

YOUTH

Very little has been written about Jerry Spinelli's life, particularly his childhood, except by Spinelli himself. His own words best describe this time: "For most of my kid years, we lived in a brick rowhouse in the West End [of Norristown, Pennsylvania]. I did the usual kid stuff: rode my bike, played chew-the-peg, flipped baseball cards, skimmed flat stones across Stony Creek, cracked twin popsicles, caught poison ivy, wondered about girls, thought stuff that I would never say out loud."

EDUCATION

Spinelli attended Stewart Junior High School and Eisenhower High School, both in Norristown. He was a popular student, active in sports and school government. After graduating from high school, Spinelli attended Gettysburg College in Gettysburg, Pennsylvania, earning his bachelor's degree in English in 1963. The following year, he earned a master's degree in creative writing at Johns Hopkins University in Baltimore, Maryland. He then briefly attended Temple University in Philadelphia, Pennsylvania, taking classes and teaching as a graduate assistant for one semester. After leaving Temple, Spinelli joined the U.S. Naval Air Reserve. He attended boot camp and military school in Memphis, Tennessee, and Denver, Colorado, in late 1965 and early 1966, and continued serving as a "weekend warrior" with the Naval Air Reserve until 1971.

CHOOSING A CAREER

Spinelli had first decided to become a writer while still in high school. As he tells it, "When I was 16, my high school football team won a big game. That night I wrote a poem about it. The poem was published in the local newspaper, and right about then I stopped wanting to become a major league shortstop and started wanting to become a writer.

"But first I became a grown-up. And I thought, as most grown-ups do: okay, now on to the important stuff.

"So I tried writing grown-up novels about important stuff. Nobody wanted them."

FIRST JOBS

Spinelli's career has turned out a bit different from what he now says he originally envisioned. While a student, he planned to become a writer and professor at an "ivy-covered New England college, sort of J.D. Salinger." But his teaching experiences at Temple University proved to be so time consuming that he changed plans. From 1966 to 1989, he worked at the magazine publisher Chilton Co. as an editor of *Product Design and Development*, a trade journal. As he describes it, "I wrote pieces about new products, like a valve, a new transistor, just little product descriptions. Most people are looking for an interesting, exciting, glamorous job. I looked for just the opposite, something that was routine and wouldn't leave me exhausted at five o'clock." Whenever he had the chance—on his lunch hours, at home each night, even while on guard duty in the military—he would use every bit of free time to write, working on his grown-up novels.

He continued this way for over ten years. And all he had to show for it was four unpublished manuscripts and a stack of rejection slips from publishers. But his next book, inspired by a late-night refrigerator raid by one of his own children, changed all that. As he tells it, "One night one of our angels snuck into the refrigerator and swiped the fried chicken that I was saving for lunch the next day. When I discovered the chicken was gone, . . . I wrote about it.

"I didn't know it at the time, but I had begun to write my first published novel, *Space Station Seventh Grade*. By the time it was finished, hardly anything in it had to do with my grown-up, 'important' years. It was all from the West End days [of my childhood]."

At first, Spinelli submitted the book to publishers as an adult novel. More rejections came, though, when they objected to his use of a child's point of view in an adult novel. But then his literary agent suggested that he submit the book as a young-adult novel. Success! Spinelli's first published novel, *Space Station Seventh Grade*, appeared in 1982.

CAREER HIGHLIGHTS

Since that time, Spinelli has become a successful author of contemporary novels for young adults. His works are widely praised for their accurate characterizations and dialogue. Often told by the teens themselves, these novels typically present realistic situations from teenagers' lives. Although the situations themselves are often serious, Spinelli leavens his work with humor. Some of the topics in his books have proved controversial, and reviewers have questioned the appropriateness of some crude references to drinking, swearing, farting, teen sexuality, and racial issues. But other commentators have emphasized his

nonjudgmental depictions of many of the awkward and embarassing moments that can occur during adolescence, praising his respect, compassion, and deep affection for his audience.

Maniac Magee (1990) is widely considered his best work to date. This captivating novel tells the story of 13-year-old Jeffrey Lionel Magee, a legendary character who can run faster and hit farther than anyone. Orphaned at age three, sent to live in a loveless home with an estranged aunt and uncle who never speak to one another, "Maniac" Magee is literally on the run, searching for a loving home. Along the way he meets a rich cast of characters, good and bad, black and white. Often described as a fable or folktale, this story confronts the issue of racism, showcasing a divided community and contrasting the actions and attitudes of two families, one white and one black. Maniac's greatest feat, if he can do it, is to bring his divided community together. Maniac is, according to Spinelli, "a hero, a kid who's a hero to other kids."

Maniac Magee has won numerous awards, including the prestigious Newbery Medal, whose awarding body was inspired to remark: "The best of Spinelli's irresistible poetic prose keeps time with the slap, slap, slap of Maniac's sneakers as he runs in search of a home. Through Maniac's encounters with an extraordinary cast of characters, the reader not only sees the world as it is, but as it could be."

MARRIAGE AND FAMILY

Spinelli married the writer Eileen Mesi on May 21, 1977, and became stepfather to her six children: Kevin, Barbara, Jeffrey, Molly, Sean, and Benjamin. Most of the children are now grown and living away from the family home in Phoenixville, Pennsylvania.

HOBBIES AND OTHER INTERESTS

Spinelli enjoys reading, traveling, playing tennis, listening to country music, and collecting antiques.

One of Spinelli's favorite pastimes is caring for his pets, a chinchilla and a rat. Certainly, these are unusual choices for a pet. But as Spinelli tells it, "I was looking for a low-maintenance pet. I kind of wanted a companion around the office, but I didn't want one that would be a lot of trouble. I wanted a pet that I didn't have to take for a walk everyday and that [wouldn't] poop on the rug . . . . That kind of leads you to the little rodents—the gerbils, hamsters, and guinea pigs, you know, creatures like that. And every book I read had a chapter on the rat as a pet. And they all said that among these animals, the rat is the most intelligent, the friendliest—it had all the recommendations, except it has a bad image . . . . And I can tell you from experience that once you live with a rat for a couple of months, they just begin to look as ordinary as a dog or a cat." Spinelli got his current rat, Daisy, last Christmas Eve, moved by the sentiment of the season; his first rat, Bernie, who has since died, is known to his readers as Bernadette in *There's a Girl in My Hammerlock*.

WRITINGS

Space Station Seventh Grade, 1982
Who Put That Hair in My Toothbrush? 1984
Night of the Whale, 1985
Jason and Marceline, 1986
Dump Days, 1988
The Bathwater Gang, 1990
Maniac Magee, 1990
Fourth Grade Rats, 1991
There's a Girl in My Hammerlock, 1991
Bathwater Gang Gets Down to Business, 1992
Do the Funky Pickle, 1992

SCHOOL DAZE SERIES

Report to the Principal's Office! 1991 (No. 1)
Who Ran My Underwear Up the Flagpole? 1992 (No. 2)

HONORS AND AWARDS

Boston Globe-Horn Book Award: 1990, for *Maniac Magee*
Notable Children's Book (American Library Association): 1990, for *Maniac Magee*
Best Book for Young Adults (American Library Association): 1990, for *Maniac Magee*
John Newbery Medal (American Library Association): 1991, for *Maniac Magee*
D.C. Fisher Award: 1992, for *Maniac Magee*

FURTHER READING

BOOKS

Something about the Author, Vol. 71
Who's Who in America, 1992-93

PERIODICALS

Horn Book Magazine, July/Aug. 1991, pp.426, 433
Reading Teacher, Nov. 1991, p.174

ADDRESS

Scholastic Books
730 Broadway
New York, NY 10003

Denzel Washington 1954-
American Stage and Screen Actor
Starred in *Malcolm X, Mo' Better Blues,*
Glory, Cry Freedom, and *A Soldier's Story*

BIRTH

Denzel (pronounced den-ZEL) Washington was born on December 28, 1954, in Mount Vernon, New York. His father, the Rev. Denzel Washington, Sr., was a Pentecostal minister who worked at the water department during the week and then preached on Sunday. His mother, Lennis Washington, was a singer in the church choir and a beautician who owned several beauty shops. The second of three children, Denzel has one brother and one sister. Their parents divorced when Denzel was fourteen.

YOUTH

Mount Vernon, where Washington grew up, is a suburb just north of New York City, in Westchester County. This multiracial community was described in *New York* magazine as "one of those good/bad neighborhoods where some kids go to college and some kids go to jail." Of Denzel's three close friends, two ended up in jail, and one ended up dead. But the senior Washingtons worked hard to keep their children on the "good" side of the neighborhood. Denzel now says that his father taught him the importance of integrity, hard work, and responsibility, while his strong-willed mother kept him from "becoming a sure-nuf gangster." As he says, "My mother's love for me and her desire for me to do well kept me out of trouble. When it came to the moment of should I go this way or do that, I'd think about her and say, 'Naahh, let me get myself outta here before I get into trouble.'"

But all that changed when Denzel was fourteen and his parents got a divorce. That event affected him deeply. "I rebelled and got angry and started beating people up at school," he said. "I rejected everything." Soon afterward, hoping to curb this rebelliousness, his mother pulled him out of the public schools and sent him to the Oakland Academy.

EDUCATION

The Oakland Academy, which Washington describes as "very rich and very white," is a private college prep school for boys in New Windsor, a town in upstate New York. He was a top athlete, going out for baseball, basketball, football, and track; he also played in the band. But he was an indifferent student with a barely adequate grade point average. As he recalls, in his junior year one teacher wrote in his yearbook, "Keep your individuality. But maybe cut down on the noise." Washington graduated from the Oakland Academy in 1972.

He then enrolled in the pre-med program at Fordham University in New York City. He soon felt unsuited to that program—he couldn't even pronounce the names of his biology classes, let alone pass them, he now says—and switched to a journalism major. One summer, while working as a YMCA camp counselor, he appeared in a talent show and immediately got hooked on the stage. On returning to Fordham, he signed up for a drama workshop with Robinson Stone, an actor and respected professor who became his mentor. Washington appeared in several college productions, including Eugene O'Neill's *The Emperor Jones* and Shakespeare's *Othello*, and Stone predicted that "Denzel had a brilliant career ahead of him. He played Othello with so much majesty and beauty but also rage and hate that I dragged agents to come and see it." While still a college senior, Washington won his first professional role in the television movie

Wilma (1977), based on the life of Olympic track star Wilma Rudolph. Washington ultimately graduated from Fordham University with a bachelor's degree in drama and journalism.

In 1978, Washington was accepted at the prestigious American Conservatory Theatre in San Francisco. Convinced that he could learn more about acting by working than by studying, he left after his first year there. He moved to Los Angeles to "test the waters," but soon returned to New York.

FIRST JOBS

Although he struggled during his early years in New York, and was no stranger to the unemployment line, Washington was able to build a serious stage career there. He had great talent, but he also had the good fortune to be starting out in the late 1970s, a time when black theater companies were thriving and when large, mostly white groups were creating multiracial ensembles and trying nontraditional casting. He appeared in a wide range of productions, including *The Mighty Gents, Spell #7, Coriolanus, Ceremonies in Dark Old Men, One Tiger to a Hill, Man and Superman, Othello, Split Second*, and *Every Goodbye Ain't Gone.*

Like so many aspiring actors in New York, there were times when Washington was unable to find work. Broke and discouraged, he gave up on his dreams at one point and took a job with the county recreation department. His wife, Pauletta Pearson, a professional singer and actress herself, convinced him to keep trying. Her advice paid off. He soon landed a part in *When the Chickens Come Home to Roost* (1981), in which he portrayed Malcolm X. The part focused on his relationship with Elijah Muhammad, the leader of the Nation of Islam, or Black Muslims. Although the show only ran for 12 performances, Washington earned a great deal of recognition, as well as additional roles.

Washington next won a part in a production by the Negro Ensemble Company, a renowned troupe that he had long hoped to join. He appeared in *A Soldier's Play* (1981), Charles Fuller's critically acclaimed drama about the racial tensions on a segregated army base during World War II. Washington won an Obie Award for his portrayal of Pvt. Melvin Peterson, the quiet but embittered killer. He also reprised the role in the movie version, re-titled *A Soldier's Story* (1984).

CAREER HIGHLIGHTS

By that time, Washington's dramatic career was firmly established. He had already made a name for himself on the stage and on television, and although he has continued in those venues, he has also added feature films to his credits. In *Carbon Copy* (1981), he played the illegitimate son of George Segal. Although the film was unsuccessful, he earned praise for his performance. That role brought Washington to the attention of television executives casting the part of Dr. Philip Chandler, a Yale-educated doctor, for the new TV series "St. Elsewhere." This comedy/drama series was set at St. Eligius, a fictional Boston hospital. Washington was uncertain about accepting the part, but assumed the show would run only thirteen weeks. Instead, "St. Elsewhere" became a great success, airing for six seasons, from 1982 through 1988. Because Dr. Chandler was a secondary character on the series, though, Washington was able to continue taking on additional work.

Throughout much of the 1980s and into the 1990s, Washington has continued to act in feature films. He has been particularly careful to select scripts that meet his high standards for depicting African Americans. Following A Soldier's Story, his next important movie role came in the 1987 film Cry Freedom. He played Stephen Biko, the slain black South African activist. Many reviewers objected to the film's focus on the white newspaper editor, Donald Woods (played by Kevin Kline), who publicized the story, rather than on Biko himself. Still, there was near-unanimous praise for Washington, who received an Academy Award nomination for Best Supporting Actor.

After returning to the New York stage in 1988 to appear in Checkmates, a comedy about two unrelated black couples, one young and one old, who share a house, Washington went on to appear in the movie Glory (1989). This Civil War epic focuses on the Fifty-Fourth Regiment of the Massachusetts Voluntary Infantry, the first black unit to fight for the Union army. Washington portrayed the soldier Trip, an angry and illiterate fugitive slave. He devoted himself to research before the filming, reading historical accounts and personal narratives from the Civil War era. For his intense and charismatic performance, Washington won both an Academy Award and a NAACP Image Award for Best Supporting Actor.

With his next project, Mo' Better Blues (1990), Washington moved from an historical to a contemporary setting. In this Spike Lee movie, he plays Bleek Gilliam, a self-absorbed trumpeter who is sought after by two women. According to critic Elvis Mitchell, "Mo' Better Blues is Washington's chance to carry a movie, and he gives what is undeniably a complex and mature movie-star performance." In fact, Spike Lee wrote this film with Washington in mind, hoping to expand his opportunities as a lead actor. Both Lee and Washington have frequently lamented the limited choices available for black actors, especially leading roles. Many reviewers have felt that Washington has that certain star quality—looks, talent, humor, charm, personal magnetism, and sex appeal—to become a leading man in romantic films, a status that has been routinely denied black actors. He is often compared to Sidney Poitier, the last black actor to become a romantic lead in Hollywood films—a comparison Washington disdains, despite his respect for Poitier, as an attempt to categorize him, as if there is a single leading man role open to black actors. After *Mo' Better Blues* and a stint in the lead role in a Shakespeare in the Park production of *Richard III*, Washington made *Mississippi Masala* (1992), an inter-racial love story of a romance between an African American man and an East Indian woman in a small town in Mississippi.

Recently, Washington appeared in the lead role in *Malcolm X* (1992), another Spike Lee production. This film biography documents the slain leader's life, from his early days in Boston, to his criminal exploits in Harlem, his years in prison, his conversion there to the Islamic faith, his work preaching in New York and eventually around the country as a Black Muslim, his subsequent break with Elijah Muhammad and the Nation of Islam, his pilgrimage to Mecca, and, finally, to his assassination in 1965. Tremendous publicity was generated by Lee and the press before the film's release, and tremendous expectations as well. Many said that no film could satisfy all who felt a stake in Malcolm, and wondered how Lee would portray his constantly evolving views. And indeed, critical reaction to *Malcolm X* has varied widely: some reviewers have heaped lavish praise on the film for its accuracy and on Washington for his complex, inspired, intense, and even humorous performance. Others charged that the film's depiction of the revered leader was false or biased, and still others have expressed disappointment that the film failed to live up to all the media hype.

Since then, Washington has been working on two films. One is a film version of Shakespeare's *Much Ado about Nothing*, directed by Kenneth Branaugh and co-starring Emma Thompson. The other, tentatively titled *Philadelphia*, is directed by Jonathan Demme. Washington plays a conservative attorney who represents another attorney (played by Tom Hanks) who is fired from his job after he develops AIDS. The film is expected to be released in late 1993.

MARRIAGE AND FAMILY

Washington lives in Los Angeles, California, with his wife, Pauletta Pearson, and their four children: David, Katia, and the twins, Olivia and Malcolm. Washington and Pearson first met in 1977, when they both had parts in the TV movie *Wilma*; they started seeing each other two years later, when they ran into each other at a party, and were married in 1983.

Washington often speaks of his great admiration and respect for his wife: "Pauletta's sacrificed a lot of opportunities to build her own career. She was doing Broadway shows. My wife was a child prodigy, a concert pianist. She's competed in Van Cliburn competitions, and she's been all over the world. I told her I want her to do whatever she wants to do for her career, but she's really committed to family and to helping and supporting me. I don't know what I'd do without her 'cause I'm all over the place, and she's my foundation and my stability. I have the utmost respect for her."

HOBBIES AND OTHER INTERESTS

When he is away from the set, Washington cherishes the time he is able to spend with his family. He also enjoys playing sports, including skiing, basketball, touch football, tennis, running, and weight-lifting, as well as reading, cooking, and listening to music by female vocalists.

CREDITS

STAGE

Ceremonies in Dark Old Men, 1981
When the Chickens Come Home to Roost, 1981
A Soldier's Play, 1981
Checkmates, 1988
Richard III, 1990

FILM

Carbon Copy, 1981
A Soldier's Story, 1984
Power, 1986
Cry Freedom, 1987
Glory, 1989
The Mighty Quinn, 1989
For Queen and Country, 1989
Heart Condition, 1990
Mo' Better Blues, 1990
Ricochet, 1991
Mississippi Masala, 1992
Malcolm X, 1992

TELEVISION

Wilma, 1977 (TV movie)
Flesh and Blood, 1979 (TV movie)
"St. Elsewhere," 1982-88 (TV series)
License to Kill, 1984 (TV movie)
The George McKenna Story, 1986 (TV miniseries)

HONORS AND AWARDS

Audelco Award: 1981, for *When the Chickens Come Home to Roost*
Obie Award: 1981-82, for *A Soldier's Play*

Academy Award: 1989, for *Glory,* for Best Supporting Actor
Golden Globe Award: 1990, for *Glory,* for Best Supporting Actor
NAACP Image Award: 1990, for *Glory,* for Best Supporting Actor

FURTHER READING

BOOKS

Who's Who in America, 1992-93
Who's Who among Black Americans, 1992-93

PERIODICALS

American Film, Aug. 1990, p.26
California, Sep. 1990, p.76
Current Biography, July 1992
Ebony, Sep. 1990, p.80
Essence, Nov. 1986, p.54
GQ, Oct. 1988, p.312
Interview, July 1990, p.66
New York, Aug. 13, 1990, p.34
New York Times, Nov. 18, 1992, p.C19
New York Times Magazine, Oct. 25, 1992, p.36
Washington Post, Aug. 25, 1989, p.D1

ADDRESS

PMK Public Relations
955 S. Carrillo Dr., # 200
Los Angeles, CA 90048

Keenen Ivory Wayans 1958-
American Comedian, Actor, and Filmmaker
Creator of the Hit TV Series "In Living Color"

BIRTH

Keenen Ivory Wayans was born in Harlem in New York City on June 8, 1958. His father, Howell Wayans, was a supermarket manager; his mother, Elvira Wayans, was a homemaker who later returned to school to become a social worker. Wayans was the second of ten children.

YOUTH

When Keenen was about six, the family moved to the Fulton housing projects in the Chelsea section of Manhattan. The family of twelve shared a four-bedroom apartment, and space was always tight. "Each [bedroom] had a closet. The closet was like our 'office.' We would go there for privacy. At dinner, my mother would count us, and if one was missing she would go into the closet and see who had fallen asleep." Money was tight, too—their father's salary barely stretched to meet the needs of his large family. And discipline was tight as well. Howell Wayans was a member of the religious group Jehovah's Witnesses, and he closely monitored his children's activities. They weren't allowed to hang out with other kids, and they soon learned to rely on one another. Although the family was poor, Wayans believes that he and his sisters and brothers were better off than many other kids he knew: "We had a mother and father, and we had to eat as a family. All washed up, we sat down at the table at six o'clock. We had structure."

It was at the dinner table that Wayans developed his sense of comedy. Dinner in the Wayans household was loose, loud, and funny. "Anything that happened that day, that's what the jokes were about. We'd start snappin' on each other. Everybody had a twisted sense of humor. We cracked jokes about [our] most painful experiences. A lot of it had to do with being alienated, being different from other kids." Wayans was doing impressions by the age of four, starting with a neighborhood wino. Two years later, he saw Richard Pryor on television and decided to become a comedian. Throughout their childhoods, Keenen and his brother Damon would create characters and then act out funny stories about them. Many of them, including the Homeboys, appear on "In Living Color."

EDUCATION

In school, Wayans was always the class clown. "Our first audience was the class," he once said. "If I had missed a day of school, when I came in the next day I would get a round of applause." Yet he was also a responsible kid: he worked long hours as a manager at McDonald's, contributed his earnings to the family income, helped out around the house, looked out for his brothers and sisters, and earned good enough grades to win a scholarship to college. He graduated from Seward Park High School in 1976.

Wayans studied engineering at Tuskegee Institute in Alabama. After growing up in Manhattan, small-town Southern life was a surprise. "I had such culture shock down there. I was used to the city, man. They'd say, 'Let's go downtown and have some fun,' and you'd get downtown and it wasn't nothing but a pharmacy and a Goodwill store." It was in that environment that Wayans started performing stand-up comedy routines, telling stories to fellow students near a fountain on campus. "There weren't a lot of kids from New York down there, and everyone was fascinated with New York. And I would tell all these stories about

New York and do all the characters—a lot of the characters you see on ["In Living Color"]. They were like my practice audience." After three-and-a-half years, Wayans decided to leave Tuskegee Institute to become a comedian. He was just a few credits short of completing his engineering degree.

FIRST JOBS

During Wayans's first year at college, a student told him about the Improv, a New York comedy club that showcases new comedians. That first summer vacation, at the age of 19, he auditioned there. While he failed that audition, it wasn't a total loss—he met fellow comic Robert Townsend, who would later become a collaborator and a celebrated filmmaker. Wayans then passed the audition on just his second try. After leaving Tuskegee, Wayans returned to New York and began performing stand-up routines at the comedy clubs there. He soon moved to Los Angeles, again working the clubs and also trying out for acting roles in movies and TV. He won parts on "Benson," "Cheers," "CHiPs," and "A Different World," had a regular role on the series "For Love and Honor," and made his feature film debut in *Star 80*. Yet he was also frustrated by the limited opportunities for blacks in Hollywood: he felt that casting, for blacks, was consistently dictated by stereotypes. His next major project, *Hollywood Shuffle* (1986), parodied this very system.

CAREER HIGHLIGHTS

Since the 1980s, Wayans has had a varied career as an entertainer, both in front of and behind the camera. He has done stand-up comedy, acting, scriptwriting, directing, and producing, in live performances as well as TV and films. To all these activities, though, he brings a satiric and distinctly African-American perspective. The first project to bring Wayans to national attention was the movie *Hollywood Shuffle*, which he co-wrote with his friend Robert Townsend. This film, in which Townsend, Wayans, and others portray black actors trying to get work, is a satiric look at stereotyping in the Hollywood casting system. While noting some flaws, critics called it inspired. Wayans worked with Townsend again in 1987, when they co-wrote and co-starred in the cable TV special "Robert Townsend and His Partners in Crime." That same year, Wayans co-produced and co-wrote *Eddie Murphy Raw*, the highest grossing concert film ever.

In 1989, Wayans made his directing debut with *I'm Gonna Git You Sucka*, which he also wrote, produced, and starred in. This film, an outrageous spoof of black exploitation and kung fu movies from the 1970s, features Wayans as Jack Slade, a decorated Army veteran with a medal for shorthand. He returns home after ten years in the service to find his brother dead—O.G.ed—from wearing too many gold chains. The parody continues with such absurdities as a "Pimp of the Year" contest, where bikini-clad men compete in platform shoes, and a "Youth Gang Competition," similar to a track and field contest, where gang members compete in races to strip cars and steal TVs, complete with Doberman pinschers at their heels. Wayans was quick to explain the movie's intent: "I'm not satirizing black people but bad moviemaking. The inspiration came from *Airplane!* I'm a big fan of that movie. I was sitting around watching old Superfly movies, and I realized they were ripe for humor." While many reviewers considered the quality of the movie uneven, they agreed that much of it was wildly funny.

The financial success of *I'm Gonna Get You Sucka*—it cost only $3 million to make and has grossed over $20 million—quickly brought Wayans to the attention of the movie-making community. He arranged advance screenings of his next movie and invited film executives to attend, hoping a studio would fund his next movie. Instead, Fox TV executives came and challenged the whole direction of his thinking. "I really wasn't interested in television," Wayans has said. "But they said the magic words, 'You can do anything you want.'"

"IN LIVING COLOR"

What Wayans wanted to do was a comedy/variety show with sketches from a black perspective, and Fox gave him the opportunity. He created "In Living Color," working as its executive producer, head writer, and host. The show is funky and urban, with a predominately black ensemble of comedians (including his brother Damon and sister Kim), a team of hip-hop dancers (the Fly Girls), and a house deejay (his brother Shawn, or SW1). Each half-hour show contains a mix of comedy sketches, dancing, short films, and music. Some of the sketches feature recurring characters, like Homey D. Clown, Little Miss Trouble, the Hedley family, the "Men on ..." pieces, "Snackin' Shack," and the "Homeboy Shopping Network," while others lampoon celebrities, like Arsenio Hall, Oprah Winfrey, Jesse Jackson, Whitney Houston, and Louis Farrakhan, to name just a few.

"In Living Color" was a popular and critical success following its debut in April 1990. Although the show originally aired during a later time slot on Saturday nights, it was changed to 8:00 p.m. on Sundays. Considering the show's content, that time period, during TV's family viewing hour, has caused problems. Many of the pieces have become controversial. Some people consider the "Men on . . ." pieces anti-gay, the Buttman sketches offensive, the Fly Girls demeaning to women, and the "Homeboy Shopping Network" demeaning to blacks. For his part, Wayans takes such criticism in stride: "If I make a handful of people p----- off, but I have the support of the masses, I don't care. This is a parody show. We go for belly laughs. When you walk on the edge, you run the risk of offending some people." For this willingness to walk on the edge, to challenge television's restrictive stereotypes and create fresh and innovative comedy, Wayans has been widely praised.

Recent events have changed all that. In December 1992, a spokesperson from Fox announced that Wayans had terminated his relationship with the network and had departed as executive producer of "In Living Color." There have been unconfirmed reports that Wayans and Fox fought over censorship issues and the company's decision to show reruns of early shows without his consent.

MAJOR INFLUENCES

"Richard Pryor has always been my comedic influence," according to Wayans. "When I decided I was going to be a comedian at age six it was because I saw Richard Pryor on TV doing comedy and I said, 'That's what I want to do.' He showed me what my dream was going to be basically. I guess he was such a strong influence because the stuff he was talking about I could relate to. He grew up in an impoverished background. He had a very strict father. He talked a lot about his family and the people in his neighborhood. It was all very real to me. He made things funny that weren't funny. What I remember is him talking about getting his ass kicked by this bully and I had just run home from this dude who was trying to take my nickel. I had just run home and I'm sitting there watching him do jokes about it. I said, 'This is what I want to do.'

"I was always a weird kid, but I just couldn't figure out what was strange about me. Watching Richard Pryor I got a sense that it was my humor that made me different. There were others that I appreciated, like Red Skelton, Carol Burnett, Monty Python. I loved them. The guys who did *Airplane*. They made me laugh. But Richard Pryor was my influence. I mean, I studied Richard Pryor."

MARRIAGE AND FAMILY

Wayans, who is single, lives alone in Hollywood. After growing up as part of a large family in a cramped apartment, he values his privacy and space.

HOBBIES AND OTHER INTERESTS

Wayans usually avoids the Hollywood social scene. Instead, he likes to work out, play chess, do home remodeling projects, and hang out with his family.

CREDITS

Hollywood Shuffle, 1986 [co-writer and actor, with Robert Townsend]

Eddie Murphy Raw, 1987 [co-writer and co-producer, with Eddie Murphy]
"Robert Townsend and His Partners in Crime," 1987 [co-writer and actor, with Robert Townsend]
I'm Gonna Git You Sucka, 1989 [writer, director, and actor]
"In Living Color," 1990-92 [creator, executive producer, writer, and actor]

HONORS AND AWARDS

Emmy Award: 1990, for "In Living Color" as Outstanding Comedy/Variety Series

FURTHER READING

BOOKS

George, Nelson. *The Authorized Companion to "In Living Color": The Fox TV Series,* 1991

PERIODICALS

Cosmopolitan, Nov. 1990, p.214
New York, Oct. 8, 1990, p.28
People, Dec. 12, 1988, p.185; June 11, 1990, p.75
TV Guide, June 2, 1990, pp.2, 4
Washington Post, July 1, 1990, p.G1

ADDRESS

Bender, Goldman, and Helper
11500 W. Olympic Blvd., Suite 655
Los Angeles, CA 90064

Dave Winfield 1951-
American Baseball Player with the Minnesota Twins
National and American League All-Star
For Twelve Consecutive Years

BIRTH

David Mark Winfield was born October 3, 1951, in St. Paul, Minnesota, the son of Frank Winfield, a railroad porter, and Arline Vivian Allison Winfield, an audiovisual department worker for the public schools. His brother Steve, who is one year older, now coaches amateur teams and works for the David M. Winfield Foundation for underprivileged youth.

YOUTH

Dave remembers little of life with his father, although he does have vague recollections that his parents had trouble getting along. His father worked the St. Paul-to-Seattle line and was often absent from home. When Dave was three, his parents were divorced, Frank moving out west and Arline staying in St. Paul to take care of the little boys. She had help from the children's maternal grandmother, Jessie, and from her other relatives in the area.

Arline Winfield was what would now be called a "supermom"—she worked full time, brought up two boys, and was active in such community organizations as Cub Scouts and PTA. Dave remembers that his mother always involved him and his brother in family decisions. "I feel that it was valuable that she thought to consult us," he has said, "to make us feel that we had some say in our lives." Though poor, the Winfields had a rich family life that emphasized church, education, humor, and values. Dave still points out how his mother was the source of his fascination with language, and how her example of hard work and a positive attitude has helped him to form his successful life.

Winfield began playing sports when he was still quite young. His first position was third base, but he soon became enamored of the greater action at shortstop and began alternating between the two positions. A new coach, Bill Peterson, soon came to the all-black neighborhood to supervise the Oxford Playground down the street from the Winfield home. Peterson was such a fine coach that he molded a group of poor youths, none of whom had ever skated, into St. Paul's championship hockey team. In the summer, he taught Winfield and the other neighborhood kids how to concentrate on baseball fundamentals and develop a winning attitude. Peterson put them through so much work that, says Winfield, had he heard the "natural athlete" tag that haunts so many black stars, he "would have laughed his head off."

EARLY MEMORIES

Although St. Paul was a relatively progressive city in the fifties and sixties, Winfield nevertheless remembers feeling separate because of his race. He calls it, however, "background stuff, on the fringes of a childhood that was never bothered much by the color issue." The civil rights struggle, though, was important to the family because of its larger implications, and Dave remembers the trauma caused by the assassination of Martin Luther King, Jr. "Most of all, I was frustrated and angry," he says, having been convinced that King's nonviolent approach was indeed the best route to a just society. "More than a bunch of black militants," Winfield argues, "his assassination created a bunch of black cynics, which I think may turn out to be a whole lot more dangerous . . . . I remember seeing black leadership founder, and asking myself, 'Now, whom do I look up to? Whom do I respect?' For a while the answer was simply no one."

EDUCATION

At Central High School in St. Paul, Dave Winfield was an average student who concentrated on sports. Having made the All-City and All-State teams in baseball, and excelling in basketball despite playing only in his junior and senior years, he had two options. Most of his friends thought he should sign the contract offered by the Boston Red Sox, but he was reluctant to start out in the "boondocks" atmosphere of minor-league baseball's farm club system. Instead, Winfield opted for a half-scholarship at the University of Minnesota, across the river in Minneapolis. There he majored in African-American studies and political science. His academics improved after a slow start, but his focus was still athletics.

A brush with the law in the summer after his freshman year gave him an education in life that he's not likely to forget. He and a friend were caught stealing snow-blowers. Winfield ended up with a three-year suspended sentence. "I was lucky," he told *Sport* magazine. He says he tells the story now so that kids will know "what a terrible feeling it is to do something so stupid and so wrong."

In baseball, Winfield had switched to the pitcher's mound. He went 8-3 in his sophomore year at Minnesota with an ERA of 1.48, the lowest in the Big Ten. Summers he played in the semipro Alaska Summer League, working on both pitching and hitting. He also made the basketball team in his junior year, helping the Gophers to their first Big Ten championship in 38 years. The physical exertion, though, took a toll on his body. He was unable to pitch that year, and some coaches worried that his baseball career might be in jeopardy. But that summer in Alaska he proved himself a good enough hitter to have value even if he couldn't pitch.

Pitch he did in his senior year—Winfield posted a 13-1 record with a 2.74 ERA, while hitting .385. Although the Gophers lost a heartbreaker to USC in the College World Series, two beautifully pitched games made Winfield the series' Most Valuable Player. Dave left school a few credits short of graduation, but was one of the finest Gopher athletes ever.

CHOOSING A CAREER

At that point, Winfield had a selection of professional sports careers available to him. In basketball, he played well enough to be drafted in the fifth round by the NBA's Atlanta Hawks. In the baseball draft, he was chosen in the first round by the San Diego Padres. And though he'd never played a down of high school or college football, he was a 16th-round pick of the NFL's Minnesota Vikings, who felt that this outstanding athlete could excel in any sport. Winfield chose the job he had wanted since following the Minnesota Twins as a boy: major league baseball player.

CAREER HIGHLIGHTS

SAN DIEGO PADRES: 1973-80

The conversion from pitcher to outfielder, a process that began with his college injury, continued for Winfield because the Padres wanted him as an everyday player. He soon realized that he needed to sharpen his skills to remain in the league. A stint over the winter in the Mexican League, where he found the living and playing conditions intolerable, convinced him to work on his conditioning stateside. He hooked up with an independent batting instructor named Bill Allen, and they studied videotapes of successful hitters. This, along with extensive physical work, brought the opportunity for everyday play. Winfield responded, blasting 20 home runs and driving in 75 base runners in his second season.

Established as one of the stars of the Padres, Winfield labored in obscurity throughout the seventies, far from the notice of the media and pennant races. His speed and powerful arm made him one of the best defensive outfielders in baseball, while his line-drive power and intelligence assured that he continued to be a feared hitter. After hitting over .300 for the first time in 1978, he decided that he needed either more money or more exposure. In 1979 he hit .308 with 34 homers and 118 RBIs, and decided it was time to test the free-agent market. Winfield played without a contract in 1980, making only 80 percent of his 1979 base pay, but he was free after that year to seek contracts with more generous clubs.

NEW YORK YANKEES: 1981-90

Foremost among the high rollers was George Steinbrenner, the "Boss" of the fabled New York Yankees, the most successful franchise in the history of sports. A series of deft moves by Winfield's agent, Al Frohman, led to a Yankees pact that gave Dave $20 million over ten years, a figure that was then a record amount. This meant exposure in the country's largest market—fame, fortune, and incredible pressure. It also meant an adjustment in Winfield's batting style, for Yankee Stadium's "death valley," the 430-foot space to the wall in left-center, was exactly the spot that represented the right-handers' power alley. Winfield shortened his stroke and compensated sufficiently that first year with the Yankees to aid the team in grabbing their 33d American League pennant. But he had a terrible World Series, going 1-for-22 at the plate as the Dodgers beat the Yankees in six games.

Winfield didn't know it at the time, but it would be 11 years before he would get a chance to redeem himself in a series. He continued, however, to play well on both offense and defense, compiling Gold Glove awards while hitting close to .300 and regularly socking 20 or 30 home runs. In 1984, he and teammate Don Mattingly staged a season-long battle for the batting title. Winfield lost on the last day of the season, hitting a career-high .340 to Mattingly's .343. And while the Yankees played extremely well after the All-Star break, they could not catch the red-hot Detroit Tigers. Three years without a pennant was too long for the Yankee faithful, and especially for their mercurial, sometimes vindictive owner. Steinbrenner had dubbed Winfield "Mr. May" to contrast his strong early-season play with the clutch play of "Mr. October," Yankee hero Reggie Jackson.

The tension between Steinbrenner and Winfield was not confined to baseball-related matters. Part of the long-term Yankee contract stipulated that the club would contribute to the David M. Winfield Foundation, set up by Dave to help underprivileged children. Winfield filed suit three times to force the Boss to pay. Steinbrenner counterattacked by charging that Winfield had consorted with gambler and felon Howard Spira. More charges and countercharges followed, turning up the heat in the already fiery atmosphere in the Bronx. Both the courts and the commissioner sided with Winfield, verifying that Steinbrenner had paid off Spira to discredit his outfielder and barring Steinbrenner from the team's day-to-day operations. Neither man came out unscarred, and the public was left with the impression that the Bronx Bombers were associating with gamblers and mobsters. Yankee fans knew with certainty what was, to them, more important: neither the flamboyant owner nor the clean-up hitter had produced a World Championship in nearly a decade.

All this tends to obscure what Dave Winfield *did* accomplish with the New York Yankees—the more than 200 home runs, the batting average close to .290, the outfield assists, and the very real contribution the Winfield Foundation made to children in New York's poorest neighborhoods. Were it not for an ego clash of monumental proportion with the team's owner and, in a sense, with the city itself, Dave Winfield would be remembered fondly in New York. Except for a year lost to injury (1989), he played consistently at a level that made him an All-Star every year.

CALIFORNIA ANGELS AND TORONTO BLUE JAYS: 1990-92

A trade to California during the 1990 season released Winfield from the climate of ill will and distrust surrounding his years with the Yankees. While many feared he was washed up at the age of 38, he performed creditably for almost two years with the Angels. He played 150 games for them in 1991, as outfielder and designated hitter, batting .262, knocking 28 homers, and driving in 86 runs. That performance gave him the opportunity to play for the perennial contenders, the Toronto Blue Jays, in 1992. Here might be a chance to smash the "Mr. May" label.

In Toronto's Skydome, the best hitters' park he has ever played in, Winfield had ample occasion to demonstrate his offensive prowess. He hit .290, slammed 26 home runs, and drove in 108 runs—his best total in seven years. When the Jays advanced to the World Series, Winfield responded in the clutch, driving in three runs. Most importantly, his two-run double in the 11th inning of Game Six won the series for the Jays—the first time a championship traveled north of the border. In his 20th major league season, Dave Winfield won his first championship ring. He also shucked a label that unfairly marked him as a choker in big games.

Winfield has signed a contract with his hometown Minnesota Twins for 1993 and 1994. There he will get a chance to extend his career statistics. At this point, he has 2,866 hits and 432 home runs to go along with his seven Gold Gloves. Winfield is almost certain to be elected to the Baseball Hall-of-Fame.

MAJOR INFLUENCES

Winfield, it is true, got his attitude toward life from his family, and his athletic work ethic from his early coach, Bill Peterson. But the man the public sees—the fighter of newspaper stories, the extraordinary negotiator, and the player who stood up to George Steinbrenner and won—was shaped by his agent and close friend, Al Frohman. He taught Winfield about business and negotiation and was a loyal and dear friend until his death from a stroke in 1987.

"He spent more time with me than any grown man ever did," Winfield said in a eulogy. "Under him and with him I grew in wisdom, ability, and stature." In his autobiography, Winfield writes: "No man ever meant or will mean as much to me as Al Frohman." Just over a year after Frohman's death, Winfield was to suffer another blow when his mother, Arline, succumbed to cancer.

MARRIAGE AND FAMILY

Dave Winfield married Tonya Faye Turner, a real estate agent, in New Orleans in 1988. They live in the Minneapolis area, where Winfield has maintained a home for several years. He has a nine-year-old child, Lauren Shanel, from a previous common-law marriage to stewardess Sandra Renfro. Winfield insisted that the two had never lived together as husband and wife, but a Texas jury decided otherwise. The judgment was thrown out on a technicality, and a new trial is pending. Winfield acknowledges Lauren as his daughter.

HOBBIES AND OTHER INTERESTS

Winfield says that he watches a few selected television programs on PBS. He also enjoys theater, biography, jazz, fishing, and fine clothes.

WRITINGS

Winfield: A Player's Life (with Tom Parker), 1988

HONORS AND AWARDS

National League All-Star Team: 1977-80
YMCA Brian Piccolo Award for Humanitarian Service: 1979
American League All-Star Team: 1981-88
Rawlings Gold Glove Award: 1979-80, 1982-85, 1987
One of Ten Outstanding Young Americans (Jaycees): 1984
Outstanding Designated Hitter: 1992

FURTHER READING

BOOKS

Winfield, Dave (with Tom Parker). *Winfield: A Player's Life*, 1988

PERIODICALS

Current Biography Yearbook 1984
People, Apr. 18, 1988, p.50
Sport, Oct. 1986, p.92; Aug. 1991, p.85
Sports Illustrated, Apr. 11, 1988, p.36; Oct. 10, 1990, p.34; June 29, 1992, p.58

ADDRESS

The Minnesota Twins
The Metrodome
501 Chicago Ave. South
Minneapolis, MN 55415

Photo and Illustration Credits

Arthur Ashe/Photo: Photograph by Jeanne Moutoussamy-Ashe.

Avi/Photo: Coppelia Kahn. Cover: Copyright © Orchard Books.

Kathleen Battle/Photos: AP/Wide World Photos.

Boutros Boutros-Ghali/Photo: U.N. Photo 178980/Milton Grant.

Chris Burke/Photos: Bob D'Amico/ABC; Bonnie Schiffman/ABC.

Dana Carvey/Photo: NBC Photo.

Cesar Chavez/Photos: AP/Wide World Photos.

Jacques Cousteau/Photo: AP/Wide World Photos.

Cindy Crawford/Photo: Jay Strauss, MTV: Music Television.

Macaulay Culkin/Photo: Andy Schwartz.

Lois Duncan/Photo: Kait Arquette. Cover: Copyright © 1981 by Lois Duncan.

Marian Wright Edelman/Photo: Copyright © Rick Reinhard 1984.

Sara Gilbert/Photo: Edie Baskin/ABC.

Dizzy Gillespie/Photos: Frank Micelotta.

Cathy Guisewite/Cartoon: CATHY copyright © Cathy Guisewite. Reprinted with permission of UNIVERSAL PRESS SYNDICATE. All rights reserved.

Jasmine Guy/Photos: NBC photo by Gary Null; NBC photo by Paul Drinkwater.

Anita Hill/Photo: Copyright © 1992 Jeff A. Kowalsky.

Ice-T/Photo: Harrison Funk.

Appendix

This Appendix contains updates for individuals profiled in Volume I, Issues 1 through 4, 1992.

* WAYNE GRETZKY *

Wayne Gretzky began the 1992 hockey season believing he would be out of the game indefinitely—and perhaps for good—due to a herniated disk in his back. But he was only out for 39 games and returned to lead the Kings to the Stanley Cup finals, where they lost to the Montreal Canadiens.

* BO JACKSON *

When a football injury forced Bo Jackson to have hip replacement surgery in 1991, many in the sports world thought his career was over. But he proved the doomsayers wrong. In 1993, Jackson helped the Chicago White Sox reach their first American League Pennant race in ten years. Despite injuries, Jackson played in 81 games in the regular season, hitting .244 for the year.

* MICHAEL JORDAN *

On October 5, 1993, Michael Jordan shocked the sports world by announcing that he was retiring from professional basketball. Jordan's father, James Jordan, was murdered in the summer of 1993. Jordan said that neither his father's death, nor the intense media scrutiny that followed it, had anything to do with his decision. Rather, he claimed that he had "lost the heart and the desire to play," and said of basketball, "I don't need it to live." He did not, however, rule out the possibility of someday returning to the game.

* MARIO LEMIEUX *

In January 1993, Mario Lemieux was diagnosed with Hodgkin's disease, a form of cancer. He received radiation treatments that appear to have been completely successful. After missing only 23 games, Lemieux returned to hockey one month ahead of schedule, and by the time the season ended, he had once again captured the NHL scoring title, his fourth in a row. He was also named the league's Most Valuable Player for the second time.

* THURGOOD MARSHALL *

Thurgood Marshall, who retired from the Supreme Court in 1991, died January 24, 1993, at the age of 84 of heart failure. As a tireless champion of civil rights, both in presenting arguments before the Court and later as a justice, he was remembered throughout the country. His legacy was summed up by *The New Yorker*: "Thurgood Marshall had as great an impact on the history and deliberations of the United States Supreme Court as anyone who has ever lived."

* EMILY ARNOLD McCULLY *

Emily Arnold McCully won the 1993 Caldecott Medal for her most recent book, *Mirette on the High Wire*. The award is given by the American Library Association to the best illustrated children's book of the year. In accepting the award, McCully called it a "splendid honor," and noted the importance of libraries to her life: "As an author of children's books, I am the adult version of a child who learned about the world in libraries. . . . Libraries must be adequately funded and esteemed or our future is compromised."

* ANTONIA NOVELLO *

Antonia Novello left her post as Surgeon General in July of 1993. President Bill Clinton did not ask her to stay on as Surgeon General, nominating Joycelyn Elders, who has since been confirmed, to take her place. Novello will now serve as a special representative for UNICEF and will work on the problems of health and nutrition, particularly as it affects women, children, and young adults.

* ROSS PEROT *

Ross Perot continues to be involved in the national political scene. In the past year he has used his own money to buy air time on network television to promote his policies for solving the problem of the deficit. Most recently, he has published a book and gone on a nation-wide tour to protest NAFTA—the North American Free Trade Agreement—which would remove trade restrictions among the U.S., Canada, and Mexico. Whether his political aspirations include another run at the White House remains to be seen.

* COLIN POWELL *

Colin Powell retired from his position as Chairman of the Joint Chiefs of Staff on September 30, 1993. He now enters civilian life and plans to write his memoirs, reportedly for six million dollars. Both political parties would like Powell to run for president on their ticket in 1996, and news organization such as CNN have taken hypothetical polls that indicate that Powell would beat Clinton if the elections were held today. But Powell himself is not making any commitment to a political career at this time.

* YITZHAK RABIN *

In September 1993, after months of secret negotiations, Israel and the PLO (Palestine Liberation Organization) came to terms outlining peace between their peoples. In a move that took the world by surprise, Yitzhak Rabin, as the Prime Minister of Israel, and Yasir Arafat, Chairman of the PLO, notified each other in writing of their recognition of the other's right to exist. On September 15, 1993, in a ceremony on the White House lawn that united dignitaries from all over the world, Rabin spoke of the toll of the years of war: "enough of blood and tears." When he met the extended hand of Yasir Arafat it was a handshake that many around the world thought they would never see. The peace negotiations will center around the issues of contested occupied lands and Palestinian self-rule.

* NOLAN RYAN *

Nolan Ryan, the pitcher who threw more strike outs and no-hitters than anyone in the history of the game, retired from baseball in September 1993, after a season plagued with injuries. He pitched his last game in Seattle in September, when he felt his elbow "pop like a rubber band." "This whole year has just been a nightmare," Ryan said in leaving the game. But his 27 seasons as a major league pitcher and his record of seven no-hitters and 5,714 strikeouts insure his fame and his legacy to the sport.

* BORIS YELTSIN *

In September and October 1993, Boris Yeltsin faced and defeated the strongest challenge to his leadership of the new Russian state. In September, a coalition of opponents, including former Communist hardliners and nationalist forces, tried to take over the nation. In retaliation, Yeltsin disolved the Parliament. On October 4, after days of fierce fighting in which many innocent civilians were killed, troops loyal to Yeltsin stormed the Russian Parliament where the rebellion's leaders were headquartered and ended the uprising. In seeking to strengthen his control of the Russian nation, Yeltsin banned the opposition parties and closed opposition newspapers, including *Pravda*. Elections are planned for December.

Name Index

Listed below are the names of all individuals profiled in *Biography Today,* followed by the date of the issue in which they appear.

General Index

This index includes subjects, occupations, organizations, and ethnic and minority origins that pertain to individuals profiled in *Biography Today*.

Places of Birth Index

The following index lists the places of birth for the individuals profiled in *Biography Today*. Places of birth are entered under state, province, and/or country.

Birthday Index

January

2 Asimov, Isaac (1920)
4 Naylor, Phyllis Reynolds (1933)
8 Hawking, Stephen W. (1942)
9 Menchu, Rigoberta (1959)
25 Alley, Kirstie (1955)
28 Gretzky, Wayne (1961)
29 Winfrey, Oprah (1954)
   Gilbert, Sara (1975)
31 Ryan, Nolan (1947)

February

1 Spinelli, Jerry (1941)
   Yeltsin, Boris (1931)
4 Parks, Rosa (1913)
7 Brooks, Garth (1962)
12 Blume, Judy (1938)
15 Groening, Matt (1954)
17 Jordan, Michael (1963)
20 Barkley, Charles (1963)
   Crawford, Cindy (1966)
24 Jobs, Steven (1955)
25 Voigt, Cynthia (1942)

March

1 Rabin, Yitzhak (1922)
2 Gorbachev, Mikhail (1931)
   Seuss, Dr. (1904)
3 Joyner-Kersee, Jackie (1962)
10 Guy, Jasmine (1964)
16 O'Neal, Shaquille (1972)
17 Nureyev, Rudolf (1938)
18 Queen Latifah (1970)
20 Lee, Spike (1957)
25 Steinem, Gloria (1934)
26 O'Connor, Sandra Day (1930)
30 Hammer (1933)
31 Chavez, Cesar (1927)
   Gore, Al (1948)

April

2 Carvey, Dana (1955)
4 Angelou, Maya (1928)
5 Powell, Colin (1937)
12 Doherty, Shannen (1971)
14 Rose, Pete (1941)
28 Baker, James (1930)
   Duncan, Lois (1934)
   Hussein, Saddam (1937)
   Leno, Jay (1950)
29 Agassi, Andre (1970)
   Seinfeld, Jerry (1954)

May

9 Bergen, Candice (1946)
18 John Paul II (1920)
21 Robinson, Mary (1944)
26 Ride, Sally (1951)

June

4 Kistler, Darci (1964)
8 Bush, Barbara (1925)
   Edelman, Marian Wright (1939)
   Wayans, Keenen Ivory (1958)
11 Cousteau, Jacques (1910)
12 Bush, George (1924)
14 Graf, Steffi (1969)
16 McClintock, Barbara (1902)
18 Van Allsburg, Chris (1949)
19 Abdul, Paula (1962)
21 Breathed, Berke (1957)
23 Thomas, Clarence (1948)
27 Perot, H. Ross (1930)

July

1 Diana, Princess of Wales (1961)
   Duke, David (1950)
   McCully, Emily Arnold (1939)
2 Marshall, Thurgood (1908)
5 Watterson, Bill (1958)

July continued

10 Ashe, Arthur (1943)
11 Cisneros, Henry (1947)
12 Cosby, Bill (1937)
Yamaguchi, Kristi (1972)
18 Mandela, Nelson (1918)
21 Reno, Janet (1938)
Williams, Robin (1952)
29 Dole, Elizabeth Hanford (1936)
Jennings, Peter (1938)
30 Hill, Anita (1956)

August

11 Haley, Alex (1921)
Hogan, Hulk (1953)
12 Martin, Ann M. (1955)
Myers, Walter Dean (1937)
13 Battle, Kathleen (1948)
Castro, Fidel (1927)
14 Johnson, Magic (1959)
19 Clinton, Bill (1946)
22 Schwarzkopf, H. Norman (1934)
23 Novello, Antonia (1944)
26 Burke, Christopher (1965)
Culkin, Macaulay (1980)
28 Priestley, Jason (1969)

September

1 Estefan, Gloria (1958)
5 Guisewite, Cathy (1950)
15 Marino, Dan (1961)
21 Fielder, Cecil (1963)
25 Pippen, Scottie (1965)
27 Handford, Martin (1956)

October

3 Winfield, Dave (1951)
5 Lemieux, Mario (1965)
7 Ma, Yo-Yo (1955)
11 Perry, Luke (1964?)
13 Rice, Jerry (1962)
15 Iacocca, Lee A. (1924)
17 Jemison, Mae (1956)
18 Marsalis, Wynton (1961)
Navratilova, Martina (1956)
21 Gillespie, Dizzy (1956)
26 Clinton, Hillary Rodham (1947)
27 Anderson, Terry (1947)
28 Gates, Bill (1955)
29 Ryder, Winona (1971)
31 Pauley, Jane (1950)

November

2 lang, k.d. (1961)
3 Arnold, Roseanne (1952)
14 Boutros-Ghali, Boutros (1922)
29 L'Engle, Madeleine (1918)
30 Jackson, Bo (1962)

December

7 Bird, Larry (1956)
23 Avi (1937)
28 Washington, Denzel (1954)

People to Appear in Future Issues

Actors
Trini Alvarado
Dan Aykroyd
Valerie Bertinelli
Mayim Bialik
Lisa Bonet
Matthew Broderick
Candice Cameron
John Candy
Cher
Kevin Costner
Tom Cruise
Jamie Lee Curtis
Ted Danson
Tommy Davidson
Geena Davis
Matt Dillon
Michael Douglas
Larry Fishburne
Harrison Ford
Jody Foster
Michael J. Fox
Richard Gere
Tracey Gold
Whoopi Goldberg
Graham Greene
Melanie Griffith
Tom Hanks
Mark Harmon
Melissa Joan Hart
Michael Keaton
Val Kilmer
Angela Lansbury
Christopher Lloyd
Marlee Matlin
Bette Midler
Alyssa Milano
Demi Moore
Rick Moranis
Eddie Murphy
Bill Murray
Leonard Nimoy
Ashley Olsen
Mary Kate Olsen
Sean Penn
River Phoenix
Phylicia Rashad
Keanu Reeves
Julia Roberts
Bob Saget
Fred Savage
Arnold
  Schwarzenegger
William Shatner
Christian Slater
Will Smith
Jimmy Smits
Sylvester Stallone
Patrick Stewart
John Travolta
Damon Wayans
Bruce Willis
B.D. Wong

Artists
Mitsumasa Anno
Graeme Base
Maya Ying Lin

Astronauts
Neil Armstrong

Authors
Jean M. Auel
Lynn Banks
John Christopher
Arthur C. Clarke
Beverly Cleary
John Colville
Robert Cormier
Roald Dahl (obit)
Paula Danziger
Paula Fox
Jamie Gilson
Rosa Guy
Nat Hentoff
James Herriot
S.E. Hinton
Stephen King
Norma Klein
E.L. Konigsburg
Lois Lowry
David Macaulay
Stephen Manes
Norma Fox Mazer
Anne McCaffrey
Gloria D. Miklowitz
Toni Morrison
Joan Lowery Nixon
Marsha Norman
Robert O'Brien
Francine Pascal
Gary Paulsen
Christopher Pike
Daniel Pinkwater
Ann Rice
Louis Sachar
Carl Sagan
J.D. Salinger
John Saul
Maurice Sendak
Shel Silverstein
R.L. Stine
Amy Tan
Alice Walker
Jane Yolen
Roger Zelazny
Paul Zindel

Business
Minoru Arakawa
Michael Eisner
William Ford, Jr.
Anita Roddick
Donald Trump
Ted Turner

Cartoonists
Lynda Barry
Roz Chast
Jim Davis
Greg Evans
Nicole Hollander
Gary Larson
Charles Schulz
Art Spiegelman
Garry Trudeau

Comedians
Tim Allen
Dan Aykroyd
Steve Martin
Eddie Murphy
Bill Murray

Dancers
Debbie Allen
Mikhail
  Baryshnikov
Suzanne Farrell
Gregory Hines
Gelsey Kirkland
Twyla Tharp
Tommy Tune

**Directors/
  Producers**
Woody Allen
Steven Bochco
Ken Burns
Francis Ford
  Coppola
John Hughes
George Lucas
Penny Marshall
Leonard Nimoy
Rob Reiner
John Singleton
Steven Spielberg

**Environmentalists/
Animal Rights**
Marjory Stoneman
  Douglas
Kathryn Fuller
Lois Gibbs
Wangari Maathai
Linda Maraniss
Ingrid Newkirk
Pat Potter

Journalists
Ed Bradley
Tom Brokaw
Dan Rather
Nina Totenberg
Mike Wallace
Bob Woodward

Musicians
Another Bad Creation
Joshua Bell
George Benson
Black Box
Edie Brickell
Boyz II Men
James Brown
C & C Music Factory
Mariah Carey
Ray Charles
Chayanne
Kurt Cobain
Natalie Cole
Cowboy Junkies
Billy Ray Cyrus
Def Leppard
Gerardo
Guns N' Roses
Whitney Houston
Ice Cube
India
Janet Jackson
Jermaine Jackson
Michael Jackson
Kitaro
Kris Kross
KRS-One
Andrew Lloyd Webber
Courtney Love
Madonna
Marky Mark

Branford Marsalis
Paul McCartney
Midori
N.W.A.
Sinead O'Connor
Teddy Pendergrass
Itzhak Perlman
Prince
Public Enemy
Raffi
Bonnie Raitt
Red Hot Chili
  Peppers
Lou Reed
R.E.M.
Kenny Rogers
Axl Rose
Run-D.M.C.
Carly Simon
Paul Simon
Michelle Shocked
Will Smith
Sting
TLC
Randy Travis
2 Live Crew
Vanilla Ice
Stevie Wonder

**Politics/World
Leaders**
Yasir Arafat
Les Aspin
Bruce Babbitt
Lloyd Bentsen
Benazir Bhutto
Jesse Brown
Ronald Brown
Pat Buchanan
Jimmy Carter
Violeta Barrios
  de Chamorro
Shirley Chisolm
Warren Christopher
Edith Cresson
Mario Cuomo
F.W. de Klerk
Robert Dole
Mike Espy
Louis Farrakhan
Alan Greenspan
Vaclav Havel
Jesse Jackson
Jack Kemp
Bob Kerrey
Coretta Scott King
John Major
Wilma Mankiller
Imelda Marcos
Slobodan Milosevic

Manuel Noriega
Hazel O'Leary
Major Owens
Leon Panetta
Federico Pena
Robert Reich
Ann Richards
Richard Riley
Phyllis Schlafly
Pat Schroeder
Aung San Suu Kyi
Donna Shalala
Desmond Tutu
Lech Walesa

Royalty
Charles, Prince of
  Wales
Duchess of York
  (Sarah Ferguson)
Queen Noor

Scientists
Sallie Baliunas
Avis Cohen
Donna Cox
Stephen Jay Gould
Mimi Koehl
Deborah Letourneau
Philippa Marrack
Helen Quinn
Carl Sagan
Barbara Smuts
Flossie Wong-Staal
Aslihan Yener
Adrienne Zihlman

Sports
Jim Abbott
Muhammad Ali
Sparky Anderson
Michael Andretti
Boris Becker
Bobby Bonilla
Jose Canseco
Jennifer Capriati
Michael Chang
Roger Clemens
Randall Cunningham
Eric Davis
Clyde Drexler
John Elway
Chris Evert
Sergei Fedorov
George Foreman
Zina Garrison
Florence Griffith-Joyner
Rickey Henderson
Evander Holyfield
Desmond Howard

Brett Hull
Raghib Ismail
Jim Kelly
Petr Klima
Bernie Kozar
Greg LeMond
Carl Lewis
Mickey Mantle
Willy Mays
Joe Montana
Jack Nicklaus
Greg Norman
Joe Paterno
Kirby Puckett
Mark Rippien
David Robinson
John Salley
Barry Sanders
Monica Seles
Daryl Strawberry
Danny Sullivan
Vinnie Testaverde
Isiah Thomas
Mike Tyson
Steve Yzerman

**Television
Personalities**
Downtown Julie
  Brown
Andre Brown
  (Dr. Dre)
Phil Donahue
Linda Ellerbee
Arsenio Hall
David Letterman
Joan Lunden
Dennis Miller
Jane Pratt
Martha Quinn
Diane Sawyer

Other
Johnnetta Cole
Jaimie Escalante
Jack Kevorkian
Wendy Kopp
Sister Irene Kraus
Mother Theresa
Eli Weisel
Jeanne White